AF386390

AMERICA'S
FAVORITE WARLORD

Those who believe in Allah and the Last Day ask thee for no exemption from fighting with their goods and persons. And Allah knoweth well those who do their duty.

Quran, Sura 9, verse 44, Yusuf Ali Translation

AMERICA'S FAVORITE WARLORD

The Life and Death of General Raziq of Kandahar

JACOB HAGSTROM

Pen & Sword

MILITARY

AN IMPRINT OF PEN & SWORD BOOKS LTD.
YORKSHIRE - PHILADELPHIA

First published in Great Britain in 2025 by
PEN AND SWORD MILITARY
An imprint of
Pen & Sword Books Limited
Yorkshire – Philadelphia

Typeset in Times New Roman 10.5/12.5 by
SJmagic DESIGN SERVICES, India.
Printed and bound in the UK by CPI Group (UK) Ltd.

The Publisher's authorised representative in the EU for product safety is Authorised Rep Compliance Ltd., Ground Floor, 71 Lower Baggot Street, Dublin D02 P593, Ireland.
www.arccompliance.com

For a complete list of Pen & Sword titles please contact
PEN & SWORD BOOKS LIMITED
George House, Units 12 & 13, Beevor Street, Off Pontefract Road,
Barnsley, South Yorkshire, S71 1HN, England
E-mail: enquiries@pen-and-sword.co.uk
Website: www.pen-and-sword.co.uk

or

PEN AND SWORD BOOKS
1950 Lawrence Rd, Havertown, PA 19083, USA
E-mail: uspen-and-sword@casematepublishers.com
Website: www.penandswordbooks.com

CONTENTS

ACKNOWLEDGEMENTS

This book resulted from the efforts of many people. I take pleasure in thanking some of them here.

Thaddeus Fox introduced me to the story of General Raziq. He contacted my first informants, who then provided others in a snowball method of research. I owe Thad an enormous debt, not only for his help with this project, but for his steadfast friendship throughout the years and across continents.

Many more veterans agreed to serve as interview subjects, despite the difficulties that recalling their experiences sometimes caused. I am grateful for their support and for the sacrifices they made while serving overseas. I wish to highlight the efforts of Afghans who served as linguists.

They often took tremendous risks to enable operations, and they continue to hazard retribution against family members who now live under Taliban rule. For this reason, many interpreters who participated must remain unnamed, though their contributions were crucial to the research. Dr. Carter Malkasian has long been a role model for recording the history of the American War in Afghanistan. After I reached out for advice, Carter revealed that he was one of four double-blind reviewers who read an earlier version of the manuscript. His suggestions made this book more accessible to a lay audience. Thanks are due as well to the other three anonymous peer-reviewers for their insights.

I appreciated the professionalism of the staff at Pen and Sword Publishing. Thanks to copy editor George Chamier for making the text easier to read and the phrasing more elegant. The attention and care of commissioning editor Tara Moran and production editor Harriet Fielding allowed this book to see the light of day.

I started writing about General Raziq while I was teaching at the Citadel, the Military College of South Carolina. Many thanks to history department chair Dr. Joelle Neulander for mentorship, and to Professor David Preston for his encouragement. Special thanks to Dr. Kerry Taylor for his guidance on oral history research. I finished writing this book in Brazil. I am grateful to my wife, Gabriela, for her warm welcome to this country.

Thanks to the many readers who pointed out errors in the text. Thanks also to family members and friends who read rambling first drafts and endured many conversations about Afghanistan. I accept full responsibility for any faults that remain. I hope this work is but an early step in understanding General Raziq, his environment, and his times. *Insh'allah.*

POMEGRANATES (JULY 2010)

Kandahar Province is known for its pomegranates, whose value has been evident since ancient times. Hippocrates recommended pomegranate treatments for ailments ranging from eye infection to indigestion. Alexander's soldiers who invaded Afghanistan knew the fruit as a versatile life-cycle symbol, which could indicate fertility as well as death. The Quran describes heaven as abundant in pomegranates, rather than milk and honey. The red fruit was Kandahar's first cash crop, before hashish and opium became its predominant trade products.[1]

Abdul Raziq counted the pomegranate among his favorite foods. He was a small man, about 1.68m tall and under 70kg in weight. He did not indulge in the edible luxuries befitting him as the leader of 200 families of the Achakzai tribe. At the feasts he hosted on a regular basis, the best *kebab* meat always went to his guests.[2]

On quiet nights, Raziq slipped away from his office to walk the perimeter of the police compound and talk with his troops. In some places, Afghans stood alongside Americans at the outposts that overlooked Taliban sanctuaries across the border. Raziq offered them lighthearted jokes and words of encouragement. Three years from now, he would work only with high-ranking officers, colonels and generals. But in 2010, his partners comprised the captains, lieutenants and noncommissioned officers who ran the war on the ground. Raziq was already the most effective leader of the Afghan Republic's security forces in the southern part of the country. He was also notorious for the allegations against him of corruption, torture, and summary executions.

Raziq and an American company commander looked out to the east from the roof of a Border Police station. The flat, dusty earth of Kandahar was indistinguishable from neighboring Pakistan, except at night. When the sun set, the city lights of Chaman outshone the stars; the Afghan side of the line was distinguishable by its darkness.[3] Raziq knew this terrain intimately, but the foreigner could not distinguish the intricacies of the border line across the distant landscape. Instead, the American's eye fell on a towering painted stone edifice, reminiscent of the Arc de Triomphe, known as the Friendship Gate. It had become an ironic name, as the gate was shuttered by a chain link fence. Relations at the time between the Afghan and Pakistan governments were guarded rather than friendly. In daylight hours, a steady traffic of oil tankers, military vehicles, and brightly decorated 'jingle' trucks lurched around the gate's massive stone pillars on a makeshift dirt road. Now, in the dead calm of night, there was little to obstruct views of the ground, covered in fine dirt that shone in the moonlight.

Raziq and his American partner tore into the pomegranates as they gazed eastward. Raziq liked to mix the sweet kernels with a pinch of salt. Together they talked about their lives outside the war. When the American turned to thoughts of home, Raziq contemplated his escape plan.

By then, he was an energetic colonel in his early thirties. Most of his contemporaries had already begun to call him by his preferred honorific: 'General Raziq.'[4] He had amassed a vast security empire. Nearly 4,000 Border Policemen, plus hundreds more sources of intelligence, made him a lynchpin of operations throughout the southern region. Raziq's American counterpart that evening, a captain in command of eighty cavalrymen, was only a few years younger than his Afghan host. In terms of their responsibilities, the men were worlds apart. But Raziq's enthusiastic demeanor allowed soldiers all the way down the chain of command to feel their own importance in his presence. Raziq assured those around him, Afghan followers and foreign partners alike, that their struggle had meaning. Together, they fought for a better Afghanistan, free from the tyranny of the Taliban.

Raziq had been under arms for almost a decade by this point. As a result, he had acquired enough wealth to retire from war and relocate – to an Emirate in the Persian Gulf, somewhere in the Balkans, or maybe to America. At times, Raziq had mulled these options with his foreign advisers. But in the end, perhaps because of what he learned about his American friends, Raziq knew that Afghanistan was his home. He would never abandon it. After all, he had three wives and more than a dozen children to look after. Millions more people depended on him to stem the tide of insurgent soldiers, recruited in Pakistani religious schools and sent across the border to bring death and destruction to his homeland.[5]

Introduction

BIOGRAPHY OF A POLICE CHIEF

This is not a typical biography. The subject left no written records, due to his illiteracy, and he was assassinated before researchers could conduct formal interviews with him. Instead of a traditional life story, what follows is a case study of military partnerships, a collective account of colleagues. From 2001 until his death in 2018, Abdul Raziq Achakzai emerged as one of the most valuable Afghan partners of the American-led Global War on Terrorism. Yet many observers demonized him as a corrupt agent who encouraged torture and extrajudicial killings.

Why did foreigners continue to work with this partner, given his grievous reputation? The short answer is that from a military perspective he was competent. But speaking of General Raziq with his former comrades revealed that competence in counter-insurgency took on a distinct number of connotations. Raziq not only captured and killed Taliban fighters; he also provided intelligence, recruited and organized manpower and gave outsiders a way into the complex tribal politics of Kandahar Province. Above all, his charisma and energy inspired hope in his military partners, along with wide swaths of the population of Kandahar. Almost everyone who met Raziq remarked on the force of his personality, which took on cult status in his last years.

On paper, he was merely the Police Chief for one of Afghanistan's thirty-four provinces. But when people spoke about General Raziq they often inflated the man to mythic proportions. He had the President of his country on speed dial, owned businesses abroad and sent his children to study in Dubai. His soldiers wore patches on their uniforms that depicted his face. Crowds of locals throughout the South, gray-bearded men and scrawny boys, swarmed round him in the streets as they posed for selfies, tugged on his sleeves, and lunged to kiss his hands. He decided civil disputes and distributed vast sums of foreign aid money across a war-torn region. A few years before his assassination, vendors at Kandahar Airfield began to sell T-shirts emblazoned with his image above the caption 'What Would Raziq Do?'[1]

This life story is one of fame and power. Raziq's critics castigated him as a typical 'warlord,' in the tradition of regional strongmen who have dominated Afghanistan for the past four decades.[2] But a closer look at Raziq's environment sheds light on how military leaders came to participate in Afghan politics after 2001, much as Americans have turned in the past to charismatic authoritarians to establish justice in the face of uncertainty. What separated Raziq from the other strongmen who worked with the US-led coalition, what enabled his rapid rise to power, were his youth and his origins in Kandahar Province.

Most Afghan leaders in the Global War on Terrorism had personal ties to the earlier Soviet occupation of the country. These experiences tended to make Afghans cynical about outsiders and skeptical of Kabul-based government projects. Raziq, on the other hand, proved not only willing to embrace democratic reforms, but willing to conduct operations in person, a trait that endeared him to the military leadership.[3]

Raziq further benefited from his roots in Kandahar, where a group of Pashtun elders had founded the Taliban during his youth. Most US allies were not Pashtun, but Tajik and Uzbek men from the north. Raziq, as a home-grown US client, brought about a new era in partnership. Instead of peeling back the Taliban from the outside, as in the early years of the war, the Americans who cultivated Raziq in Kandahar attempted to root out the insurgents from within. Raziq's tenure as Chief of Police established an alternative to both the Taliban and to ethnic outsiders who dominated the Afghan National Army (ANA). He came to represent, for his foreign sponsors, a legitimate third force for the new republic: against the insurgents and apart from the Communist-tainted past.

Still, Raziq was an unlikely candidate for leadership in Kandahar. He did not come from one of the two powerful clans of the province. The strongest members of his own family had been murdered by the Taliban during their initial rise to power in the 1990s. Raziq spent his late adolescence as a refugee in Pakistan, where he found work as a mechanic and small-time smuggler.[4] His fortunes turned when Americans and their NATO partners arrived in the region after the Al Qaeda attacks of 11 September. Clandestine US agents renewed old friendships with the powerful families of Kandahar that had originated during the Soviet era. Over time, Raziq worked his way up this revitalized hierarchy through a combination of tribal politics, leverage with American partners, and a personal reputation built on martial effectiveness and brutality. When the US troop surge arrived in 2009, he had become the region's indispensable military partner.[5] As the foreigners drew down their troop levels over the ensuing years, Raziq emerged as a stabilizing presence in politics.

Finally, what set Raziq apart from many of his peers in the Afghan republic was his survivability. He navigated a seven-year term as Kandahar Chief of Police despite dozens of assassination plots against him, as well as an attempt by US agents to remove him from power. Raziq's long career makes him a good lens through which to view foreign attempts at counter-insurgency and state-building in one of Afghanistan's most strategic provinces.

The Setting: Kandahar

Americans have tended to view Afghanistan spatially from the north, as Soviet invaders did a generation before. In late 1979, the heavy army divisions had rolled across the border. In late 2001, the George W. Bush administration airdropped a lean contingent of Special Forces. These few American ground forces lent substantial airpower to Afghan militias, known as the Northern Alliance, united only by their opposition to Taliban rule.[6] But after this initial invasion from the north, the military center of gravity shifted to the south, where first the Canadians and then the Americans surged troops. Logistics became dependent on the Pakistani port of Karachi and its closest border crossing at Raziq's home district of Spin Boldak.

The South has been the historic cradle of Afghan leadership, the homeland of the Pashtun clans that have ruled the region for centuries. Kandahar Province was the birthplace of both Hamid Karzai, the first president of the

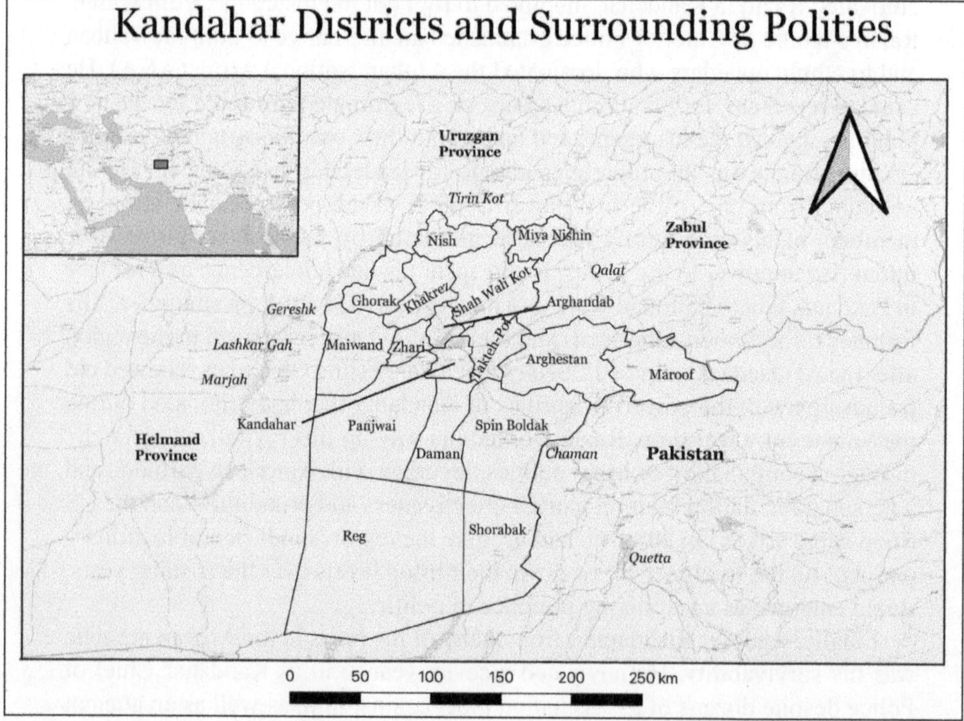

Afghan Republic, and Mullah Omar, the first leader of the Taliban. Before the Soviet era, the entire south-eastern quarter of Afghanistan had been known as Greater (*Loy*) Kandahar. As the state apparatus grew, new political units stripped Kandahar of what are now its neighboring southern provinces.

By the time of the American invasion, the province comprised some 55,000 square kilometers of territory, about the size of Croatia or West Virginia. The northern part abuts the jagged peaks of the Hindu Kush mountains, while the southern half is the Registan (sandy country), a vast plain of red ridges that shift with the wind. Most of the population, some 1.2 million people, lived in two major urban centers: the ancient imperial capital of Kandahar City (500,000) and the booming border town of Spin Boldak (100,000). The rest, modest farmers and herders, occupied small villages that lined the mighty Arghandab river and its tributaries.[7] Others moved camp seasonally in nomadic caravans, large families who drove larger herds of donkeys, sheep and camels, all laden with the fine sinews of Central Asian trade. This population often found itself hostage, caught in a deadly triangle of foreign coalition, Afghan republican and insurgent forces.

Counter-insurgency Paradox

On 22 May 2024, *The New York Times* published two pieces about Abdul Raziq that demonstrate his controversial legacy. Though the texts share a publication date and an author, journalist Matthieu Aikins, they arrived at opposing conclusions. The shorter article argued that Raziq's abuses drove the population of Kandahar into the arms of the Taliban. Partnership with him was a self-defeating course of action. The longer, more nuanced magazine piece claimed that Raziq's violence was effective, though it gave the lie to US claims about fighting a 'better war' of counter-insurgency. Raziq's systematic torture and execution of prisoners intimidated the population and dissuaded them from aiding insurgents, perhaps the only possible route to success.[8] So, was this partner more help or hindrance? A third possibility remains more likely: that human rights violations had little bearing on Raziq's effectiveness. His harsh policies were mere byproducts of Central Asian history – part of the region's cultural landscape, but not a causal factor for the outcome of the war.

The paradox of Raziq's effectiveness is difficult to unravel, but one may begin with a brief review of counter-insurgency theory. Aikins, like many pundits, accepts the premise that counter-insurgency was designed to win 'hearts and minds' rather than to unleash brutality. COIN doctrine does contain an aspiration to wage war through minimally destructive means, but the difference is in degree rather than in kind.[9] Violence in conventional combat is meant to be overwhelming, whereas violence in counter-insurgencies is supposed to be limited and precise.

Yet COIN doctrine admits that killing is necessary. The relevant Global War on Terrorism field manual warns, 'There will be times when an overwhelming effort is necessary to destroy or intimidate an opponent.'[10] Speaking of General Raziq revealed the diversity of opinion among his foreign partners about what counter-insurgency actually meant in practice, as emphasis shifted between protecting the population, encouraging economic development, enabling governance, gathering intelligence and training Afghan forces. Furthermore, individual commanders differed in their willingness to embrace these new tenets, as opposed to the older, more straightforward approaches of employing firepower against suspected threats.

In fact, counter-insurgency advocates sold their strategy with 'better war' rhetoric, but their true purpose was to fight a different kind of enemy, one that relied more on local people than on a bureaucratic state for legitimacy and logistical support. Political scientist Jacqueline Hazelton concluded that 'good governance' has never been a successful counter-insurgency strategy. What has worked, instead, is 'compellence.' Counter-insurgents do not compete for support of 'the people' as a whole; they recruit a narrow set of elites to wage violence against a rival armed force.[11] The population's hearts and minds may be won in the long term, but until enemy fighters are defeated, local people must be controlled rather than courted. In practice, this emphasis on kinetic operations over nation-building was consistent throughout the Global War on Terrorism, despite what generals and politicians said in press conferences.[12]

Theorists tend to distinguish between kinds of warfare by the distinct goals of their practitioners. In this typology, irregular wars are contests for the political loyalty of a population, whereas regular combatants seek to gain physical territory. But here again, the differences are of degree rather than kind. Territory remains important for counter-insurgents, though its meaning in military terms does shift. In conventional combat, a hill is significant if it can be fortified, defended and weaponized against nearby enemy units. In counter-insurgency, that same hill may require occupation for surveillance over a nearby road or village, or it may be significant in cultural terms for the buildings standing on it. Either way, territoriality remains significant.

Indeed, as political scientist Stathis Kalyvas concluded in a landmark study, the level of violence in civil wars depends more upon the emplacement of opposing forces than the morality of the commanders. Land may be 'segmented' through local monopolies of control or 'fragmented' in overlapping zones. Violence is most likely to escalate when one side turns fragmented space into a zone of 'near-hegemonic control,' since this is when the demand for information about enemy forces meets a supply of civilians who have access to both sides.[13] Afghanistan's history of diverse sources of political authority – religious, state, and tribal – encouraged the fragmentation of loyalty. When momentum shifted toward one side or another across this territory, incentives for violence against civilians abounded.[14] Almost every Afghan military leader confronted allegations of human rights abuses during the Global War on Terrorism; few organized violence as competently as Abdul Raziq.

Nevertheless, Raziq's official recognizance through promotions to Border Police commander and provincial Chief of Police did present strategic choices, decisions that split the strands of the foreign coalition in Afghanistan. In broad terms, military agents were more likely to dismiss accusations of Raziq's human rights abuses as hyperbolic rumor, given the police chief's capacity to keep the Taliban insurgency from overrunning outposts across the South. But even within the military, some worried about concentrating power in an individual leader rather than an enduring system.

Most representatives from the State Department and the Non-Governmental Organizations (NGOs) sent to Afghanistan believed it was a mistake to empower Raziq. Instead, foreigners should have sidelined him; more attention and funds could have supported governance projects, rather than security forces.[15] By this logic, inclusive political institutions result in peaceful, wealthy societies. Others counter that a degree of wealth must precede representative government. It is a chicken-or-egg conundrum. Which came first: dollars or democracy?

In Raziq's case, some observers feared too much foreign money might make its recipient immune from legitimate local grievances. Americans grew concerned that, like British colonizers before them, their policies encouraged 'local despotism.' Their actions empowered an individual strongman, rather organizations such as provincial or district councils, chambers of commerce and nonprofit organizations.[16] None of these alternative options was democratic – councils tended to be dominated by the old, tribal aristocracy, whereas a narrow technocratic elite made up the business and nonprofit sectors. But many Westerners perceived institutions as an alternative to the warlordism that military partnership with Raziq seemed to risk.

Warlords and their Discontents

Americans and their allies disagreed about what support to Raziq would yield. While some held that he was an impressionable young man who could reform as he aged, others believed that foreign support to him could only cultivate a 'warlord' unaccountable to the people of Kandahar and empowered with external resources to exploit them.

A warlord, in the most basic sense of the definition, is someone who uses command of armed forces to gain political and economic power over a given region. In theory, they govern by personal coercion and patronage rather than through impersonal laws and institutions. They tend to be motivated by private gain rather than ideology. While some scholars describe warlordism as distinct from state rule, either prior to its emergence or in the wake of its failure, others claim that the warlord has been a foundational figure in state formation around the world.

The first usage of the term is instructive. In the nineteenth century, Ralph Waldo Emerson denigrated the English aristocracy's transition across the ages, from 'the war-lord to the law-lord . . . the privilege was kept, whilst the means of obtaining it were changed.'[17] Following this literary observation, scholars Max Weber and Charles Tilly have described state-building in early modern Europe as the mastery of violence by regional strongmen, the nobility of the sword, who maintained relative autonomy until monarchs came to dominate the continent and organize it into 'nation states' over the course of the early modern era.[18] Warlords may have served in this manner as transitional figures who, by staving off anarchy and foreign conquest, created space for more impersonal, rule-based systems to emerge over time.

According to political scientist Kimberly Marten, the crucial difference between the warlordism of the early modern period and that of recent times consists in the changing norms that emerged during the intervening centuries. In the early period, warlords were not surrounded by strong states. This vacuum of sovereignty gave feudal nobles motivation to develop self-sufficiency: to innovate with respect to their armed forces, and to create political and social institutions. But in recent centuries, the centralized state has become the normative political unit. Warlords, now hemmed in by mature political entities, cannot aspire to statehood. So instead they play what Marten describes as a 'parasitic' role on the edges of states.[19]

Other academics counter that Marten's definition owes more to theory than practice. Throughout history, most states did not attain true monopolies of violence. More often than not, autonomous local militias, if not active rebellions, have contested the legitimacy of government claims to territory. State forces themselves have become extractive and abusive of the populations they are meant to serve. Furthermore, it is difficult to distinguish the legitimate grievances of revolutionaries from the illegitimate greed of criminals. Political scientists Ariel Ahram and Charles King, rather than identify warlords by their lack of legitimacy, recommend they be defined by their ability to navigate across borders – not only the political boundaries that separate states, but the conceptual gray areas between legal and illegal economic activity, sovereignty and dependence. 'Warlords are not necessarily the state's foil,' Ahram and King summarize, 'rather, they may also become the state's de facto deputy.'[20] Raziq's many supporters characterized him in this way, not as a parasite but a productive middleman between the central state and its unwieldy periphery.

Few countries in the world can claim such troublesome peripheries as Afghanistan. A running joke held that the president's authority extended about as far as that of the Mayor of Kabul. Afghanistan did not develop into a modern state like those of Europe through a monarch's conquest over a region's noble class. Instead, foreign patrons have dominated the country for the past two centuries: first the British and then the Soviets. These agents supplied funds from abroad for the King (Emir) in Kabul to maintain power by patronage to tribal and religious authorities, whose loyalty to the government was relational rather than fixed.

The country was divided, not only by sources of political authority, but also by physical geography. The towering Hindu Kush mountains split the land into two distinct cultural spheres. The Persian north and west contain the ethnic minorities of the country: the Tajik, Uzbek, Turkmen and Hazara peoples. The south and east are dominated by Pashtuns, who form a tribal confederacy of segmented lineages. Tribal institutions (*jirga*, council) and tribal norms (*Pashtunwali*, the way of the Pashtun) moderate governance. For this reason, prominent researcher Antonio Giustozzi has claimed that true warlords are a phenomenon of the non-Pashtun north-western regions, and that a 'tribal warlord' is in fact a hybrid category.[21]

Warlordism in Afghanistan proliferated following the Soviet invasion and its associated flood of foreign military funds. Whereas the old aristocracy came to power through its capacity to organize people by tribal, civic, or religious means, a new class of leadership emerged by converting external aid into military might. When the war against the Soviets ended in 1989, the patchwork of warlords who had opposed foreign occupation fell apart in the midst of civil war. The Taliban emerged during this period of chaos in Kandahar. It was here, where Pashtun commanders were divided, weak, and subject to tribal constraints, that the Taliban movement grew. Opposition to the theocratic upstarts came from the stronger, non-Pashtun warlords. These forces formed the Northern Alliance, the manpower for the 2001 US invasion that pushed the Taliban into exile in Pakistan.

None of these men referred to himself as a warlord, a term Westerners employed for specific purposes. Prior to the conflict against the Taliban, the label served to justify foreign intervention; during the war, critics denoted allies as warlords in order to bolster the accomplishments of Western agents; and throughout the long reconstruction of the Afghan government after 2002, Westerners deflected criticism of their own efforts by pointing to troublesome warlords.[22] While the term has taken on connotations of cruelty and greed, the concept might be shorn of these moral judgments and refer simply to a military figure who has assumed political authority. In this way, warlords form a useful category of analysis in Afghanistan, as distinct from other types of leadership: tribal aristocrats and new technocrats. Raziq's story lends evidence to recent work by political scientists, who have noted the productive roles that warlords played in Afghanistan during the Global War on Terror.[23]

The recent history of Kandahar challenges basic theoretical assumptions about warlords – that they are authoritarian, unpopular and incapable of reform. Raziq rose to power as a hybrid figure, as he gained authority through military and tribal accolades. This hybridity helps to explain why his leadership was more flexible and inclusive than authoritarian in nature. He began his career as a narrow tribal militiaman, but he ended it as a coalition-building nationalist. He was widely admired in Kandahar throughout his time as Police Chief, and he attained celebrity status throughout the country in his last years. He adopted Western reforms when they did not threaten to upend the republican government. Upon his death, Raziq inspired heartfelt artistic commemorations. Such a life contradicts the popular image of the warlord.

The Oral History Method

Over the course of the pandemic years, in which archives were closed and homebound folks were more likely to accept calls, I conducted more than one hundred interviews with individuals whose paths intersected with Raziq's. Twenty sources are Afghans, five are Canadians, and fifty-three are Americans. Perhaps the most significant informants were former officials of the Afghan republic.[24] Pashto linguists were helpful as well, since they understood subtexts often lost on foreigners. On the American side, most sources were captains, majors and lieutenant colonels when they spent time with Raziq. They were with him as he policed the dusty border crossing, trekked across hills and dug up explosives among the rows of vines. As such, these informants gained different insights into the man than those who read dispatches about him in air-conditioned oases at Kandahar Airfield, or worse still, in Kabul or Washington.

Oral histories can sometimes be self-serving. They often come riddled with rumor and fogged by 'forgettery.'[25] But despite their deficiencies, spoken interviews produce profound benefits, as they allow for preservation of folklore, ways of speech, and mindsets of the masses who, for whatever reason, do not write about their experiences. Oral testimony allows for a more democratic representation of the past. Because much of Raziq's life is undocumented, his story is prone to myth-making. Speaking of General Raziq allowed for the arrangement of myths in chronological order: from good village boy, to brave commander, and finally to martyr. Labeling these stories allows for analysis, the separation of facts from the fictions they contain.

Research by oral history interview was necessary for a practical reason in this case as well. Documents that refer to Raziq have been destroyed by the Taliban since their takeover of 2021, or remain classified by the US government. Military agents, unlike in past generations, did not create a massive paper trail during the War on Terrorism. Documents were stored on electronic servers 'wiped' clean at the end of rotations overseas. This lack of text constituted a limit for the research. No existing document can prove how much money Raziq made, or how much he spent on his businesses or humanitarian interests. All that could be done, at the time of writing, was to gather testimony from those who observed his organization and found themselves willing to recall it in good faith. What follows, in a sense, is annotated hearsay.[26]

Journalists who wrote about Raziq for popular media outlets tended to ask a moralistic 'why' question. Why did United States agents work with Raziq, tarred as a 'torturer in chief'?[27] The question was rhetorical, since whatever answers his partners supplied became excuses for errant logic. But if one shifts the framing of the question, different answers emerge. Rather than ask why foreigners worked with him, one might instead ask how Raziq gained power. This question not only avoids the moral angst that can obscure analysis, it restores some agency to Raziq. Though he lacked the material resources of his foreign patrons, his familiarity with the borderlands and their diverse populations granted him the autonomy of a valuable guide, a middleman without whom outsiders could become lost.

The foreigners sent to Kandahar often compared their areas of operations to the 'Wild West'. For these newcomers, Kandahar represented another 'Indian Country' characterized by the absence of order, a place that demanded surveillance and firepower to hold back the 'barbaric' foe.[28] The concept of the Wild West was malleable in Afghan contexts. It was elastic enough for some Americans to see Raziq as a kind of 'Lone Ranger,' an authority whom they could entrust with power and exit with safety. Others imagined him as 'Tonto,' a trusty scout who could enable some foreigners – Special Forces, intelligence agents and elite contractors – to remain in the country as senior partners for an indefinite period.

At the beginning of the Global War on Terrorism, Raziq was a young man in a country of elderly statesmen, an illiterate individual surrounded by hyper-literate Westerners. Yet his presumed defects allowed the commander space to maneuver. Some elder Afghans believed they could act through young Raziq, like pulling the strings on a puppet. American partners thought that this unschooled man might be impressionable, a blank slate upon which to draw their imagined futures for Afghanistan. But Raziq flouted these expectations as he cultivated a multitude of competing sources of allegiance in Kandahar, with the CIA and with Blackwater, with US Special Forces and with regular army units, with members of his own clan and with refugees from other parts of Afghanistan who flocked to his district of Spin Boldak for safety. This last group, the internally displaced people of the country, formed Raziq's bedrock of independent support, the key element in his transformation into a nationalist political leader.

In order to understand Raziq's rise to power, it is necessary to know about the world into which he was born. Part I introduces the concept of tribe in the context of Kandahar and follows Raziq's tribal predecessors in power: a fellow Achakzai during the Soviet era, and his uncle during the subsequent civil war. Part II explores Raziq's rise to power, which began with partnership efforts during the Global War on Terrorism by American, French, and Canadian agents. The American surge arrived in 2009, and Raziq employed its influx of aid to augment his patronage network and create oases of security, first in Spin Boldak District and then across greater Kandahar Province. Part III describes Raziq's fall from power, amid the drawdown of US troops and efforts to reform the Afghan forces. The epilogue reveals the fragmented legacy that Raziq left in the wake of his assassination in 2018.

Critics claimed he was a war criminal. But his supporters had seen him as the last best hope to save the Republic of Afghanistan from a Taliban takeover. Raziq could be characterized either way with comparable truth. As such, his career exposes the moral ambiguity inherent to war, and perhaps to civil wars in particular. Foreign partners believed they were showing Afghans the way to progress. But Raziq made more significant revelations to Western observers, as he unveiled the forces and passions that supported their systems of politics.[29]

PART I

ABDUL RAZIQ'S WORLD

O ye who believe! Take not into your intimacy those outside your ranks: They will not fail to corrupt you. They only desire your ruin: Rank hatred has already appeared from their mouths: What their hearts conceal is far worse. We have made plain to you the Signs, if ye have wisdom.

Quran, Sura 3, verse 118

Chapter 1

TRIBE

The concept of tribe (*qawm*) was often invoked but little understood by visitors to Kandahar. Nearly every foreigner who spoke about General Raziq mentioned that Afghanistan was a tribal place. But what that meant was difficult to define. Even well-meaning, culturally sensitive Western eyes saw Afghan tribesmen as inscrutable, somehow other.

Whatever the precise definition, most foreign observers agreed that tribes produced formidable warriors. Military accomplishments elevated the status of young tribesmen, which helped to explain why warfare was endemic to their societies. By the end of the nineteenth century, many Britons subscribed to the theory of 'martial races,' the Social Darwinist belief that some ethnic groups produced better fighters than others.[1] Knowledge was power for imperial agents who sought to divide and conquer colonized peoples, and the British studied tribes in order to choose appropriate allies through which to subdue the rest.[2]

The Pashtun (or Pukhtun, Pathan) people attracted special attention because they ranked toward the top of the nineteenth-century British military caste system, alongside others considered natural warriors, such as the Gurkhas. Mountstuart Elphinstone, a Scottish diplomat dispatched in 1807 to oppose a proposed Napoleonic invasion of India, took his prejudices with him and concluded Afghan government bore a 'strong resemblance to that of Scotland in ancient times,' as the King managed 'the precarious submission of the nearest clans, and the independence of the remote ones.'[3] This was not quite accurate for local conditions, since physical distance counted for less in Central Asia than the figurative genealogical distance of a tribe from the royal family. Nevertheless, Elphinstone's account served for decades as the only reliable source on the region in the English language. The military officers and political agents who arrived in the region afterward adopted his 'Scottish clan' tribal mode of analysis.[4]

Early-nineteenth-century observers such as Elphinstone had linked tribes to positive qualities, such as the nobility, vigor and independence displayed by Scottish Highlanders and the Germanic conquerors of Rome. But by the end of the century, tribes came to signify backwardness.[5] Winston Churchill, during an 1897 campaign in North-west India, assessed the local Pashtun people as living 'in a state of warlike leisure' that allowed them to perfect the tactics of hill fighting: ambushes and hit-and-run raids. Churchill described the Afghan tribesman with a telling transnational comparison of colonized peoples: 'To the ferocity of the Zulu are added the craft of the Redskin and the marksmanship of the Boer.'[6] Here Churchill's language exhibits the typically negative image of ferocious and crafty tribal opponents.

For American newcomers, even those armed with the knowledge of their British forebears, the task of selecting partners among tribesmen could be opaque. Consider the case of Major Jim Gant, whom General David Petraeus once praised as the 'perfect counter-insurgent.' Gant was an experienced Green Beret who had advised Egyptian officers during the Gulf War and gained minor celebrity in military circles with the publication of *One Tribe at a Time*, an account of the four months in 2003 he spent among the Pashtuns.

Gant's primary message was that the American military leadership needed to learn about how tribal politics worked in Afghanistan. Tribe was Afghanistan's 'Rosetta Stone,' through which terrorist networks became intelligible. 'The central cultural fact about Afghanistan', Gant declared, 'is that it is constituted of tribes. Not individuals, not Western-style citizens, but tribes and tribesmen.'[7] Gant saw tribe as a concept that could unite Afghans and Americans, at least those of the US military. In his mind, the 'tribal' concepts of bravery and loyalty that formed the bedrock of Pashtun values were little different to the American 'warrior ethos.'[8] In a transcendent performance of partnership, Gant tattooed Pashto words for honor (*ghairat*) and the defense of women (*namus*) on his wrists. The American believed he was linked in spirit to the Spartans of ancient Greece. His universalized warrior world view made him feel at home among the Afghans, or so he thought.[9]

Gant's read on tribal politics produced a dramatic result, but it was not the one he had in mind. When he returned to Afghanistan in 2010 he was accused of using counter-insurgency doctrine's dictate to live among the people as cover for the ulterior motives of wooing an embedded journalist and consuming drugs. Perhaps these were indeed apt behaviors to gain the trust of Pashtun leaders. The bigger problem, though, was that Gant had based his analysis of tribe on a misreading of the social situation in his fragment of the Kunar River valley.

Nur Afzal, an elder whom Gant called the Afghan Sitting Bull, a 'proven fighter' imbued with 'charisma,' was in fact a humble state employee with scant military experience. He inherited his authority in the village upon the death of his older brother. He had limited local ties to the region, since he had spent much of his adult life in Karachi, Pakistan, a common destination of work-based migration for Pashtun men. The double irony is that if Gant *had* found an important tribal leader to assist him, that individual would likely have used the American connection to siphon weapons for his own clients to turn on their rival tribe. A bureaucrat such as Nur Afzal, though he was not a warrior, was familiar with the civic function of distributing resources from the central state to remote people of the villages. The American stumbled into the correct course and selected the proper partner by accident, despite his peculiar tribal logic.[10]

Though the Green Beret officer had cultivated genuine bonds with local leaders in Afghanistan, his noncompliance with US Army regulations resulted in a letter of reprimand, loss of rank, forfeit of his Special Forces tab, and forced retirement. Gant and the embedded reporter, Ann Scott Tyson, married and settled in the Pacific North-west. Over the years, the couple remained in contact with Nur Afzal's family, who adjusted without much difficulty to life under the Taliban regime that took over in 2021. The new local government representative had worked with Gant, as part of the latter's attempts to use tribal connections as a means of infiltrating the insurgency back in 2010.[11]

The episode suggests that many 'facts' assembled by Special Forces officers and State Department representatives, stamped with the imprimatur of authoritative reports, were in fact hastily constructed misunderstandings. As one American officer put it, remembering his arrival in Kandahar in 2005, 'You had to trust somebody. You had to figure out who' was worthy of confidence, knowing that 'everybody's got a grudge. Everybody's trying to get Americans to kill their enemies.'[12] Though Gant's experience serves as a cautionary tale, his premise on the importance of tribes to Afghan society was a sound one.

American journalist Sebastian Junger, who spent over a decade covering the Global War on Terrorism, defined tribal societies by what they lacked: attention to individual identity and material accumulation. Present-day Americans had lost their way when they shed humanity's original tribal conditions: communal and egalitarian lifestyles. Junger mentioned in passing American Indians and the !Kung of the Kalahari to provide examples of traditional values. But he reserved most of his praise for the American infantry platoon that he accompanied to the Korengal Valley of eastern Afghanistan. Junger, though surrounded by Pashtun tribes, applied tribal concepts mostly to his observations of US soldiers. These young men risked individual safety for the benefit of the unit, sacrificed food and sleep for each other, and comforted comrades in times of shared hardship.[13] It is easy to see how Junger, seeing at first hand these displays of virtue by soldiers at the outposts, became disillusioned by the rampant fraud and freeloading he observed in the United States. But the author's celebration of the American military 'tribe' as a means of critiquing a decadent home front evokes deeper questions.

How does one define a tribe? Are tribes around the world communal and egalitarian? The rise of Raziq in Kandahar demonstrated not only persistent infighting between tribes, but a complex hierarchy within them. Moreover, tribal power shifted with the arrival of foreigners.

Tribal Empire in Kandahar

Historians date the birth of modern Afghanistan to the founding of Ahmad Shah Abdali's empire in Kandahar. Abdali, like Raziq much later, came to power through a military career sponsored by a foreign partner, in his case the Persian Safavid 'pretender' Nadir Shah. Abdali and other Pashtun tribesmen helped Nadir Shah to acquire the trading hub of Kandahar in the first decade of his rule. But in 1747, the Emperor died in his tent, apparently the victim of an assassination. Military leaders from the newly conquered territories began to form their own states. Abdali had two important assets on his side: experience leading the Emperor's Pashtun armies and possession of his mobile treasury. The theme of military commanders appropriating foreign patronage is thus foundational to the history of Afghan statecraft.

Historians give another reason why Abdali was able to gain power and found his own empire: his obscurity. He was young, and he came from a minor clan of the Popalzai tribe. The myth holds that during a Supreme Council (*Loya Jirga*) to determine the leadership of the new empire, eight military chiefs of the recently slain Nadir Shah each made the case for himself to be appointed. Abdali remained quiet, so a holy man in attendance stepped in to give his blessing to the humble young man, said to be descended from Sufi saints. The other Pashtun elders agreed to compromise on Ahmad Shah, since they believed his youth would make him impressionable. The older chiefs imagined they would be able to pull strings from behind the scenes; a weak leader might allow them to gain favorable concessions for their clans. It was the same logic that Achakzai elders used more than two centuries later, when they promoted young Raziq in the wake of the 11 September attacks.

Though historians sometimes see the selection of Ahmad Shah Abdali as a seminal example of democratic government by the Pashtun tribes, this council could also be called a military junta. Abdali's appointment as Emperor, rather than consensus-building among a broad swath of equals, was the calculated move of a narrow circle of fellow commanders.[14]

Newcomers to Afghanistan often assumed that tribes were static units, their attributes fixed in time immemorial. But each community has its own history of triumphs and grievances. Nor do tribal groups conform to a single way of life. Historian Ibn Khaldun noticed that tribes produced both 'desert civilization,' characterized by nomadic herding, and the 'sedentary civilization' of farms and villages. Distinct environments encouraged divergent moral values of honor (*nang*) and taxation (*qalang*). The distinction is evident in the Pashto proverb: 'Honor ate up the mountains and taxes ate up the plains.'[15] The differences between the mountain tribes, who are often poor, nomadic, egalitarian, and hostile to central government, and the plains tribes, typically wealthier, settled, hierarchical, and connected with central government, were reinforced by the new Emperor's policies of patronage.

After he accepted the throne, Abdali took on the name 'Shah Durr-i-Durran,' the Pearl of Pearls. Each of his loyal tribes henceforth became known as Durrani.[16] Ahmad Shah broke up the dominant Barakzai tribe into two groups and granted the descendants of Achak Khan their own lands in the Toba hills.[17] The establishment of Raziq's tribe, the Achakzai, was thus commensurate with the origins of modern Afghanistan. Perhaps this historical link prompted Abdul Raziq to hang a portrait of the Durrani founder above his bed.[18] The first Pashtun Emperor was fond of the Achakzai, whom he visited when the heat of summer made Kandahar City unbearable. Raziq's kinsmen, due to their physical closeness to the Emperor, tended to be more privileged than their neighbors of the rival Noorzai tribe.[19]

Ahmad Shah, and later Abdul Raziq, demonstrated the speed with which Pashtun commanders have used tribal connections to infiltrate the state, rather than resist or break away from it. Both leaders came to power through a tribal council (*jirga*), and each ruled through a combination of patronage and warfare. The Durrani leaders were selective in distributing the spoils of their patronage system. As a result, tribe has had split effects on Afghan politics. Elite clans used their prestige as a means of access to the central state. On the other hand, marginal tribes developed networks to resist their Durrani cousins, who held the reins of state power. Most leaders of these disenfranchised tribes preferred to be left autonomous, free from interference unless interests united them against a common enemy.[20]

The growing presence of Europeans altered the balance of the 'military labor market' in Central Asia. Whereas before, Asian empires had raised cavalry armies through land grants, the East India Company introduced professional bodies of infantry and artillery, paid in cash. The large body of Afghan tribesmen formerly exported as mercenaries to India now found themselves hemmed in by Indian states fortified by technical experts from abroad. Ahmad Shah, blocked from the emerging British colonial project to the east, turned north to conquer the cosmopolitan crossroads city of Kabul in 1772. The next year, the Durrani founder died of an illness while convalescing in the highlands east of Kandahar amongst his favored Achakzai tribe.[21]

Tribal Culture and Feuds

Every foreigner who visits Kandahar hears about the way of the Pashtun (*Pashtunwali*). Whereas in the eighteenth and nineteenth centuries tribes had been a way to organize military force, by the twentieth century they had become one means of cultural identity among many. One emigrant reported that even after forty years in the United States, *Pashtunwali* was something that never left him. He underlined the point, by saying, 'It is a part of my blood.'[22] Other Pashtun informants recalled their tribal affiliation in negative terms, since it left them vulnerable to hostile Dari speakers in Kabul. Still others believed tribe to have been relatively unimportant in recent decades, and more important in the countryside than in the cities.[23] The relationships between individual Afghans and tribes during the Global War on Terrorism were personal and somewhat unpredictable.

Conflicting opinions about tribal culture are partly due to the fluidity of its practices. *Pashtunwali* is not a static system of law or a formal code of conduct, but a collection of values. Sometimes these values conflict with one another, so they must be acted out in physical context, rather than debated, codified and referenced in the abstract. The fundamental tension among the values tests individual freedom and peaceful coexistence. If individuals in a tribal setting cannot settle a dispute, they may take their problem to a council (*jirga*) of local elders. If either party deems the council's decision unacceptable, they initiate a feud. Insiders speak of acting in a just manner as 'doing *Pakhtu*' (*Pakhtu kawal*).[24]

Many Americans noticed the Pashtun value of hospitality. Raziq, like many Afghan leaders, was a great host, known for his ability to 'feed the people'. Mountstuart Elphinstone remarked on this primary quality during the first visit of a European to Afghanistan in the early nineteenth century, writing that 'an inhospitable man' was said to have 'no *Pooshtoonwullee*'.[25] Americans in the twenty-first century understood the importance of being patient with the slower pace of Afghan business, one that allowed hosts to demonstrate their generosity. Newcomers to Afghanistan often found on commander-approved reading lists the widely praised (albeit fraudulent) *Three Cups of Tea*, which described a Westerner's heroic overcoming of culture shock. Most foreigners had prepared themselves for long and aimless conversations with local greybeards.[26] Some foreign officials grumbled about the time wasted drinking *chai* tea, discussing the finer points of goat herding and cricket. But they were often even less comfortable with the fundamental Pashtun value of *badal* (revenge), in defense of one's honor, often against paternal cousins.[27]

Cousin-hatred (*Tarboorghanay*) runs so deep in Pashtun culture that a host of relevant proverbs remain in use today. 'When he is little, play with him; when he is grown up, he is a cousin (*tarboor*). Fight him.' Another counsels, 'If a cousin (*tarboor*) is good, he kills others; if he is bad, he kills us.' Still more to the point: 'Tolerate anyone but the cousin (*tarboor*).'[28] In a society of patrilineal descent, cousins are rivals for their shared grandfather's inheritance, so material factors drive the endemic intra-Pashtun feuds.

But cousins are also potential sources of shame, perhaps more important to the worldview of the typical Pashtun youth. Relatives might dishonor one another, or they might come together to avenge slights to their clan. The resolution of dishonor sometimes extended to generations-long blood feuds against the offending man and his uncles, brothers, sons, and nephews. Another proverb emphasizes the interminable nature of honor culture in the region: 'People say of the Pashtun who took revenge after one hundred years, he took it quickly.'[29] Over time, the violence of related tribal groups has split them into smaller clans that compete for prestige and resources.

On the macro level, Durrani Pashtun tribes contended with Ghilzai tribes. But on the micro level, there was competition within the Durrani clans. Even in the early nineteenth century, Elphinstone had noticed that the 'Atchukzye,' Raziq's tribe, and the rival 'Noorzyes, who inhabit the desart [*sic*] country,' were 'the tribes most addicted to rapine.'[30] Violence between closely related Pashtun groups reached its most desperate state in the mountainous and arid regions of Afghanistan, where resources were scarce and honest modes of earning a living almost impossible to maintain.

There is a certain continuity in the gaze of Western visitors upon this part of the world that connects the British agent Elphinstone's nineteenth-century description of Achakzai men with American NPR reporter Sarah Chayes's more recent impression. Elphinstone claimed the Achakzai tribe to be notorious for their 'boldness in robbery,' and noted their dirty clothes, 'their beards unclipped, and their hair long and shaggy. . . They are not hospitable; they have no mosques and seldom pray or trouble themselves about religion.'[31] Chayes similarly described the Achakzai militia types she met in 2001 as 'hard-swearing, ill-famed rogues . . . an intimidating lot . . . sporting characteristically hooked noses and great mats of hair . . . A picture out of a Persian miniature.'[32] To outsiders looking in, the roughness of the terrain – half jagged mountain passes and half scorched desert – seemed to produce equally rough men.

Americans disagreed about the intensity of the rivalry between Kandahari tribes. Some referred to a familiar example of frontier vigilantism and labeled the Achakzai and Noorzai the region's 'Hatfields and McCoys'. Others, however, used the American feud as a counter-example, to downplay the level of inter-tribal animosity they observed in Kandahar. The relationship was characterized more by old grudges and mild prejudice than active conflict.[33] In historical terms, the American family conflict was limited to the generation that followed the US Civil War. By contrast, Afghan feuds reignited frequently over the course of the nineteenth and twentieth centuries. Frequent reversals among the regional powers led to disputed claims and opportunities to reset local arrangements.[34]

Violence took place not only between Achakzai and Noorzai, but among the Achakzai clans. Raziq led just one of the three major family groups within his tribe.[35] This intra-tribal level of distinction was opaque to all but the most anthropologically aware of the foreign soldiers sent to Kandahar. The common narrative during the Global War on Terrorism claimed the Achakzai were the pro-republic tribe, and the Noorzai were pro-Taliban. Raziq himself encouraged this concept, as he told NATO officials that Taliban leadership included thirty-five Noorzai elders and only 'two or three' Achakzai. But this generalization belied important exceptions. One of Raziq's critical allies within the Afghan security forces was Noorzai, while one of the Taliban's highest-ranking members was an Achakzai elder.[36]

The disputes endemic to the region did not unite entire tribes or even clans. Instead, the participants emerged from specific family networks. In the nineteenth century, these social webs protected agricultural land and animal herds; by the late twentieth century, they controlled smuggling paths and border crossing points. The conflicts were thus local and interpersonal in nature, though they took on political consequences for international military partners. The Soviets reignited the old tribal grudges in their attempts to divide and conquer the country.

Chapter 2

SOVIET WAR (1977–1994)

Abdul Raziq was born in March 1977. He was the oldest son of a family from the village of Konchi, in Spin Boldak district. Konchi consisted then, as it does now, of a few rock-and-mud-walled compounds surrounded by sandy hills. The family could look east from their lands into Pakistani territory. There was no military checkpoint on that part of the border, so when Raziq and his three younger brothers were children they used to walk from their ancestral plot across the frontier. One brother recalled that Raziq did so frequently. These jaunts allowed him glimpses into the thriving routes of commerce, both licit and illicit, that crossed the borderlands.[1]

Incentives for illicit trade increased in the decade before Raziq's birth, with the 1965 Transit Trade Agreement. This international law allowed for duty-free imports from Pakistan to Afghanistan, resulting in a 'U-turn scheme.' Truckers sealed their containers inbound from the Pakistani port of Karachi and drove them into Afghanistan at Spin Boldak. From here, they often smuggled goods back over the line into Pakistan for sale on the black market.[2] Automobiles became a major item of trade, and Raziq learned to work on cars when he was a child. Mechanical tinkering became a lifelong hobby. 'Some Afghans enjoy dogfighting,' he used to say, 'but I prefer cars.'[3] Smuggling came naturally to the Pashtun clans of the borderlands, since tribal associates on both sides of the frontier allowed them to evade the porous administrative systems of the two states. The illicit traffic assumed higher stakes with the beginning of the Soviet invasion of 1979, as Afghan fighters and Western-funded weapons began to cross the border along with the automobiles.

To understand any Afghan participant in the Global War on Terrorism, it is essential to know about their ancestors and their roles in the Soviet war. This earlier conflict, which raged throughout the 1980s, killed more than one million Afghans out of a total population of sixteen million. The initial Soviet invasion provoked a political purge of some 60,000 people deemed enemies of the new

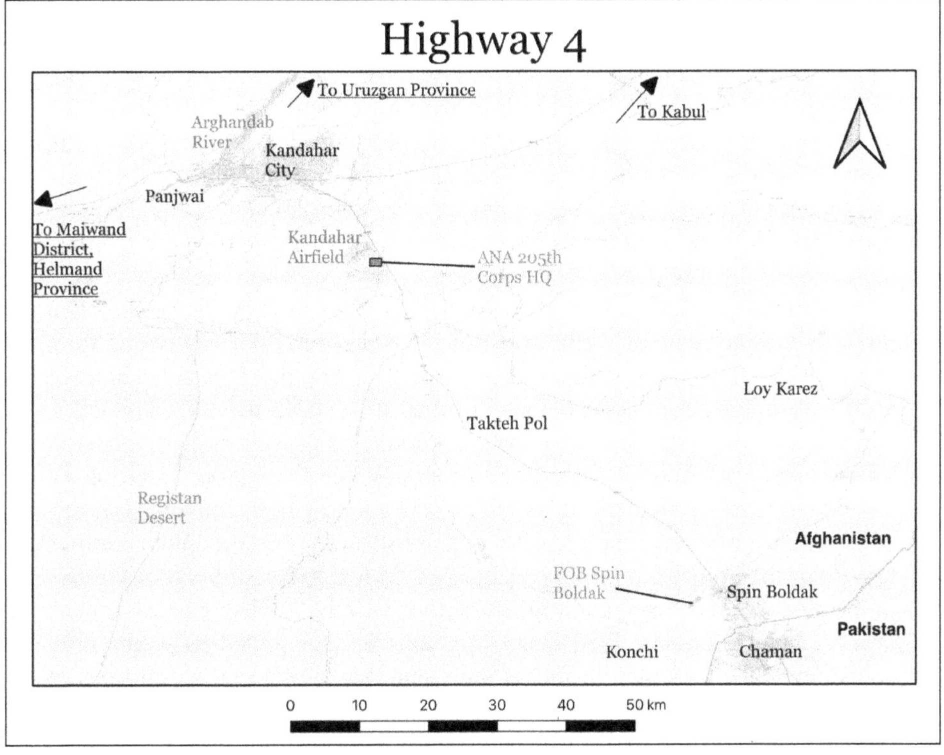

regime. Thereafter, the strategy of 'rubblization,' the destruction of infrastructure in places where insurgents took refuge, ruined half of the country's villages and displaced one out of every three Afghans.[4] Raziq's father, Mohammad Khan, became part of these grim statistics. He had been a driver along the Pakistan border. One day, he left home in his tractor and never returned. The family suspected he was killed by rival smugglers from the Noorzai tribe, but they would never find proof.[5] Raziq was then about eleven years old.

The fatherless family moved to the outskirts of Kandahar Airfield, where Raziq's three paternal uncles supported them. The benefactors were all leaders in an Achakzai militia that raised funds by smuggling goods across the border. Two of the three did not survive the Soviet war. One uncle was killed in an attempt to transport the victims of a mortar attack to safety. Locals found the corpse of another uncle tied to his motorcycle at the bottom of a large well.[6] The remaining role model in young Raziq's life was his Uncle Mansour, who was the Spin Boldak district-based lieutenant of another Achakzai militia commander, Ismatullah Muslim.

Ismatullah was a major in the Afghan Army at the time of the communist coup in 1978. He had visited the Soviet Union as both a military trainee and a prisoner convicted of drug trafficking. When the war broke out, he joined the widespread resistance to foreign occupation. But over time, the brash commander proved unable to work with the Islamist political parties through which Pakistan funneled aid. After a number of disputes, the Pakistani Intelligence Services (ISI) barred him from receipt of foreign funds in late 1983. Ismatullah promptly defected. The Soviet-sponsored Kabul government promoted him to Brigadier General and made him responsible for the defense of two critical axes: 130km of the border with Pakistan, and the highway to Kandahar City. He used his new state patronage to crush rivals and attract thousands of local soldiers, often recruited through Achakzai tribal contacts.[7]

Ismatullah's function in the Soviet system was to keep the paths clear for their military convoys. But much of his wealth and power derived from another kind of highway traffic, that of narcotics. Though Afghanistan boasted a thriving opium crop even before the war, from 1982 to 1983 production doubled to nearly 600 tons per year. War conditions drove the sharp increase. The Soviets made traditional agriculture impossible throughout much of the country by their systematic destruction of rural irrigation tunnels (*kharez*), which could serve as weapons caches or ambush sites. Because opium requires less water than other crops, poppies became critical to the survival of farmers in the absence of the irrigation infrastructure.[8] As the Soviets pushed Afghan farmers from traditional food crops, the United States pulled them into drug cultivation. The CIA plan to funnel arms into Afghanistan relied on sales of raw opium and processed heroin to help pay for the weapons.[9] After Ismatullah switched sides and turned on his erstwhile allies in the resistance, he began to acquire their territory for narcotics production and distribution.

He did nothing to indicate that patriotism motivated the construction of his security empire. On the contrary, many observers believed he acted to gratify his passions for violence, drugs, and sex. He claimed to have ten young women in his harem, in defiance of the Quranic limit of four; some of the women's families complained he had forced them to marry him. Critics accused him of torture, and abundant reports claimed he had executed dozens of innocent Kandaharis by his own hand.[10] After his promotion in January 1986 to the Revolutionary Council, he established a party palace in Kabul, where he hosted orgies of dancers and prostitutes. In the fall of 1987, he broke up a national council (*Loya Jirga*) with gunfire that killed fourteen bystanders.[11]

Ismatullah held on to power, despite his personal indiscretions, so long as he had the support of the Soviet Army. It was only in 1988, after the withdrawal of Soviet forces from Kandahar, that he lost his Spin Boldak base to a swarm of *mujahidin* fighters. The commanders split up the territory of the province and the smuggling routes across the border. Raziq's uncle Mansour and his few dozen loyal militia soldiers held on to the airport and adjoining family lands after their patron's flight to the Soviet Union. Ismat Khan died in the USSR in 1991, and a cynical military partnership for highway security came to a close.

When the Americans arrived in Kandahar in 2001, they confronted this uncomfortable tribal history. American officials worried that giving Raziq resources would turn him into a new Ismatullah. Locals continued to associate Raziq and his militia with their Achakzai forebears, who had fought with the Soviets during the *jihad*. A State Department representative recalled meetings in Spin Boldak district at which Noorzai elders reminded him of this inconvenient truth. 'You were supporting us, the *mujahidin*,' the elders complained. 'The Achakzais were on the wrong side . . . and we're on the outs now. Now we're fighting for crumbs. And back in the day, you were supporting us. We were your allies.'[12] The Achakzai militias had adopted their traditional role in support of the central government in Kabul, whereas rivals in the Noorzai tribe had maintained their historical tendency toward rebellion. The ongoing tribal competition over resources and smuggling routes collided soon after the withdrawal of the Soviets, as a new religious movement, once again nurtured with aid from Pakistan, swept across Kandahar.

Chapter 3

CIVIL WAR (1994–2001)

After the Soviet army withdrew, several factions assumed power in Kandahar, including an Achakzai militia under Raziq's uncle Mansour. Raziq had joined the organization in 1988, following his father's death. At first, he served *chai* tea and cleaned up the guest rooms at his uncle's headquarters. Over time, Mansour gave his oldest nephew more tasks. The boy had a mechanical knack, and he took on responsibility for vehicle maintenance. Soon he also learned the basics of radio communications and accounting.[1]

At the time, the Achakzai militia competed with the forces of other petty commanders. Some of these men were freelancers, some supported national politicians, but most fell under the banners of two local strongmen, Gul Agha Sherzai and Gulbuddin Hekmatyar. Sherzai was a former bandit who had been Governor of Kandahar, whereas Hekmatyar had been an Islamist client of the United States during the late anti-Soviet war.

This patchwork of leaders established checkpoints on Kandahar's roads, where their soldiers extracted humiliating tolls from the population. By the summer of 1994, rumors reported a number of unconscionable atrocities. One story claimed that a checkpoint boss had captured several young religious students and encouraged his followers to gang-rape them. Another held that two warlords had waged a tank duel over a prized dancing boy. Yet another, reputed to be 'more credible,' claimed that a commander had kidnapped two girls, shaved their heads, and used them as sex slaves at his militia camp.[2]

It was around this time that Mullah Omar began to preach about peace in Afghanistan. Omar's Hotak clan had ruled Kandahar long ago, before the dominant Durrani tribes pushed them to the margins. Omar dreamed that the Prophet had instructed him to purify the country. His mission began with a desire to stop the perversions of the petty checkpoint commanders. But soon, Pashtun communities across Afghanistan joined the movement as a way to put their own disenfranchised clans back on top of unwanted overlords.

During the Soviet war, Omar had served under the prominent smuggler Hajji Bashir Noorzai. Omar lost his right eye in battle, and he maintained a humble demeanor that appealed to rural Pashtun people. When Mullah Omar resolved that something had to be done about the feuding commanders in 1994, he approached his wealthy patron from the Soviet days. The Noorzai elder donated about $250,000 and two pickup trucks. The two men recruited other veterans of the jihad. Soon they gathered a few dozen sympathizers to meet at a white mosque in Sangisar.[3] A movement was born.

The Taliban gathered adherents as they traveled eastward and took control of checkpoints, from Kandahar City to Spin Boldak on the border. Here, in Raziq's home district, the group's connection to Pakistan altered the course of Mullah Omar's career. Donations from Kandahari elders had been generous, but they could not sustain a sweep through Afghanistan. The Taliban therefore turned to Spin Boldak, which featured a government armory as well as the opportunity to tax goods that crossed the border.

Taliban leaders denied having received initial coaching and support from Pakistan, for fear they would be dismissed as foreign puppets. But witnesses reported that the Pakistani Frontier Corps provided artillery support for the Taliban attack on Spin Boldak. A Deobandi political party based in Pakistan sent thousands of recruits from *madrasas* to the Taliban side. One observer reported watching the fighters carrying weapons 'still in their grease,' a reference to newly manufactured rifles coated in a waxy lubricant to prevent rust during transit. These were not the old, battle-scarred pieces from the Soviet war that elders had stockpiled in their compounds.[4] They had come from the factories of government sponsors.

Pakistani officials were in the midst of sending a thirty-truck aid convoy into civil-war-torn Afghanistan, with routes planned from Kandahar west to Iran and north to Central Asia. The goal of the aid mission was to test a new trade scheme that bypassed the heaviest fighting around Kabul. The Prime Minister of Pakistan met with Afghan strongmen from the north and west of the country to encourage their support of the convoy. The one remaining question comprised the group of Pashtun commanders around Kandahar.[5]

On 29 October 1994, Pakistani officials launched the test convoy across the border. Former soldiers drove a column of vehicles led by Colonel Imam, an ISI agent known for distributing funds to the Afghan resistance during the Soviet war.[6] Taliban leaders, who had seized the gates two weeks before, met and escorted the convoy across the border. After a few days of wrangling over the terms of the transit trade, the Pakistani agents convinced the student movement that their trade was 'good for Muslims.' The Taliban agreed to ride on ahead of the convoy, according to one witness, 'cutting the chains laid across the road by toll-hungry commanders.' The Taliban assault on the fragmented powers of the region benefited not only the Pakistani truck convoy, but Afghan businessmen as well. Even those who had no material interest enjoyed seeing the 'arrogant local commanders' laid low by the pious young fighters. A prominent tribal elder in Kandahar informed the Taliban that he would not stand in their way against the predatory commanders.[7] The path to power in the south was cleared.

On 1 November, the convoy rolled up to the edge of Kandahar Airfield, the territory of Raziq's uncle Mansour. Two other commanders joined him to confront the Taliban, as they sought to take their customary bribes.[8] On the third day of a tense stand-off, hundreds of Taliban fighters from the north ambushed the local commanders. Mansour and ten of his bodyguards became stuck on the sandy roads; a spray of gunfire caught the men at close range. Raziq fled in another truck that got away just before the trap closed. Locals heard young Raziq on the radio throughout the night, calling for his lost uncle. But it was too late. Taliban fighters hanged Mansour from the barrel of a tank outside the airfield and stuffed his mouth with money, a message that greed for toll-collection had been his downfall. Within a few days, and with fewer than fifty men killed on all sides, the Taliban overran Kandahar City.[9]

Though many Kandaharis expressed enthusiasm about the new movement that promised to unite the country under Islamic law, some had reservations about the Taliban 'There have been a few too many unnecessary hangings,' one supportive elder admitted in late November 1994.[10] Was he referring to the execution of Raziq's uncle as a gratuitous example of violence? Or was Mansour a fitting target for the Taliban's initial administration of justice? Whether or not Raziq's family deserved their harsh treatment at the hands of the Taliban, they had suffered a blow that demanded vengeance. Raziq's close familial connection to the early Taliban violence impressed his early foreign allies as a good reason for mutual trust. Partners seldom questioned his loyalty to the cause of fighting the Taliban as a result of his traumatic adolescence.

Though Abdul Raziq was a mere teenager in 1994, he was thrust into responsibility as the oldest surviving nephew. Raziq stepped forward to claim Mansour's body and give his kinsman a proper funeral. From that point, Raziq took on the care of his uncle's family and served as their representative in the ongoing civil war.[11] He went first to Kabul, to fight alongside the forces of strongman Abdul Rasul Sayyaf. Then he traveled to Herat for an abortive attempt to retake Kandahar from the Taliban, before reluctantly fleeing back across the border to Pakistan. In Chaman, Raziq began to work in auto shops. Sometimes he fixed engines, sometimes he coordinated with his brother, located in Dubai, to move cars and parts around the region. He also volunteered his services to fellow tribesman Mahmood Khan Achakzai, a Pakistani politician whose party led Pashtun resistance against the Punjab-dominated central government in Islamabad.[12] During these formative years, Raziq gained a political awareness of Pashtuns as victims of the Pakistani state. So despite the Pashtun origins of the Taliban in Kandahar, Raziq continued to criticize the student movement as slaves to Punjabi government masters.

PART II

THE RISE OF PARTNERSHIP

But the treaties are not dissolved with those Pagans with whom ye have entered into alliance, and who have not subsequently failed you in aught, nor aided any one against you. So fulfill your engagements with them to the end of their term: for Allah loveth the righteous.

Quran, Sura 9, verse 4

Chapter 4

MILITIAS (2001–5)

Al Qaeda's attacks on the United States offered Raziq new opportunities. The vengeance that the Americans promised opened pathways for ambitious young Pashtun men of the region. Just a few months earlier, Raziq had had few prospects. Throughout his early twenties he struggled to establish himself as a car dealer. But in the last months of 2001, American intelligence agents began to meet with notables among the Afghan refugee communities in Pakistan, as they sought to recruit militias to help them liberate Kandahar from the Taliban.

US agents turned to Gul Agha Sherzai, son of a prominent *mujahidin* commander and former Governor of Kandahar during the civil war of the early 1990s.[1] Sherzai in turn recruited Achakzai militiamen to reoccupy their home district. In mid-November, American B-52 and B-1 bombers destroyed fortified positions along Highway 4 from Kandahar City to the Pakistan border. The targets included Mullah Omar's residence, perched on a hilltop north-west of the city center, later known to the Americans as 'Camp Gecko' for the lizards that abounded there.[2] One US Special Forces team parachuted into Afghanistan north of Kandahar City, where operators linked up with Hamid Karzai and helped him to rally local people against the faltering Taliban regime. Another team infiltrated across the border, north-east of the main highway. Mullah Omar escaped into Pakistan, while two dozen guards died in the bombing of his headquarters. Taliban fighters who had been entrenched at the frontier abandoned their posts.

After the dust settled, militia commanders entered Spin Boldak from the Afghan side in the last days of November 2001. Sherzai then turned his forces north toward Kandahar City, which fell without resistance in the first week of December. Sherzai raced to occupy his former residence at the Governor's palace. Thanks to his close relationships with the Americans, and despite the objections of Karzai, he regained his gubernatorial position for the first years of post-Taliban reconstruction.[3]

The new Afghan government formed in Bonn, Germany and transplanted to Kabul in 2002 inherited the victorious militias. The republican regime under Hamid Karzai attempted to demobilize some of these fighters, to whom they owed the Taliban's overthrow, and to fit those who remained armed into a new infrastructure for security forces. As the republican government built up its National Army (ANA) and Police (ANP) organizations, smaller institutions such as the Border Police (ABP) and the Highway Police (AHP) absorbed some of the militia units that tribal smugglers in the borderlands had raised for the initial invasion.

Raziq became one of the most active junior militia leaders in the region. He had long known about the Tarnak Farms location where Osama bin Laden established an Al Qaeda headquarters and training camp. An early operation alongside his Uncle Mansour had captured two Taliban fighters there, prior to their assistance to the Pakistani convoy late in 1994 that launched the religious students as a regional movement.[4] So Raziq was familiar with the terrain, and he served as a guide to US officials who wanted to know where the foreign fighters were in Kandahar. The area contained a grab bag of armed forces: Al Qaeda's 055 Brigade, independent Arab and Chechen mercenaries, and Special Forces officers from Pakistan and Iran. Raziq's supporters claimed that his fame originated from this time, when he made a name for himself by capturing 'many Arabs,' foreign commanders who fought for bin Laden.[5]

Sarah Chayes, former NPR reporter and founder of an Afghan women-led cooperative, rejected the notion that Raziq was promoted on his merits. To her, the military operations to which he contributed seemed to be 'fig leaf,' cover for ulterior motives among the militia commanders. Whatever limited fighting took place seemed more like gangs taking out their tribal opposition than the targeting of Al Qaeda terrorists and their Taliban hosts in government.[6]

The first commander of the Border Police was Fayda Mohammad, an Achakzai elder who promoted Raziq from ordinary soldier to lieutenant early in 2002. But this initial leader stepped down from his role after just a few months. Another Achakzai elder stepped into the lead role, but he died in an accident the following year.[7]

It is unclear how Raziq emerged at the head of the new organization, between 2003 and 2005, in the aftermath of its early leadership shake-up. By the latter date Raziq was chief of staff for the entire Border Police brigade in Kandahar, a force of several thousand men. There are three basic narratives that account for his rise, which taken together help to explain the complicated nature of power in Afghanistan. These narratives fall into three categories: tribal promotion, self-generated following, and foreign aid.

Journalist Matthieu Aikins offered the earliest version of the 'tribal promotion' explanation for Raziq's rise to power. In this explanation, leadership within the Achazkai tribe sought someone to replace Fayda Mohammad, and they settled on Raziq as a good candidate. The young man was not only bright and brave. His inexperience made elders believe they could manipulate him from behind the scenes.[8] The same logic appeared in stories about the legendary crowning of Ahmad Shah Durrani during the eighteenth-century succession that established a Pashtun empire in Kandahar.

Other versions of tribal logic may better explain Raziq's promotion. The Achakzai leaders of Raziq's own tribe often split on political matters. Instead, it was more likely that a member of a more prestigious Pashtun family, Sherzai or Karzai for example, selected Raziq as a military servant to his more established clan. The key Pashtun patron in Raziq's eventual promotion over the region's many petty commanders may have been Asadullah Khalid, who was appointed Governor of Kandahar in 2005. Raziq and Khalid had several points of contact. They had both fought for anti-Taliban militias raised by the Kabul-based commander Sayyaf in the 1990s. Further rumors connected the two men as business partners in the smuggling and drug protection rackets that were rampant in the southern borderlands.[9]

Many of Raziq's supporters describe a different pathway to power. Instead of appointment from above by a powerful patron on a certain occasion, Raziq seemed to generate followers on his own over time. One Afghan observer, a contractor from Kandahar City, described Raziq's rise this way: when the US first took on the Taliban in late 2001, 'he was just a police commander, only for five people. He has only one small station. Then after that, he became, day by day, month by month, year by year, a big man.'[10] Over the course of years, Raziq helped the Americans to locate Al Qaeda and Taliban targets. He was generous in sharing the material benefits of that relationship. His primary means of advancement was accumulation of followers and prestige.[11] Raziq's acquisition of a powerful sponsor had been the result of his independent base of power, rather than the cause of his rise.

By this logic, Raziq cultivated compound commanders as an intentional plan to gain power. While he could have attempted to build up large headquarters and centralize his operations, instead he developed a kind of franchise system. He set his supporters up in small compounds, organized in units of just a few border guards. Each commander now had a sufficient title to give him a sense of status within the Border Police organization, for which Raziq was more a figurehead than an operational leader. According to one of Raziq's early mentors, each of the compound leaders could now 'go home and tell their families: I am a compound commander in the ABP, instead of just a soldier . . . Now people think they're a big guy.'[12] Raziq's acceptance of decentralized power allowed him to gain loyal followers.

Some of Raziq's critics held that his promotion resulted less from the dynamics of Afghan patronage and clientship and more from foreign sponsors. It was the early access to external sources of money and equipment, these critics argued, that allowed Raziq to rise in status.[13] But Raziq could not have made inroads with the foreigners without the personal attributes he displayed, which won him the acquiescence of local tribal elites.

In fact, Raziq's power came from his ability to navigate between these worlds, to exchange information and resources from one domain to another.[14] His contacts with Pashtun politicians allowed him insights that CIA agents found valuable. His experience as a smuggler and junior militia leader allowed him to serve as the eyes and ears of Special Operations teams as they conducted patrols and raids. The funds that Americans gave him allowed him to pay and equip a growing network of men seeking to become militia leaders. This ability to serve as a mechanism for foreign funding only raised his profile in the eyes of Afghan tribal leaders, some of whom already respected Raziq for his connection to the former Achakzai authority, his martyred uncle Mansour. These distinct sources of authority reinforced each other. The more Raziq demonstrated his insight into tribal politics, the more foreign money and contacts arrived at his doorstep. The more access Raziq acquired to CIA money, Special Forces mentors, and Blackwater training, the more impressed Afghan tribal leaders became. At times, both sides might have exaggerated the authority that Raziq held in his other domains.

Raziq's overlapping authority, which encompassed both informal and formal realms, presented his foreign partners with a fundamental problem. Many Westerners believed Raziq capable of controlling the Pashtun militias that he paid and equipped, much like the leaders of NATO units. They looked in vain for his official position on an organizational 'block-line chart.'[15] He was not a Border Police zone commander, though some referred to him as 'chief' or 'director' of the zone that included Spin Boldak district. Nor was Raziq one of the battalion (*kandak*) commanders.[16] He was more of a figurehead than an administrative leader for the police and militias of the region. Even within the Achakzai tribe, Raziq was only popular among 200 families of his own clan. Raziq could not go into the territory of other powerful tribes and give orders to their militia leaders. Instead, he could ask for support and coordinate resources for combined action.

Raziq served as a liaison and a source of inspiration. He proved willing to put himself in harm's way in early military operations, and these displays of bravery earned him the support of many other militiamen throughout the region. Other commanders might be willing to provide him with information or rally to his side during offensives, but they did not fall under Raziq's day-to-day operational control. This confusion about authority emerged as Raziq and his Border Police became significant players among the constellation of Afghan security forces. Their first tests came in 2005, as the Taliban re-emerged from their sanctuaries.

Chapter 5

WILD WEST (2005–6)

By the summer of 2005, it became clear that the Taliban was back on the march in Kandahar. For the past two years, the movement had gone underground in Pakistan to recruit its next class of student-fighters. This new generation began to confront Lieutenant Colonel Bertrand Ges and his artillery battalion, Task Force Gun Devils, as the unit arrived in Raziq's home province.

Ges leaned on experiences accumulated during his previous deployment to Iraq, where he had been impressed with the 'lethality' of the insurgents. He explained, 'I saw some of the first tanks getting blown up in Iraq. It really caught my attention. But I can honestly say we hardly ever did *adjust fire* missions. It was always *fire for effect*.' The policy to fire artillery 'for effect' was a departure from US Army doctrine, which counseled firing one round first, rather than many, given that firing data often needs an adjustment before explosive rounds can be sent with accuracy and precision. The commander admitted that some of his peers accused him of 'recon by fire,' a disavowed Vietnam-era practice of 'harassment and interdiction' missions, in which unobserved rounds were flung into the jungle on suspected enemy locations.[1] In Afghanistan, Ges acknowledged there were risks to the fire-for-effect approach, but he accepted them in the interest of presenting an aggressive posture to the growing insurgency.

Ges's mindset required justification during the supposed reconstruction mission that Afghanistan had become, after the ouster of the Taliban in 2002 and the establishment of a new government. The Bush administration had already declared 'Mission Accomplished,' not only in Baghdad but at Bagram as well. Ges recalled discussions at his unit's train-up in Germany prior to the deployment: 'We just had an election, the war's over, success. We're moving out. Somebody said the phrase, "We're going to be giving out popsicles and ice cream sandwiches at the airport."' But when the group of incoming commanders broke down into groups by region, the outgoing division commander pulled Ges aside. Units on their way to Kandahar Province should expect a fight. It was, Ges recalled, 'a 180 from what we had heard before.' Early in the deployment, the violence predicted by intelligence reports began to manifest.

Ges recalled a meeting with an Alokozai tribal leader. After the meeting, one of the vehicles in his convoy hit an improvised explosive device (IED). The elder was a close confidant of the Karzai brothers, but he was also a former Taliban commander. His sisters had married his former comrades who fought for the insurgency. It was a perfect illustration of the gray area that Kandahar had become, some four years after the initial American intervention. In the aftermath of the IED blast, Ges found himself in the face of a difficult decision on engaging potential targets.

The US commander recalled a briefing that advised the Taliban's new techniques in Kandahar were complex attacks. These tactics began with an explosion and were followed by a motorcycle team, either to strafe the target with small arms and grenades, or to blow themselves up in what became known as martyr operations. As Ges and his men stood around the disabled Humvee, 'All of a sudden, just like textbook, this motorcycle came around. And I said, engage. And I remember somebody shot a warning shot. I said, no, shoot to kill. And we shot at the motorcycle, and we killed one person.' The casualty wore the uniform of the Kandahar Prison Guards. Whether he was actually employed by the prison or had only acquired a uniform was unclear. He also had wire-cutters and Pakistani currency, evidence he was employed by an IED cell.[2] It appeared that the snap decision for lethality had been warranted. A Canadian augmentee to Ges's battalion recalled the incident as setting the tone for the deployment. 'This wasn't Bosnia,' he'd thought to himself. Another staff officer confirmed, 'Everybody here speaks gun.'[3] It was a far cry from passing out ice cream at the airport.

Productive conversation often seemed impossible, given the conditions that troops confronted on the ground. In one incident, Ges's soldiers arrested a former District Governor who had 'black tar [heroin], hash, and weapons' in his offices, and who was believed to have coordinated an attack against coalition forces. However, the man also happened to be a close friend of Hamid Karzai. The President leaned on the Governor of Kandahar, who leaned in turn on Ges to set things right. 'I had to go back there, had to apologize to him in Kabul, give him condolence funds. It was just crazy,' Ges recalled. The drug bust gone wrong made the Gun Devils skeptical about their ability to work with hosts in the Afghan government. Though Ges repeatedly told his command that 'the Afghan people are not the enemy,' the soldiers found it difficult to be enthusiastic about partnership given ongoing events.[4]

Across Afghanistan the dilemma became widespread, as priorities shifted between objectives to eliminate insurgent fighters, train Afghan forces, and aid the development of Afghan governance and economy. Since the Cold War era, cooperation with indigenous military forces had been the provenance of the Special Forces, which referred to the mission as 'foreign internal defense' (FID). The new counter-insurgency manual, still in the drafting process in 2005, stipulated that the 'partnering' approach was distinct from the 'light footprint' approach of Special Forces. The latter involved a small cadre embedded within the local organization. Partnership, on the other hand, joined two large units in a 'union . . . designed to end as HN [host nation] forces gain the capability and capacity to stand alone.' The partners were thus supposed to act together, but not on an equal basis. Afghan units were to learn by operating alongside their more competent allies. The manual further stipulated that partnership could take place in different contexts. 'Combined action' was a true merger of forces, but was only 'appropriate in environments where insurgents lack resources and freedom of maneuver.' In areas where US agents expected combat, the manual instead counseled 'localized security activities,' the enabling of an indigenous force from afar with intelligence, supplies, and guidance rather than operations undertaken together.[5]

One US officer from outside the unit recalled that the Gun Devils approached partnership with impatience. It seemed as if meeting with locals was a 'nuisance' that interrupted more important activities. The officer explained, 'They'd pull in all loaded for bear,' and demand that the villagers take them to their chief. When a suitable elder came forward, the Americans would say, 'We're here in the area, and if you have any information, we'd appreciate it. We're here to help you out, just let us know.' After this curt introduction, the Gun Devil officer would 'turn around, get in his vehicle and drive off,' in a rush to plan the next kinetic operation.[6] The perfunctory approach toward potential allies during the early years in Kandahar contrasted with the emphasis US officers placed on relationships during the surge.

In 2005, partnership was a shoestring affair. The Gun Devils worked for the most part with Afghan National Police (ANP). Some Army (ANA) companies had been organized at Kandahar Airfield, but they were in the early stages of training. Still, some Americans believed it was better to bring along untested army units, comprised of Hazara and Tajik men from the north, rather than the more established police units formed of local Pashtun men. The better-connected locals had more opportunities for graft and betrayal.[7]

In addition to the Afghans, the Gun Devils cooperated with a Romanian infantry company, a French Special Forces group, and the incoming Canadian Provisional Reconstruction Team. The Romanians struggled early on. They had a rigid 'Soviet-style' organizational culture, whereby any changes to an operation, however minor, had to be passed up the chain of command before a subordinate leader could divert from the initial plan. Furthermore, their radios were not compatible with those of the Americans, and the US was not allowed to share its communications security codes. As a workaround, a US soldier carrying a radio had to ride in the Romanian vehicles, old Soviet-era BMPs that stank of fuel. The battalion commander had some difficulty communicating with the French, whose English skills were 'very bad,' though better than Ges's French. The Canadians were easier to talk to, but they had strict national caveats on their use of force.[8]

Taunting the Taliban

To pile onto the initial struggles, a darker event made some locals wary of their new partners in Kandahar. The incident occurred on 1 October in Gumbad, about 100km north of Kandahar City. Ges had planned another 'hammer and anvil' operation, in which his infantry companies would push the Taliban into the positions occupied by a fellow battalion from the 173rd Airborne to the north-east. But Ges ran into contact on his way north and decided to concentrate on the situation developing in his 'own backyard.' One company drove up the Gumbad valley, in order to force Taliban fighters east onto the road. There, instead of a high-speed avenue of escape, the fleeing insurgents ran into two other companies that had dropped from helicopters onto fighting positions within view of the highway. Two Taliban soldiers were killed, but the operation also resulted in the deaths of two Americans, including an experienced squad leader.[9]

Now a new question emerged: what to do with the corpses of the Taliban soldiers? The early autumn day in Kandahar was hot. As temperatures climbed and the bodies began to bloat, US officers ordered the remains to be burned. Then an attached psychological operations team began to use the battlefield cremation as an opportunity for counter-intelligence. Ges had counseled his PsyOps to be 'aggressive' in their messaging, but to refrain from insults. Nevertheless, an Australian journalist embedded with the unit recorded the team's broadcast: 'You allowed your fighters to be laid down facing west [i.e. toward Mecca] and burned. You are too scared to come down and retrieve the bodies. This just proves you are the lady boys we always believed you to be.'[10] Some Americans believed that this harsh talk would demoralize the Taliban, but others found such messages to be counter-productive. The religious and gendered insults likely stoked anti-American sentiment among the local population.

The body-burning incident was almost certainly on Lieutenant General David Barno's mind as he gave a post-tour interview. Barno had been the first theater commander to propose a holistic counter-insurgency strategy rather than narrow anti-terrorism. He recalled, 'I hammered on my PAO [public affairs office] folks, not infrequently, about mouthing platitudes that sounded relatively sophomoric about the "cowardly Taliban" and things that I thought were unnecessarily offensive culturally to these folks.'[11] The advice was in line with broader counsel to avoid cultural gaffes. Americans were not supposed to humiliate the enemy, though some believed the macho culture of Pashtun men offered a potential target for psychological operations. On the other hand, the burning of bodies and the 'lady boy' taunts might have pushed those neutral Afghans still on the fence to take the side of the Taliban as victims of intercultural abuse.

An investigation by Ges's division commander decided that the soldiers had burned the bodies for 'hygiene reasons' rather than as an intentional taunt. Two NCOs and two junior officers received administrative punishments for their insensitivity. But the army refrained from more serious punishments. Ges had to write a formal report that justified his remaining at his billet, which his command duly accepted.[12]

For the rest of their deployment, Gun Devil soldiers persisted with what they knew best: conventional operations that integrated infantry and fire support. One National Guard trainer of the Afghan Army's 205th Corps described operations like this: 'they would send out one company to try to stir up some contact and then they would send out the other two or three infantry companies to set up blocking positions or to exploit any kind of intelligence they were able to gather. The artillery battery would set out in a supporting position.'[13] The formula proved successful in terms of producing reports of enemy fighters killed, weapons captured, chatter on Taliban communications, and so on – the makings of a successful combat deployment.

By the middle of the year abroad, attacks became more frequent but less intense. The enemy shifted tactics around October 2005. Suicide bombings, IEDs, and distant rocket fire replaced the complex, direct-fire ambushes. Instead of fighting the coalition's vehicles in the valleys from perches high above, the insurgency's pattern became: 'attack, break contact.' Ges estimated that no more than twenty-five enemy fighters occupied his thousand-plus soldier task force in this desultory manner.

Wild West

As the Gun Devils persevered through a busy deployment north of Kandahar City, Colonel Raziq benefited from the conventional unit's salutary neglect of the borderlands to the east. His relationship with the coalition's Special Forces grew over the next year, as he worked alongside French Task Force Ares, a parachutist unit known as the 'scorpions' of Spin Boldak. Ges recalled hearing reports from the French about a 'very charismatic young person' who was leading the Border Police on ferocious raids against Taliban insurgents. But Ges had no direct interactions with the budding star. At this point, Raziq partnered with CIA agents and Special Forces, who paid him to rent vehicles and land for their compounds. US government agents, to give Raziq a tactical edge over the Taliban, helped to set up a Blackwater training facility at his compound.

The following summer, the French soldiers of TF Ares provided support to Raziq in Maroof District, 100km from the border crossing that was his nominal purview. The Border Policemen in the northern hills found themselves surrounded by fifty Taliban fighters, so the French embedded with them provided airstrikes by two Mirage jets. The damage to the Taliban was unknown, but French ordnance allowed Raziq to escape from the trap and live to fight another day.[14]

Some chaos in Kandahar was good for the Karzai government. More threats meant more foreign funding. The more patronage opportunities the better, so the Karzai regime often rotated Governors or promoted them to Kabul-based ministerial positions in order to make way for new clients. Asadullah Khalid, former Governor of Ghazni, was appointed Governor of Kandahar in 2005. Khalid proved more amenable than his predecessor to the President's brother, Ahmed Wali Karzai (AWK), and his land-grabbing schemes. The family network seized government properties and sold them to developers, who were flush with foreign contract dollars. So while a bit of chaos encouraged military aid, too much of it threatened to halt real estate development and fold the regime like a house of cards.

In January 2006, Governor Khalid met with notables from across the province. During the session, AWK described the security situation in Kandahar as 'out of control,' like the 'Wild West.' He added that he had recently joked with his brother, 'We might as well give it to the Pakistanis if we are not going to exercise any control over that area.'[15] In this environment, Raziq became an important tool for the Afghan government: an aggressive and loyal fighter, who worked well with foreigners, to boot. Just two months after this meeting, however, allegations of massacre threatened to derail Raziq's career, at the outset of a transition from American to Canadian commands.

Chapter 6

MASSACRE (2006)

Raziq grew up without radio or television to supply his entertainment. The tales he knew had been passed down by spoken word through the generations. The Soviets had called their opponents ghosts (*dukhi*), because they communicated by mysterious night letters, and they seemed to vanish when chased.[1] When the Americans arrived they began to tell ghost stories, too. An army patrol that went missing in 2002 was rumored to have fallen victim to a Giant of Kandahar, thirteen feet tall, with flowing red hair, six fingers on each hand, and two rows of teeth.[2] Older stories explained how travelers ended up dead in the deserts. The 'Spirit of the Waste' was a ghost that took on the appearance of an oasis. Travelers who approached the watery illusion tumbled into the Spirit's gaping jaws, which tore them to pieces.[3]

In Afghanistan, storytellers do not begin with the phrase 'Once upon a time.' Instead, they start with, 'It was and it wasn't' (*Buud, na buud*).[4] Perhaps Raziq's critics had only created some new tall tales. The dead themselves did not make trouble for the young commander. But the stories people told about the killings of 21 March 2006 would haunt him for the rest of his career. Sixteen bodies lay lifeless on the Pakistani border. The most prominent of them was Mullah Shin Noorzai. These facts everyone could agree on. But from there, the stories diverged.

Raziq claimed, in the straightforward manner of a policeman, that Mullah Shin and other members of the group had previously been arrested, on both sides of the border. They were criminals who had attempted to enter Afghanistan with illegal intent. They had been stopped after a two-hour firefight with a unit of the Border Police.

Others gave more elaborate accounts. Pakistani authorities, for example, often used such events to cast aspersions on their Afghan neighbors. A government spokesman in Chaman claimed the murdered men had been innocent refugees, on their way to a holiday celebration at Mazar-i Sharif in northern Afghanistan.[5] The Pakistanis would say anything to make Raziq look bad.

The most sensational of the accusations came from Raziq's fellow Achakzai tribesman, Mohammad Naeem Lalai. Another militia commander under the patronage of Gul Agha Sherzai, Lalai came from a rival clan within Raziq's tribe and he likely felt entitled to more of a share in the organization's power and profits than he had gotten thus far.[6] Now, Lalai was telling anyone who would listen about Mullah Shin's abrupt end, perhaps as a means of taking down his more successful colleague.

Lalai claimed to have played a central role in an episode of trickery and revenge. He had run into Mullah Shin's group of travelers in Kabul and convinced the men to join him for dinner before they pushed north for their celebration. After dinner, Lalai persuaded the group to visit another house nearby for music, to rest before they took up the road again. As the party settled into the festive atmosphere, he allegedly drugged the men's drinks, gagged them, tied their hands, and drove them in the undercarriage of a bus some 600km from Kabul to Kandahar (a full day's journey under the best of conditions). Back at the border crossing, Lalai claimed, he delivered the captives to Raziq, who wanted to execute the leader of the group. Raziq believed that Mullah Shin had killed his brother, Bacha, two years before.

About 10km outside Spin Boldak city lies Mullah Shin's family homestead, in the Milk and Water (*Shir Obi*) village. At the outskirts of the village, close to the border with Pakistan, a Border Police truck pulled up to a dry riverbed, and men in blue uniforms unloaded their human cargo. The policemen aimed automatic weapons a few feet from the mass of men and fired.[7] Mullah Shin's network had been competition for the smuggling rackets of the region. But Raziq claimed the men worked as logistical agents for the Taliban, as well. Though the history of tribal feuds created suspicion about the motive for the killings, the victims were not all from the Noorzai tribe. The group traveling with Mullah Shin included men from the Ghilzai branch and from Raziq's own Achakzai tribe. So had the killings been a matter of honor taken to extremes, the elimination of business rivals, or a crackdown on Taliban logistics?

There were others besides Raziq who wanted Mullah Shin dead. The Noorzai leader's cult of personality had grown over the past years. Mullah Shin's tribesmen saw him as an uncompromising and valiant fighter. He had been imprisoned and tortured at the infamous Maach facility in Pakistan. Rather than give up his compatriots to escape confinement, Mullah Shin organized a prison break and returned to defiant smuggling operations. As he picked his way between safe houses on both sides of the border, he dispersed the patronage of his lucrative schemes to Noorzai villages disenfranchised by the dominant family networks. Mullah Shin had presented an attractive target to many in Kandahar.

Though Raziq certainly wanted to kill the man, there was no smoking-gun evidence to suggest that he had given such an order. Perhaps Lalai sought to shield a more powerful politician and offer up Raziq as a scapegoat. In any event, Lalai's version of events, the cross-country overnight convoy, stretched credulity.[8] The incident, rather than confirm Raziq's guilt, showed how blurred the lines had become between smuggling militias, Border Police units, and their shared tribal patrons.

Kandahar Governor Asadullah Khalid placed Raziq on administrative leave while his office investigated the matter. Was this the first step to being fired? Raziq knew the Governor's deputy was a fellow Noorzai tribesman of the deceased Mullah Shin. This man might have persuaded his boss that the Border Police had engaged not in anti-Taliban violence, but cold-blooded tribal vengeance.[9]

In the midst of the Taliban offensives west of the city, Raziq soon returned from leave, thanks to the support of his Governor and President Karzai. But those outside of their power structures, civilians sent to advise the Afghan government, feared that a focus on security had created a 'culture of impunity' among Afghan commanders.[10] Michael Semple, a Pashto-speaking EU adviser, read the report that the Governor's office sent to Kabul. Semple recalled the case as 'open and shut' against Raziq. 'No reasonable person' could doubt that the killings were 'summary executions carried out by the Border Police.' Nevertheless, Hamid Karzai commented in a cryptic manner that Abdul Raziq was a 'special case,' and he remained an important leader of security forces in Spin Boldak.[11] Some observers saw the Afghan President's demurral as a sign that he condoned corrupt tribal conflict. Others suspected Karzai agreed that Mullah Shin represented a legitimate target; these opinions reinforced the theory that the late smuggler had been an ISI agent. Raziq believed the Pakistani connection. When he returned to duty after the investigation he began to cultivate refugees from Pakistan's aggrieved Baluch minority who arrived in his home district. These dissident migrants provided new means for Raziq to strike back against his enemies across the frontier to the east.

The incident demonstrated the complexity of tribal politics and the ambiguity of identity in the region. It was rival Achakzai militia commander Lalai who led the accusations, who incriminated himself in the effort to bring down Raziq, and who afterward requested a transfer to another organization, in order to investigate Raziq for corruption.[12] For those who subscribed to the Pashtun honor code, the killing of Mullah Shin had either been righteous revenge for Raziq's brother, or a betrayal of hospitality on the part of Lalai and his tribal patrons. The killing of all Mullah Shin's companions was certainly overzealous, even for the most traditional adherents to the honor code. But in a time of war, even an honest police force could mistake such a group of alleged holiday-travelers, all men of military age, for a supply run on behalf of the insurgency. Over the next two years, ambiguous incidents continued to trouble Canadian soldiers, replacements for the Americans who had shifted their collective attention to Iraq.

Chapter 7

CANADIANS IN KANDAHAR (2006–9)

Lieutenant Colonel Ges recalled the media's interest in the transition from American to Canadian forces in his area of operations. Late in the deployment, a Canadian news station sent a journalist to speak with him. The interview was meant to warn the public about the often-hidden violence ongoing in Kandahar, under the radar of world attention then fixed on Iraq. The reporter stretched her microphone toward the American officer and asked, 'Is the Canadian Army ready?'

Ges replied, 'The transition from the US forces to the Canadian forces is nothing more than a hockey line change. The same team, pushing the same puck, towards the same goal.'[1] The reporter smiled and put her mic down. Sometimes international partnership lent itself to camaraderie. If only operations could match the neatness of press release soundbites.

Canadians had many reasons to participate in the Global War on Terror, unlike Americans focused on revenge after 9/11. Canada had not been directly attacked, but there was some genuine solidarity with the American-led fight against international terrorism. In geopolitical terms, the Canadians sought to bolster their alliance credentials and abided by the NATO invocation of mutual-defense Article 5. Furthermore, Canadian military officials lobbied for the opportunity to advance their careers, which had stalled in the absence of an overseas conflict.

But perhaps the most important push for the Canadians into Afghanistan came from a desire to restore their reputation, which had been damaged by scandals of the early 1990s. In Somalia, Canadian soldiers shot a civilian in the back on suspicion of stealing from the military base. Days later, two soldiers beat another suspected thief to death upon finding him, a sixteen-year-old boy, hidden in a portable toilet. An official inquiry discovered that the Somali victim

31

had been beaten in a sadistic manner, sodomized with a broomstick, and burned on his penis. Media reports found the command of the Airborne Regiment had made racist comments to the formation, and the unit was promptly disbanded. The military remained in the spotlight through the mid-1990s due to a spate of sexual assaults within the force. Amid these atrocities, and with the end of the Soviet threat, Canada cut its military budget by a quarter.[2]

In the first decade of the new millennium, Afghanistan offered a chance at redemption. As such, the Canadian government was keen to maintain oversight and strict regulations on their armed forces. They were wary of the potential issues that could result from partnership with Afghan 'warlords.' Canadian sensitivity to abuse of civilians caused some friction with Governor Khalid, whose handling of Raziq and the sixteen massacre victims was one incident among many that worked against Canadian plans to institute good governance.

The issue of selecting proper allies came to the forefront as the Canadians stepped up their role from policing Kabul to taking over an entire Provincial Reconstruction Team (PRT) in Kandahar. Prime Minister Stephen Harper's Conservative administration was eager to consolidate military forces and show the world what they could accomplish on their own slice of Afghan territory.[3] The NATO countries backfilled for the United States, in order to free up more units for the American surge in Iraq. As the Canadians flowed southward, the Italians went west to Herat, the Germans took Mazar-i Sharif, and the British occupied Helmand. The Dutch and Australians came to share tiny Uruzgan Province, on Kandahar's northern border.

To defend its political unit, Canada sent one of its most cerebral field grade officers, Lieutenant Colonel Ian Hope, to lead a battalion-sized battle group. Hope was well versed in the American way of war. He was a graduate of the US Command and General Staff College, and from there, shortly after 9/11, he had worked for the US European command. On his first deployment to Afghanistan, he was seconded to finance minister Ashraf Ghani, a former Johns Hopkins professor who later became the Afghan republic's second and last President.

The unit under Hope, about 1,000 men strong, was taking over from a combined force twice that size. In addition to the American Gun Devils, there had been three Special Forces organizations, from France, the Netherlands, and the United States, now all on their way out of the country. The Canadians named their battle group Task Force Orion, in honor of the legendary hunter. But the unit was stretched too thin to stalk prey. Instead, the men of TF Orion spent 2006 reacting to events and putting out fires. Hope had planned to send one of his three infantry companies to the border at Spin Boldak, to take over from the French SF unit. But the Canadians were unable to spend much time there, given the insurgent offensive underway to the west of Kandahar City.[4]

The Taliban shifted strategies after their rapid flight from Afghanistan at the end of 2001. The regime's leadership spent most of the next three years hiding in safe houses in Pakistan and recruiting their next class of fighters. A 'turning point' year arrived in 2005, when the government of Pakistan eased restrictions on the group's funding, and donations from Arab states began to pour in.[5] When the Taliban infiltrated back into Afghanistan, they avoided the main gate at Spin Boldak guarded by Raziq and his policemen. One of the alternate routes of entry was through the Registan desert. Insurgents could skirt around Spin Boldak district to the south in Shorabak and then head west across the sand until they reached the Arghandab River Valley, which provided a 'green zone' of cover and concealment in its lush orchards and vineyards. From these western hideouts, they could launch attacks toward Kandahar City.

There were other paths into the country to the north of Spin Boldak. Coalition officers referred to these Taliban routes of ingress as 'rat trails.' They took comfort that Raziq at least made it more difficult to get into the country by these rugged means than on the newly-paved highway that led directly from the border to Kandahar City.[6]

The Taliban build-up in Kandahar put Western governments in a bind. NATO leaders had sold their publics on the narrative that post-2003 Afghanistan required only 'stability operations,' the mild military-led reconstructions that had been the norm through the late 1990s in the Balkans and Latin America.

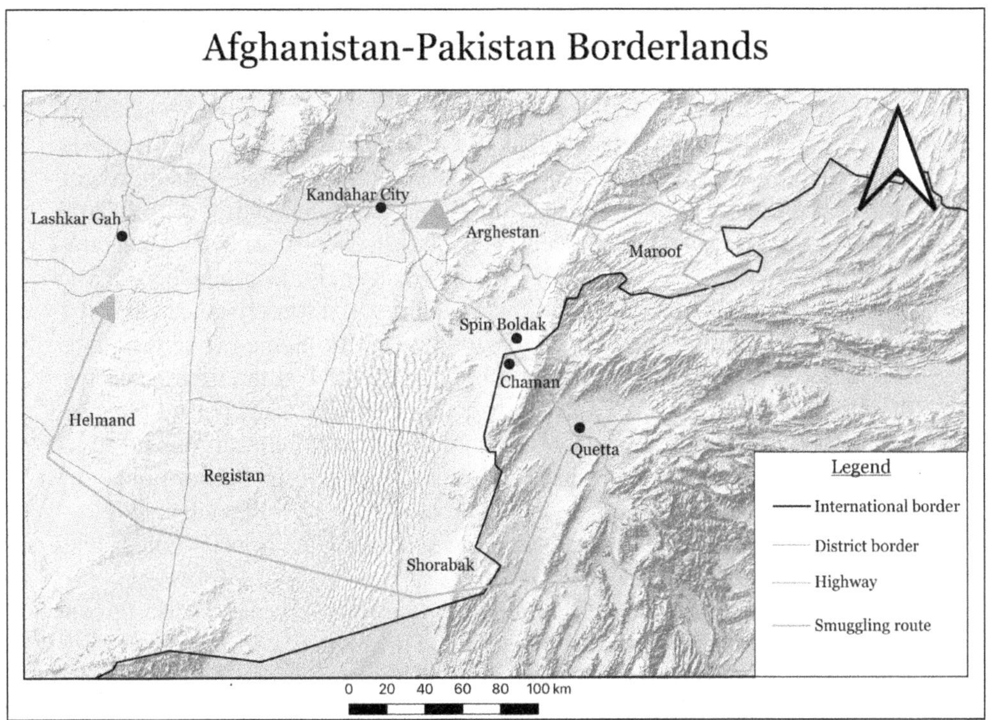

Hope recalled that the more comprehensive 'counter-insurgency' term was, 'as the Germans say, *verboten*,' an unwelcome label in 2005 among politicians and military leaders. The expansive designation threatened to inflate the war beyond the desires of most officials in the NATO alliance. When Hope arrived for pre-deployment visits in preparation to take over from Ges in August and October, he soon learned that existing measures could not solve Kandahar's security problems. He began to lobby for more assets, loosened rules of engagement, and a more offensive mindset for operations, rather than the presence patrols typical of stability operations.[7]

TF Orion became a restless unit, always on the move. The battle group was already undersized for Kandahar Province, but it had to extend further to support British positions in neighboring Helmand. Early in the deployment, the Canadians headed west to help set up Camp Bastion. They received follow-on orders back to Helmand to help the US Drug Enforcement Agency (DEA) eradicate opium crops. The battle group had no installation infrastructure besides one 'platoon house' that their American predecessors had built north of Kandahar City. Instead, the Canucks lived in their trucks, Light Armored Vehicles (LAV), which were smaller, less boxy versions of the US Strykers. Veterans of the battle group were fond of the LAV for its 25mm cannon and its protective armor. The vehicle was relatively immune to the early versions of IEDs that dotted the Kandahar landscape. The Taliban referred to the smoke-belching, machine-gun toting vehicle as 'the monster' (*bala*).[8] Other modes of transport proved to be more vulnerable.

At the moment when Hope and his unit deployed into Kandahar Province, the new Canadian PRT suffered a tragedy. Glyn Berry, the team's political leader, was a seasoned diplomat in his late fifties. He was riding in a Mercedes G-wagon on the way back to base from a meeting at Kandahar Airfield, where he had been coordinating the influx of Canadian troops with local officials. Suddenly, a silver Toyota Town Ace pulled up alongside Berry's car and detonated its load of explosives. Berry and two other civilians died in the blast. The next day, an IED-carrying motorbike exploded as it was driven into a crowd assembled to watch a wrestling match at Spin Boldak. Some two dozen more civilians perished. One source who worked at the PRT at the time suspected the second suicide attacker's target had been Abdul Raziq, but he escaped unharmed.[9] Just four years since his appointment to a junior leadership position in the Achakzai militia, Raziq had become a Colonel of the Border Police. In this time, he had built a reputation as one of the most prolific adversaries of the Taliban, through a series of operations with coalition Special Forces and intelligence-sharing with US CIA agents.

The assassination of Canadian diplomat Glyn Berry served as a wake-up call for his government in Ottawa, which now had to accept that its personnel were in for more of a fight than anticipated. The PRT shut down for two months as all Canadian civilians pulled back from Kandahar to the ISAF bubble of security in Kabul. American intelligence had estimated Taliban strength in Kandahar Province at only 200 regular fighters. By May, estimates had soared to 400 in Panjwai district alone. It appeared that the Taliban had hit on a successful strategy: to embarrass the NATO countries and expose their divisions as new forces filled in for the Americans. Radio traffic from the Taliban reported, 'Canadians are good fighters, but their politicians are weak.'[10] A public outcry in the NATO countries might have convinced their governments to pull out. If the United States became isolated and over-extended, they might be chased from the region for good. The strategic thinking turned out to be sound.

The Taliban's operational leader in Southern Afghanistan who implemented the new offensive was Mullah Dadullah Akhund, known as 'the Lame' after the loss of a leg to a landmine. Dadullah boasted that in addition to a 1,000-man force of regular fighters, formed into fourteen groups of platoon or company size, he also had his choice of some 500 'martyr volunteers,' mostly teenagers who had trained to be suicide bombers. Over half of the 119 suicide attacks launched in Afghanistan in 2006 took place in Kandahar Province.[11] The Canadian soldiers of TF Orion sought to prevent their deadly progress.

The battle group's main concern was a lack of partners from the Afghan security forces. Ges's Gun Devil battalion had cooperated with four army battalions (*kandaks*) during its deployment. Higher headquarters assigned TF Orion just two. A third battalion that was supposed to work with Hope was reassigned to a Canadian Special Forces unit. The idea was to create more elite Afghan commando units. But from what Hope could tell, the Afghans mostly undertook base security so that foreign coalition operators could conduct direct-action raids.

Hope initially ordered each company to maintain a relationship with one designated battalion. But due to the pace of operations, the policy shifted to allow any Afghan unit, whether Army, National Police, or Border Police, to accompany Canadian patrols. Even this became a policy in name only by the middle of the deployment. One company commander recalled the Afghan units as variable in their competence. The units that had Embedded Training Teams (ETT) of American advisers tended to be at least fairly competent. Those without trainers spanned 'both ends of the spectrum,' from 'great' to 'terribly led.' Much of what the Afghan units did in those early days depended on the experience of their commanders, whether they were seasoned and motivated *mujahidin* fighters, jaded paycheck collectors, or political appointees.[12]

In the spring of 2006, the Taliban shifted their efforts from the districts north of Kandahar City to the western agricultural 'green zone' around Panjwai. On 11 April, Governor Khalid informed the Canadians that Taliban fighters had returned to Sangisar village in Maiwand, the site of Mullah Omar's home mosque. Hundreds of fighters had been seen moving along Highway 1 less than 40km from Kandahar City.[13]

The accumulation of supplies and fighters attracted the attention of the Canadian patrols, which began to focus west of the city by the summer months. Hope had only three infantry companies to maneuver around Kandahar Province. One patrolled the northern part of the province, where Ges's battalion had encountered most of its resistance. Another company remained in Kandahar City. A third was supposed to be deployed to Spin Boldak, but only spent a few weeks at the border post. The French Special Forces unit at FOB Spin Boldak had to extend through July in order to ensure some NATO presence at the border outside of US CIA agents and Blackwater contractors. The Canadians who had planned to occupy Spin Boldak pulled back to support their sister companies. Hope, in the midst of coordinating these movements, had a chilling run-in with Raziq.

On the night of 2 August, Hope found himself surrounded by staff officers at Patrol Base Wilson, located at the Zhari district police headquarters. They were planning an operation to cross the Arghandab River to hit a small cluster of villages where a white schoolhouse doubled as a Taliban headquarters and weapons cache. Raziq sidled up to Hope during the meeting and told him to spread the LAVs at 100m intervals and to locate his personal vehicle at a certain grid square. Hope had not been to the location and wanted to press Raziq on the suitability: 'Are you sure it's a good one? Because my communication is very sensitive. It can't be everywhere.'

Raziq responded with a big smile and a customary wag of his head, 'Oh, it's absolutely perfect.'

Hope considered, but in the end he demurred on the offer to move his vehicle.

The next day, just after high noon, the Canadian battle group commander spotted Taliban mortar fire. He called his artillery battery for confirmation, 'Where's that coming down?'

The response was: 'That's coming down on that [same] grid square. That's exactly where they wanted me to be.'

Hope was unsure if Raziq had intended to offer him up as a sacrifice, a 'pawn' in secret negotiations with the Taliban. But he recalled the incident as 'Sopranos-ish,' a mafia story in the Afghan borderlands.[14]

Raziq's presence continued to be controversial through the summer of 2006, as TF Orion headed out of the country and was replaced by a new Canadian task force. As they swapped units, the Canadians used Raziq's Border Police as an advance party on the roads west of Kandahar City. Instead of instilling order and finding the IEDs in the roads, Raziq's forces provoked the populace. Rumors spread that Raziq was there not to hunt the Taliban, but to massacre local Noorzai people for the benefit of their Achakzai neighbors. One member of Kandahar's provincial council admitted, 'This was a bad idea, to bring Abdul Razik [*sic*]. One village had ten or twenty fighters against the government before he came, and the next day, maybe two hundred.' The local Taliban commander advised the Achakzai leader that if he entered Sperwan village he would ignite a tribal uprising. Raziq did so anyway, and his forces walked into a firefight on the western edge of the settlement. After taking casualties, the Border Police backed out, a retreat that marked the limit of government control over the valley.[15] In these early years, Raziq's forces were still experiencing some growing pains.

It is debatable whether NATO forces achieved any more than their Afghan partners in the ensuing weeks. Canadian forces under Hope's replacement, Brigadier General Omer Lavoie, fought a harrowing multi-day battle in Operation Medusa against hundreds of insurgent fighters. The Canadians had their backs to a wall, as they faced a 'frontal offensive' from Panjwai. The attack exposed a troubling lack of resolve in other NATO allies, who refused to send troops to the operation. One Canadian officer recalled, 'We were basically told: you're on your fucking own for a while.' What the Canadians could fall back upon was American air superiority. They called in strike after strike, using helicopters, jets, and bombers on vineyard defenses and mud huts where the insurgents hunkered down. When the dust settled, the Canadians claimed some 300 fighters killed, in addition to eighty captives taken from the battlefield. Canada lost six soldiers killed in action, and the coalition suffered fifty more injuries, most from the friendly fire of an American A-10 Warthog plane.[16]

Beyond the skewed casualty count, the effects of Operation Medusa were more difficult to assess. In a matter of weeks, the Taliban regrouped in southern Afghanistan. Most of its leadership remained intact and able to raise more student-fighters at will. Insurgents killed two more Canadian soldiers on 14 October as they defended a construction crew building a four-kilometer 'combat road' between the Panjwai and Zhari district centers. The existing road had become an 'indefensible IED alley.' The same day, Kandahari elders returned requests for aid following the destruction caused by NATO bombs. Three villages produced a total of 227 claims for civilian deaths or damage to property.[17]

The long-term result of NATO's bombing of Panjwai district was to drive out its local population. One local elder reported after the campaign, 'They killed our children, they killed our families. Every canal is collapsed. Every field needs water. We don't have enough food.'[18] In stemming the Taliban tide, the foreign coalition perhaps created more enemies than it eliminated. The foreign bombs made it more likely, in the calculus of insurgency, that displaced refugees would look the other way when the Taliban returned to Panjwai in search of food or shelter. Hundreds of insurgents had returned to the district by 2007. When they arrived, the Taliban shifted tactics from standing and fighting to the use of IEDs and suicide operations.

Raziq, despite his recent setback to the west of Kandahar City, continued to serve as a source of stability at the border crossing, and as a willing partner for other missions out of sector. Though the human rights community petitioned the government to replace the controversial military leader in the wake of the March 2006 massacre, the Canadian military learned to tolerate him. The coalition's more sustained push for reform was to replace Kandahar's Governor.

Asadullah Khalid endured continuous accusations from his coalition partners. Even amid successes, he raised eyebrows. After the coalition's May 2007 killing of Taliban commander Dadullah 'the Lame,' Khalid displayed the enemy's corpse on his palace veranda for members of the press to admire.[19] One diplomat recalled hearing that the Governor ran a torture dungeon under one of his guest houses. Many alleged that he had operated a similar set-up during his previous tenure in Ghazni Province. Both there and in Kandahar, he used his official position to arrest business rivals and extort money from them. Khalid had connections to Afghanistan's national intelligence service (NDS), which was known for torturing detainees.[20] In addition to prisoner abuse, there was evidence that Khalid was helping to run a narcotics racket in Kandahar, and that he had ordered an attack on a UN NGO that killed five international workers.[21]

When the Canadian Foreign Minister visited Afghanistan in April 2008 he made headlines by suggesting that Karzai fire Governor Khalid as part of an effort to stem corruption. This faux pas was an affront to Afghan sovereignty.[22] Nevertheless, the public display of disaffection signaled Khalid's fate. He could not remain long at the Governor's post alongside his Canadian patrons. In August 2008, he left Kandahar for Kabul, where he went on to serve as Minister for Borders and Tribal Affairs. Though Raziq lost a patron in Khalid, he now became an established authority in the region compared to the new political appointees. Khalid's interim replacement in Kandahar was then dual-hatted as the commander of the 205th Army Corps. With his substantial military credentials, the interim Governor began to balk at orders issued by the pampered Ahmed Wali Karzai, a former Chicago restaurateur. In late 2008, the Karzai regime finally found someone more palatable to the Canadians.

An Afghan-Canadian Governor

Tooryalai Wesa was a native of Kandahar. His family's farm is in Kuhak, on the banks of the Arghandab River. But he had spent much of the past two decades in Europe and Canada, where he was an agricultural extension professor at the University of British Columbia. Rumors claimed that Wesa could be a pushover; some alleged he could hardly control a classroom of undergraduates, let alone an Afghan province on the brink of Taliban invasion.[23] But an itinerant life had taught him to persevere through adversity, and to succeed in unfamiliar circumstances.

Wesa had an appropriate family pedigree for leadership in Kandahar. Since his grandfather's generation, the family had been close to the nearby Karzai clan. Wesa's father was a well-connected former District Governor. But young Tooryalai learned primarily from one of his uncles, who oversaw the family's hundred-acre farm. It was there that he gained his appreciation for scientific farming. His uncle was the first farmer in the valley to use a tractor. By the 1970s, Tooryalai began to seek ways to apply science to the growing of crops.

He began his graduate studies at the American University of Beirut, but the program postponed courses due to political instability in Lebanon. USAID then sponsored Wesa at the University of Nebraska. He finished his degree at the end of 1977, about a year before a coup replaced the Afghan monarchy with a Soviet republic. Toor Wesa and his brother Zalmay both thrived under the new Soviet regime. They were part of Afghanistan's growing technocratic class, equipped with foreign degrees and cosmopolitan contacts. In 1989, Wesa helped to found Kandahar University, where he served as president.

About a year later, following the Soviet withdrawal, the civil war began to intensify in Kandahar. Wesa, who feared for his family's safety, took them first to Kabul. A few months later, they decamped again. His wife, a medical doctor, had a heart condition that needed attention. The couple took their three young daughters with them out of the war-torn country, crossing the northern border into the crumbling Soviet Union. Over the next few months, they made a series of desperate treks by train: to Moscow, Budapest, and Zurich. Finally, Wesa gained acceptance to the University of British Columbia, and the family settled in Canada.

Wesa returned to Kandahar in 2004 and 2006, after more than a decade as an agronomist in the Pacific Northwest. By then, he barely recognized the province amid the destruction and aid dollars that the foreigners had dished out. Wesa had come as an academic consultant for various government aid organizations. But on the second trip, he reconnected with the Karzai family, and his life underwent a dramatic change, during a chat 'over veggies and cherry juice,' from academic to politician. First Ahmed Wali and then Hamid Karzai leaned on him to take over as Governor in Kandahar. The President asked for a three-month term until he could find another candidate. After all, Karzai reasoned, Wesa knew how to get along with Canadians.[24] The three-month interim period stretched into six years in office.

As Governor, Wesa encouraged foreign partners to direct resources toward ordinary Kandaharis. The Canadians developed several signature projects in Kandahar, including the distribution of polio vaccine. The Governor encouraged the broadcast of pro-vaccine messages in mosques, schools, and at family gatherings. Wesa remembered a trip to Dubai, during which Bill Gates congratulated him for helping to eliminate the disease from his province.[25]

The most significant Canadian project was the rehabilitation of the Dahla Dam, which had provided power and moderated the Arghandab River before it fell into disrepair. Wesa's training as an agronomist made him especially enthusiastic about the project, conceived for its potential to draw workers out of the narcotics economy and into legal pursuits.[26] But none of these development projects could proceed if the Taliban committed enough violence to drive away civilian experts. As a trained academic, Wesa did not have the security background of his predecessor Khalid. This meant Raziq's skills and resources as a provider of military force became more valuable in the provincial hierarchy.

Stalemate

As plans for development continued, the Taliban fought the Canadians to a stalemate in the Arghandab River valley. Canadian troops built outposts and roads farther down the valley toward the 'horn' of Panjwai, ever more distant from Kandahar City, out into the desert borderlands that flanked the river. The Taliban responded by occupying bombed-out villages and creating mazes of IEDs. Insurgents exerted just enough force to prevent the Canadians from implementing the kind of clear-hold-build strategy that depended upon stable government and economic opportunities. The Canadians sought to ensure that the population would not turn back to the insurgents after foreign soldiers returned to their FOBs, so the presence of indigenous Afghan forces became essential. By 2008, in addition to the battle group, the Canadians fielded partnership-focused Operational Mentoring and Liaison Teams (OMLT, pronounced 'Omelet').[27]

The Canadian training teams operated in distinct groups, based on the type of Afghan trainees they engaged. Afghan Army (ANA) companies received one officer, one warrant officer, and two soldiers. At the battalion (*kandak*) level, Canadians sent a field grade officer, a sergeant major, a medic, and a radio operator. Each National Police (ANP) substation in the area of operations further received two military police soldiers. Early mentorship operations took place at Patrol Base Wilson in Zhari district. From there, the footprint expanded to the south-west down the Arghandab valley.

Afghan companies rotated between the bases to maximize their exposure to Canadian trainers. The Canadians rotated for relief from the conditions of the new outposts. One officer in 2008 recalled FOB Sperwan Gear as being the end of the line in terms of comfortable lodging. His that his soldiers spent time there had to rest and refit between stints at more austere patrol bases farther west, mere 'dust holes' surrounded by 'HESCO bastion and sandbags' for a thin wall of security. Within the outposts, the comforts of home were limited to 'buckets to piss in.' Soldiers at Patrol Base Mushan erected a large wooden sign that read 'The Alamo.'[28] The Afghans they worked with in the river valley, locals in the ANP and outsiders from Kandahar's 205th Army Corps, spanned the gamut from self-motivated and competent to corrupt beyond help. Junior leadership often made the difference between capacity and dysfunction.

While the Canadian OMLT trained Afghan National Army and Police units, Raziq led elements of his Border Police on operations throughout the southern part of the country. Governor Wesa relied on Raziq as a 'very active' force against the Taliban. Wesa described Raziq as a good manager, 'straightforward' and with 'no diplomacy. He'd say, 'This is what we should do,' and that was the end of the conversation. People started to move. Though he could be brusque in giving orders, Raziq was close to his subordinates. They knew that if they were injured or killed, the boss would support their families. In those days, Raziq was paying for some seventy children of his fallen comrades to attend school in India.[29]

Wesa measured Raziq's effectiveness in terms of his own increasing ease of transport. At the beginning of his tenure, the Governor could only visit outlying districts by Blackhawk helicopter. By the end of 2009, however, he was able to drive in relative safety out of Kandahar City to historically troublesome districts in the north.[30]

Yet Raziq could only do so much against Taliban encroachment, given recent turns in Kandahar politics. In October 2007, Alokozai strongman Mullah Naqib died from a heart attack. He had suffered poor health since the previous March, when he was the target of an insurgent explosion that destroyed a canal bridge. Naqib had been a moderating force on Kandahar's political scene since the early days of the Taliban. Now that he was gone, the floodgates appeared open to the insurgency. Hamid Karzai, in order to consolidate his power and block more adept rivals, flew south from Kabul to crown Naqib's inexperienced son as his political heir. Weak district leadership stood to benefit the Karzai regime, since the vacuum allowed the Karzai brothers to persuade local elders to include them in their graft projects, to supplant the existing networks with a new layer of tribal patronage.[31]

But the lack of political establishment stood to benefit the insurgents, too. Between February and July 2008, Taliban assassins killed two government officials and two more Karzai-affiliated elders in the valley. In June, Taliban soldiers on motorcycles coordinated a complex attack with an explosive-laden tanker-vehicle to break open Sarposa Prison, a feat which liberated over a thousand inmates, of whom four hundred had been confined for aiding the Taliban. In September, two insurgents detonated suicide vests at a Kandahar City police station during a visit from Raziq. He escaped 'with only minor wounds,' as was his wont. Though his intelligence network kept him one step ahead of the Taliban, episodes such as these also demonstrated Raziq's luck. Six other police officials died in the attack.[32]

Early in 2009, the Canadians deployed their maximum level of combat power in Kandahar. At the same time, they began to seek a way out. Ottawa found its exit path with Washington's renewed attention to Afghanistan, after a years-long distraction in Iraq. The US retook the lead in Kandahar by mid-2009, though vestiges of the Canadian force remained in the form of Special Forces teams and small infantry units designated as quick reaction forces.

One of the last major operations by the Canadian Army was to send an infantry company to relieve a counterpart of the 101st Airborne Division on their fifty-third consecutive day of patrols in Panjwai district. The Americans had air-assaulted in mid-September 2010 for a planned week-long mission. As the days passed, they became ensnared in a maze of IEDs at a river-junction village called Zangabad.[33] After seven weeks of incoherent explosions and desultory ambushes, the Canadian company that arrived in support was a sight for sore eyes. But just a few months later, by 2011, all Canadian forces had moved to Kabul to focus on advising the Afghan Army and government ministers at the national level. Canada transferred the PRT in Kandahar back over to the authority of the United States.

To the Canadians involved at this stage, the changing of the guard did not feel like Bert Ges's metaphorical hockey line change. It felt like a playoff series; as one junior officer put it, 'Lose and you're out. You don't want to leave the game feeling you could have done more.'[34]

THE ARRIVAL OF THE SURGE (2009)

Since the beginning of the war, Russia had allowed the American-led coalition to use its airspace from the north. Most foreign personnel flew by this route into Kabul.[1] But the more efficient way was by sea from the south. For this route, the Americans needed Pakistan. Afghanistan's eastern neighbor increased in significance as the American surge arrived in phases from the end of 2009 through early 2012. The bulk of supplies – shipping containers full of equipment, enormous tanks of fuel, oil, and water – had to enter the region through the port of Karachi and then overland through Pakistan.

The busiest border crossing point into Afghanistan was at Torkham Gate, closer to the capital. But the terrain there formed a narrow mountain pass that was easy to surveil. Those who crossed had to present documents.[2] On the dusty plain at Spin Boldak district, an occasional pat-down was all that stood between migrants and the international boundary. As a result, men, women, children, camels, horses, and donkeys crossed in formless masses rather than in the ordered lines that formed at Torkham.[3]

Compared to the Canadians, the Americans came in greater numbers, and they brought more stuff. The more supplies and equipment crossed the international boundary at Spin Boldak, the more military strategists sought to secure the border district. Raziq used the augmented security aid to reinforce his dominance on Highway 4. The incoming American unit spent more than $10 million to make the frontier more defensible, as they built observation towers, set up concrete barriers and wire fences, and laid gravel on dirt tracks. Raziq was essential in this process for buying the necessary land, and for resettling those who had lived in houses and attended schools that were demolished in the name of improved security.[4]

US aid, along with Raziq's own mastery of the border, carried him to the position of Kandahar Chief of Police. By the end of the surge, Raziq gained a promotion from Spin Boldak district to Mandigak Palace, named for an ancient

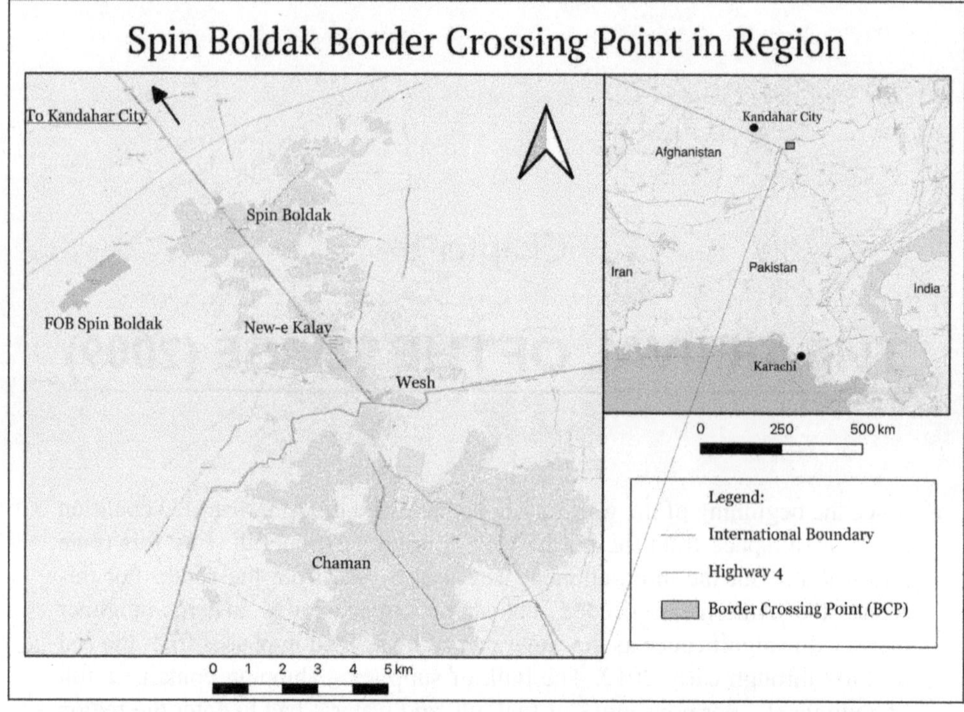

Kandahari civilization that predated Alexander's armies. A Greek analogy may help to frame the ongoing partnership. American contracts were like the wax-sealed wings of Daedalus, tools of artifice that permitted Raziq to fly closer to the sun.

The highway solidified Spin Boldak's significance as the pre-eminent border crossing point in the south. There were many places where one could travel from Pakistan to Afghanistan and back, but none outside of Raziq's home district was attached to a high-speed route to a major metropolis. Highway 4 connected Kandahar City to the port of Karachi. The route was a spur off Highway 1, the ring road that linked Kandahar to Kabul in the north-east and Herat in the west, a vital connector that enabled the movement of military personnel and supplies across the country. The Canadians had tried during their tenure to improve the section that ran through Spin Boldak city, but it was only with the investment of more American dollars that Highway 4 became paved in a uniform manner throughout its length.[5]

Foreign personnel in Afghanistan typically moved in such small numbers as to be able to find an airlift within a day or so. But the massive quantity of the surge's war materiel had to be shipped overland on military convoys and civilian 'jingle' trucks, through the spindly and vulnerable road system of the Afghan borderlands. The foreign coalition spent enormous sums and employed countless thousands of men in the manning of checkpoints and mobile patrols along the highway, to ensure its continuous operation.

Highway 4 became a double-edged sword to the US units that arrived during the surge. They benefited from the flow of NATO supplies that arrived down the road. But the task of highway clearance exposed them to explosive devices. The Americans relied on the continuous function of a massive logistics scheme to acquire material advantages on the battlefield, while the Taliban waited for opportunities to disrupt those logistics with bombs hidden under or alongside the road. A well-worn expression emerged to describe the situation: 'the Americans had all the watches, and the Afghans had all the time.'[6]

The insurgents used the border to their advantage, as well. Many attacks on supply convoys took place on the Pakistani section of the road, where conventional American troops could not respond. From their Afghan Border Police checkpoints and from their massive Stryker vehicles, equipped with magnifying optics, American partners sometimes watched without recourse as fuel convoys destined for coalition FOBs burned on the far side of the border.[7]

The Stryker

The Stryker was an imposing, armored hulk of guns, computers, and radios. Up close, the vehicle was ugly to behold. It was as if J.R.R. Tolkien's legendary 'mind of metal and of wheels' had been made manifest.[8] The truck sported cages and nets to deflect rocket-propelled grenades, sometimes lobbed from afar at inviting rectangular sides that measured 7m long by 2.67m high. Antennae, sensors, and microwave responders stuck out at irregular intervals, giving the Stryker a jagged profile.[9] The exterior took on patches of oil, dust, and grime that radiated from the wheel wells, coating the vehicles in a foul crust.

But from an appropriate distance, a formation of Strykers rumbling across the plain attained a kind of grace, like ships on the ocean. Their camouflage canopies fluttered like sails in the desert air as the huge trucks traversed in packs of four, though they cut wakes of dust rather than sea foam. The lead vehicle in the formation had a mine roller attached to its front, which kicked up billows of fine earth particles that showered the trailing formation.

The Stryker, unlike the buttoned-up MATVs and MRAPs used by infantry units, could be opened to the elements. Two air hatches – one in the front for the vehicle commander, one in the rear for a secondary weapons platform – allowed for interaction between the crew members and their environment.[10] The hatches gave troopers the ability to wave a jolly 'ahoy' to surrounding Afghans, or to gaze on them with silent imperium, like an old ship's captain upon benighted island dwellers. To the Afghans, the Stryker and its human appendages emerged out of the desert from unpredictable directions, rather than from known harbors. They proved not to be the ancient ghosts (*djinn*) of the wasteland, but some new, devilish cyborgs, bristling with machine guns and grenade launchers. Each machine spewed helmeted, dark-goggled, sand-coated men from its orifices.

The nature of the Stryker dissuaded potential enemies from challenging 8-1 CAV with direct fire. Instead, insurgents turned to the indirect method of improvised explosive devices. They weaponized the roads that provided access to Afghan villages. On paved highways, where the Taliban could not dig into the dirt, they adapted to vehicle-borne (VBIED) or suicide-vest explosive devices (SVIED).

The Americans in their vehicles were quite vulnerable to these blasts, but not nearly as much as the Afghans in soft-skinned Humvees and pickup trucks, who in turn suffered in fewer numbers than civilians, who depended on the highway as a means of trade and sustenance. Unlike the Strykers that traveled in packs of four, the Border Police often ventured out in single or paired vehicles, providing inviting targets. An IED that caused damage to a Stryker's exterior and concussion to the men inside could launch the ABP's green Ford Ranger pickup trucks high into the air. Policemen who survived the blasts suffered broken legs and fractured spines from landing on the desert floor after parabolic flights through the air.[11] As the years passed, Highway 4 became a graveyard containing the skeletal remains of ABP vehicles.

8-1 CAV

Lieutenant Colonel Bill Clark confronted a daunting task. His cavalry squadron was the first conventional US military unit stationed at FOB Spin Boldak. He had spent hours before arrival poring over maps, drone imagery, and the reports of clandestine agents who had preceded him at the border. But without having been there in person, on the ground, Clark remained wary of potential dangers. 'We didn't know what we didn't know,' he shrugged, in a folksy adaptation of Donald Rumsfeld's 'unknown unknowns.'[12] Without clear knowledge of what they would find, the Americans surged in Spin Boldak district through a series of experiments, tests, and trials.

The Canadians in Kandahar had been limited to one battle group, a battalion-sized element of about 1,000 soldiers. This relatively small number of troops could only do so much in a province the size of West Virginia. They relegated themselves to securing Kandahar Airfield and using a company or two (about 100 soldiers each) to make sporadic visits to surrounding districts. For brief stretches, a Canadian platoon of some thirty men camped out at FOB Spin Boldak, then a tiny outpost located a few kilometers from the district center and population hub. When the Americans surged in 2009 they brought an entire brigade, more than 4,000 strong, to Kandahar. The increase in manpower meant that a squadron of more than 400 cavalrymen could station themselves permanently in Raziq's district of Spin Boldak. The outpost, which had been home to just a handful of French Special Forces and US intelligence agents, grew into a robust compound. When the second wave of the surge arrived in 2010, Spin Boldak became the headquarters location for its own brigade, a new hybrid organization that combined cavalry and intelligence units.[13]

The American generals running the war wanted troops at the border to safeguard the delivery of supplies required for the surge in the South. Most of the fighting was taking place west of Kandahar City. But the coalition conducting operations there depended on a logistical train that made landfall in Pakistan and came up through the Spin Boldak border crossing. By the height of the surge, more than one hundred ISAF trucks per day rumbled over the frontier, past the Friendship Gate and the gaze of Raziq's police force.[14] Most of the 30,000 additional US troops that deployed came to the southern part of Afghanistan. This trend made Spin Boldak more important than ingress points farther north.

The increasing significance of the southern border crossing increased Raziq's opportunities for patronage. But more power brought more attention, in turn, to Raziq's methods. In December 2009, the same month that Barack Obama defended the rationale of the surge, Canadian journalist Matthieu Aikins published a landmark piece entitled the 'Master of Spin Boldak.' Aikins had been backpacking across Central Asia when he ran into a 27-year-old opium dealer in Quetta, Pakistan, who wanted to make a Western friend. The local trader began to regale Aikins with stories about the newest power player gaining followers across the region.

The Canadian interloper's subsequent article portrayed Raziq as the second coming of Soviet-era strongman Ismatullah Muslim, an illiterate thug, one of the 'corrupt and brutal' men propped up by the Western mission in Afghanistan, a rising star among the country's constellation of 'unpopular warlords.' Aikins traced the history of governance from the Soviet era up to the present and concluded that Raziq represented a 'classic Afghan narrative: the sudden ascent to power through violence and foreign patronage.' Though the reporter got most of his information secondhand, he did meet the notorious commander for a brief moment on this first trip. On the basis of a handshake in a greeting line, Aikins provided insights into the aura that captivated so many newcomers to Kandahar:

> He looked even younger than his thirty years and had a boyishly handsome, guileless face with a square jaw and clear eyes. It was not at all the face of a fire-breathing warlord. A tuft of short hair poked out from under his hat in what was nearly a widow's peak. He was dressed simply, in a white cotton *shalwar kameez* and a gray pinstriped waistcoat. Only his full mouth, with its crop of slightly crooked, strong-looking teeth, gave any hint of his great vigor and violence.

The article accused Western military figures in Kandahar of enabling and legitimizing this charismatic criminal, who was rumored to earn between $5 and $6 million per month from smuggling rackets. Aikins concluded by noting that Raziq's Border Police had overseen the recent presidential election, which tallied more than 8,000 votes for Karzai and only four for his opponent.[15] The article soon became required reading for the American officers, like Bill Clark, who pondered how to manage the fraught relationship, now thrust into the spotlight of international media.

The Army's doctrine counseled officers to think in terms of systems rather than individual personalities. Decision-makers acted to maximize the function of the Pakistan border: to allow for the free flow of legal goods and the interdiction of Taliban fighters, weapons, and narcotics. Raziq was a key part of that system, but as a unique human agent he was difficult to categorize. His leadership offered security at the border and along the highway to Kandahar City, but his methods threatened to undermine the legitimacy of the Afghan government, encourage black market trading, and lead to human rights violations. Prior to the surge, NATO allies had removed other corrupt agents: the British sacked a problematic Helmand Governor in December 2005, and the Dutch refused to participate in operations in Uruzgan Province until President Karzai removed a fellow Popalzai elder from the Governor's post.[16] Did Raziq fall into the same category? Was he more policeman or criminal? Clark became the first of a series of conventional US military partners who had to grapple with these questions.

Clark received little guidance on partnership from his boss, Colonel Harry Tunnell, a rare African American brigade commander and a skeptic of counter-insurgency. Tunnell wanted his unit to focus on 'killing people,' as he rejected the army's recent emphasis on nation-building. The commander distributed, rather than the new field manual on counter-insurgency, old copies of the army's 1986 counter-guerrilla manual, which concentrated on pursuit of enemy fighters.[17] To his critics, Tunnell was hotheaded and stubborn, a 'toxic leader' who had been scarred by a previous deployment to Iraq. Though Tunnell's strategy and style alienated Clark, other subordinates in the 5/2 Stryker Brigade came to admire his realism about combat in Kandahar. Tunnell was in some respects a 'soldier's commander,' one who understood the urgent need of his men to demonstrate their willingness to kill and their competence as killers.[18]

The geographical focus for Tunnell was west of Kandahar City, in the Arghandab and its tributary river valleys. The terrain there dictated that infantrymen had to dismount from armored vehicles and patrol on foot. The 'green zone' was a place of shaded refuge from which *mujahidin* fighters had attacked the Soviets and their puppet government a generation before. Southeast of the city, the desert plains that led to the Pakistan border provided scant cover. This open ground was more suited to Strykers than dismounted infantry.

Still, Spin Boldak district presented a steep learning curve for Clark. Raziq and his Border Police seemed to have a good hold on the border crossing point itself and on Highway 4. Outside of this narrow strip of country, Raziq had less sway, which Clark discovered to his chagrin through a series of IED attacks at the beginning of the deployment.

Just a few days after the ground convoy from Kandahar Airfield to Spin Boldak, a devastating explosive device ripped into one of the 8-1 CAV Stryker vehicles. Two officers had to be evacuated out of theater due to severe injuries. In the weeks that followed, two more roadside bombs disabled American vehicles and wounded soldiers inside. Clark himself had been present at an incident in October; he had met with Noorzai elders in a village called Loy Karez, some 20km north-east of the highway, located on one of the rat trails through the foothills that extended to the Pakistan border. When the meeting adjourned, Raziq was nowhere to be found. He had taken an alternate route out of the valley. The American convoy, without its Border Police escort, hit an IED a few kilometers outside the village.[19] Clark believed that Raziq, whose intelligence network had enabled his rise to power in the area, was holding out on his American partners.

Clark had an understandable focus on his own unit and the protection of his subordinates, but the Afghan Border Police at the time struggled with their own issues of force protection. Raziq's lieutenant, a Noorzai outpost commander, had lectured his fellow tribal elders in Loy Karez about their responsibilities to the government. The tirade may have been a show for Raziq and his American partners, and the locals were not impressed. Less than a week after the meeting, the outpost commander and four policemen suffered an ambush as they came out of a bath house. A handful of insurgents set upon the unsuspecting men with AK-47 and PKM machine guns, rendering them 'unrecognizable' in photos that captured the carnage.[20]

One 8-1 CAV platoon leader recalled than even aid projects were unwelcome in Loy Karez. Toward the end of his deployment, the American lieutenant was walking through the village with local elders who had come to thank his unit for funds that had enabled the local water source to be dredged. 'Thank you for cleaning the water,' the elders said, 'now we never want to see you here again.' They were afraid that by accepting the help of government forces, they had made themselves targets for the insurgency. If the United States was not prepared to stay 'for the long haul,' they risked leaving the beneficiaries of their aid 'to face Taliban violence alone.'[21]

A critical question for the surge troops emerged: how far off the highway could they venture? The further the Americans spread their inkblot of security and economic development, the more they risked diluting their resources and alienating people who abhorred any connection to Kabul. Loy Karez and many other towns in the Afghan countryside had existed for centuries without the benefits – or the interference – of a central government. Could a few years of American troops and development dollars shift the mindsets of these independent communities? Or was it better to limit the focus of development to Highway 4?

Sex and Suicidal Attacks

The explosive devices that Clark's unit encountered represented the preferred tactic of insurgents, though this was a recent development. It was not until late 2004 that the Taliban began to employ mines and suicide attacks. Their manned defense of positions in Western Kandahar during Operation Medusa two years later was perhaps the last stand of the Soviet-era light infantry tactics. While insurgents made 2,000 IED attacks in 2006, the number alongside the American surge mushroomed to over 7,000 by 2009. Iraqi and Palestinian mentors coached Afghan insurgents on the most recent designs and methods of emplacement.

Afghans considered the suicide attacks to be controversial. Whereas martyrdom culture blossomed in the Middle East, locals tended to shudder at the practice. Rumors held that Pakistanis, rather than Afghans, were the only ones who would do such a thing. Others said that suicide bombers, if they were Afghans, were not in their right minds. They must have been brainwashed during their time in *madrasa*, or mentally challenged, or traumatically abused.[22]

One story about the Taliban's suicide soldiers scratched the surface of an Afghan taboo, *bacha bazi* or 'boy play.' In 2008, a few months before Clark's unit arrived, Border Policemen captured an attempted suicide bomber, one of twenty-eight who came for Raziq over the course of his career. Attackers almost always killed themselves before they could be captured, so this was a unique chance for Raziq to learn about his enemies. He arrived on the scene to find his policemen beating the bomber. A suicide vest was hanging up on the wall, still intact. Raziq ordered his men to stop harming the suspect, clean him up, and invite him to a wedding celebration set to take place that evening. The attempted suicide became Raziq's guest of honor. After the party, the man became a close confidant. He revealed that older boys at his *madrasa* had used rape as a means to shame him into becoming a martyr.[23] This controversial recruiting anecdote belies the Taliban's image as a movement for religious purity.

In public, Taliban leaders took great pains to punish sodomy wherever it was found. For example, when a prison guard in Kandahar was caught abusing inmates he was sentenced to the *sharia* prescription for homosexuality: death by stoning. Executioners pushed a wall onto the offender's prone body.[24] When the US and its allies replaced the Taliban in local governance, many Kandaharis noted that the practice of *bacha bazi* began to flourish again. One of Gul Agha Sherzai's first orders as Governor of Kandahar in 2002 was to ban boys from living with his forces, though enforcement proved to be difficult and sensitive.[25]

Social scientists speculate that same-sex acts become common in places where women are absent or forbidden. At religious schools, chauvinistic leaders often taught misogynistic themes. Older students remained on campus rather than depart for marriage, since high dowry prices resulted in few opportunities. Sodomy became rife in the *madrasa*, as in other adolescent male-exclusive societies such as boarding schools, prisons, and ships at sea. Afghan military and police barracks proved not to be an exception. In 2009, the Afghan Ministry of Interior recorded twenty-eight cases of child rape among government forces, though anecdotal evidence suggested the number was 'much higher.'[26] Separate from the bleak *madrasa* and barracks bullying, a more glamorous underworld of 'dancing boys' flourished. Rooms full of dark-whiskered, heavy-set men competed with waved handfuls of cash for the attention of nimble, long-necked boys who sported flowing dresses, rouge, and eyeliner, spinning around to the beat of drums.[27]

Foreigners had noticed 'boy play' in Kandahar since the early nineteenth century, when the British recorded Pashtun marching songs that hailed the beauty of male dancers. The singers of these marches, then and now, do not consider themselves to be homosexual, which is forbidden by Islam. Their narrow definition of homosexuality is romantic love for another man. To use a boy for sexual pleasure is considered a mere indulgence, but no mortal sin.

The Taliban prided themselves on reducing sodomy during their time in power, though the frequency of such practices is impossible to confirm. Anecdotes suggest that homosexual relations had been more common before the Taliban regime, at *mujahidin* camps in Pakistan and during the civil war in Afghanistan, as orphaned children trickled into encampments looking for food and work. War may have accelerated this process, but similar stories about sex with boy-apprentices emerged from the highway system in the previous generation. Since the 1960s, children had served as driver's helpers or mechanic's aides. They rode along with the smugglers and trucking mafia of Central Asia, which had been the dominant economic forces since the advent of western-built highways. The best-liked boys in these arrangements often stayed and married into the families of their older partners. The rest drifted on to a nearby urban center, with hopes of making fresh starts after their beards grew in.[28]

A recent change to the Taliban code of conduct further demonstrated the complicated nature of childhood in Afghanistan. In 2009, Article 50 stated 'Youngsters (those without beards) are not allowed to be taken for jihad.' The following year, the statute was revised: 'Youngsters (those without beards) are prohibited from living in *mujahidin* residences or administrative centers.' This change implied that children could be recruited as soldiers, but not kept for sex.[29] There are two potential reasons for the edit. It was possibly intended to distance the Taliban from ongoing allegations against Afghan government officials. Then again, the amendment may have resulted from a recognition that the practice had become an issue in the Taliban ranks and needed to be addressed in doctrine. On the foreign coalition side, ISAF command issued an order in 2010 for personnel to look out for underage recruits in the Afghan forces. Governor Gul Agha Sherzai's office fielded questions about heavily made-up teenage boys who often accompanied him; his spokesman responded that nothing untoward was happening.[30]

Feelings of foreboding have dominated the historical memory of the American frontier. The spirit of The Alamo contained a fear of being overwhelmed, a sentiment that was never far from the surface at outposts in Afghanistan. In this atmosphere, Bill Clark's 'we didn't know what we didn't know' took on ominous connotations. Westerners shuddered as they overheard the well-worn phrase, 'Women are for children, boys are for fun.' 'Man-love Thursday' was rumored to be a sexual free-for-all prior to the holy day of the week on Friday.[31] Some cavalry troopers believed the mustache to be a defense against unwanted advances by local men. Pashtun practices provoked a tension among the US soldiers that resonated with the homosocial pasts of their own borderlands. The concept of the frontier as an unsavory place was embedded in the American psyche, as male sexual vulnerability formed a central theme of iconic Western fiction: from *Red River* (1948), to *Blood Meridian* (1985), to *Brokeback Mountain* (2005). This additional threat reinforced a central tenet of the American military mindset in Afghanistan: that violence was required to pacify lawless regions.

Many of the NATO leaders who interacted with the shadowy figures adjacent to Raziq's organization, Pakistani truckers, low-level Taliban commanders, and junior ISI agents, compared their experiences to a mafia crime story. But one senior NATO official disagreed: Kandahar was more like *Deadwood* than *The Sopranos*. The former is a western story whereas the latter is an eastern. Westerns are based on an absence of order, whereas eastern stories deal with a rotten system. Newcomers to Kandahar saw no order to be corrupted as in the eastern mafia stories, only an empty void toward which they could aim money and ordnance.[32]

Chapter 9

AIRSTRIKE (2009)

---

9 November 2009: 1945 hours

Raziq was still getting used to the new US soldiers, cavalry troopers with black Stetson hats. He liked their equipment and their never-ending flow of contract dollars, but sometimes they took things too far. Raziq approached the Americans like he had the Canadians before – give them what they wanted, as long as it suited his own priorities. If they could increase the power and security of his patronage network, why not try to make them happy? Every once in a while, Raziq included his new American neighbors in his operations.

On the evening of 9 November, Raziq called Lieutenant Colonel Clark's headquarters to ask for support.[1] He let the Americans know about a house that belonged to someone who was behind on his protection payments. It didn't matter who owned the house. The important point was that they were making money on hash and cutting Raziq out of his share of the spoils.[2]

Everyone knew about the unofficial tax on drug crops. Opium and hashish were technically forbidden. Still, many Kandaharis deferred to regional rather than religious custom. Authorities looked the other way, and the crops flourished. Bribes, or protection payments, had been the rule in Kandahar since the days of Raziq's strongman predecessor, Ismatullah Khan, a fellow Achakzai tribesman. But unlike Soviet patrons before them, the Americans now began to vocalize opposition to the international drug trade. The rules of the superpower sponsor had changed. The Afghan government, now endowed with its partner's massive resources for surveillance, could seize drugs at any time. The crops now needed protection, which came at a cost.

Raziq's plan was simple. He would seize the drug house and evict the previous owners if they were slow enough to get caught. He would then have a new property to dispense as patronage to one of his more loyal followers. Raziq knew that the Americans would want in on the drug bust, because the house was within a couple kilometers of their base. He would enjoy revealing to the Americans what had been going on under their noses. In addition, he could use their explosive ordnance disposal (EOD) team to destroy the house. It would be a win-win. The message to the Americans would be: Raziq is a good partner, he knows the right intelligence, and he is always sharing it with us; he appreciates the resources we can provide to him; he knows how to leverage American assets. The message to local farmers around Highway 4 was: beware of missing payments to Raziq's Border Police.

9 November 2009: 2257 hours

Clark's men, a platoon from B Troop, arrived at the drug house and set up a perimeter for the explosives disposal team. But they did not stop there. The troopers nodded at Raziq's men in their green ABP pickup trucks parked in front of the house and then began to look around. This was not supposed to happen. But these were reconnaissance soldiers, after all.

One of the cavalry troopers, wearing night vision goggles and shining a red-lens flashlight over the dusty ground, discovered a trap door that led down to an underground bunker. 'You wouldn't notice that it was there unless you stepped on it,' Captain Erik Aadland recalled. 'They were growing something. There looked like there were furrows, but they had doors in the ground with ladders.' Aadland, the Charlie troop commander, saw the mission as a distraction. He would rather be hunting down terrorists than confiscating their drugs. Still, this was more than a routine patrol. He recalled, 'There was some machinery down there. We weren't experts in what they were doing, but there was a cache of hashish . . . they were pressing it and rolling it within this facility.' The discovery kicked off further searches.[3]

Just before 11.00 pm, about 200m from the house reported by Afghan Border Police, the Americans found more evidence. Plastic bags contained over 2,000kg of raw cannabis buds; another pile featured eighteen huge packages, each holding 90kg of processed hash. Another platoon arrived around midnight in relief. They set up positions to scan the desert, in the hope that the owners of the drugs would show up to claim the produce. By now, however, the Americans had kicked up enough dust to warn off anyone intending to return.

The next day, the drug bust continued to spiral. More US soldiers arrived on the scene and spread out the perimeter around the house. Around midday, cavalry troopers found two more holes containing drugs, including a 10m trench, covered with a tarp and camouflaged with bushes, that contained more than 360kg of hashish. Forty minutes later, the Americans reported a mud hut about 100m away with over 450kg of cannabis plants. Another two caches yielded 400kg more. The Afghan Border Police got in on the game and revealed a few bags of opium poppy seeds. Perhaps the owner of the field was looking to expand into opium next planting season, if he was able to evade attention to his hashish operation.

In the middle of the afternoon, Raziq arrived at the scene.[4] He had heard the Americans were up to something, but maybe he could stop them from overreacting. Initial guidance from Clark had been that EOD could not blow the bunker that contained the processing facility. US troops were to wait for the Afghan Counter Drug Insurgency Team to collect evidence and burn the materials on site. As the Americans waited for the Afghans to assemble, Clark from his office on the base looked for other ways to destroy the processing equipment: 155mm artillery? 120mm mortars? Rules of engagement restricted the use of indirect fire assets, due to the proximity of the field to FOB Spin Boldak and Pakistan. Clark's Air Force liaison checked for the feasibility of a precision air strike.

Raziq asked Captain Aadland through his interpreter what was going on. He replied with the options that Clark was mulling over, and Raziq's smile turned into an incredulous laugh. Aadland remembered that Raziq 'thought it was kind of funny when I mentioned that we may destroy the drugs.' During the extended discussions between headquarters about the fate of the seized drugs, the Afghan police commander acted, Aadland recalled, as if 'it was all a big joke. He was kind of laughing about it.'

Around this time, the Afghan Counter Drug team, a special unit of the National Police, arrived with another of Clark's platoons. Raziq planted some second thoughts in Aadland's mind. Did he know how much those drugs were worth? It seemed like a waste to use artillery or the air force for this task. Raziq waggled his head in his customary way. 'Well, if you want to go ahead with it, I won't stop you,' he chuckled.

By 5.00 pm, the Afghans had consolidated the drugs into a big pile, thousands of kilograms of cannabis, some in green, leafy form, some processed into flat brown bricks. Aadland stepped up to toss a thermite grenade onto the fuel-soaked pile, when he glanced at his soldiers behind him. Some, typical soldiers, wanted to be as close to any explosion as they could. A few perhaps wanted a better position from which to inhale the resulting bonfire. Aadland stopped and told his noncommissioned officers to back the troops up behind a 1km standoff.[5]

As the fire blazed, two Navy F-18s, call sign GRAPHIC, checked on station. The pilots were always happy to lend a hand. In a conflict without an enemy air threat, they were eager for missions. Rules of engagement had been satisfied under category 421 – 'Attack anyone demonstrating hostile intent – not constituting an imminent attack.' GRAPHIC 34 lobbed a dumb 500lb bomb that landed about 30m from the bunker with a low crump. The bunker did not appear to be damaged despite the heavy ordnance. For good measure, GRAPHIC 33 and 34 each dropped another bomb on the drug processing facility, this time 'smart,' precision-guided GBU-12s. The earth shook and the concrete-and-mud structures crumbled.[6]

A convoy of white SUVs tore across the dirt road that connected the drug field to Highway 4. It was only a couple of kilometers from the bombing site to FOB Spin Boldak. Raziq stormed up to Clark's Strykers, parked in a circle outside the American colonel's tactical operations center (TOC). Clark did not allow Raziq to enter the TOC without an invitation, and he had not been expecting this meeting. He had received a phone call a few minutes before and heard Raziq's enraged voice. He handed the phone to his interpreter, Najib.

'Raziq's coming to the FOB, and he's pissed,' Najib translated.

Clark gathered some of his staff officers and ushered them out of the operations tent toward the ring of Stryker vehicles that provided an informal outdoor arena.

Raziq was upset about his partner's lack of coordination, the unconsidered second and third order effects of the F-18 strike. He pointed his finger in Clark's face and shouted, 'What the hell are you doing dropping these bombs? If you're going to do this, you need to talk to me first. I control this ground.'[7]

He never let Clark know whose drugs had been destroyed. Had they belonged to a Taliban leader? To an ordinary farmer who had missed protection payments? Or to someone closer to Raziq?

Clark sensed that Raziq's anger implied the drugs had belonged to one of his political or tribal bosses, likely Ahmed Wali Karzai. But Clark, rather than accuse Raziq, saw the emotional outburst as an opportunity to flex American power.

He spun the argument around and said, 'I had three Strykers get hit by IEDs. That's not acceptable. I had soldiers get injured.'

Clark paused. That evening, he was due to pin a Purple Heart on one of his troopers. A couple of weeks before, Clark's own convoy had hit an IED after a meeting. Raziq's forces departed from the event by another route that happened to be clear.

Clark resumed to Raziq, 'If you don't want your stuff blown up, my Strykers better not hit an IED again.'

Clark used his control of airpower in the region to insist on closer partnership. He wanted Raziq to provide more intelligence, to help fix his IED problem.

'A lot of people are going to be upset about your airstrikes,' Raziq responded in a cryptic manner.[8]

As he stamped off, Raziq considered this new American presence in Kandahar. He had worked well with foreigners before. In the aftermath of 9/11, small teams of Special Forces had brought their night vision, their high-powered radios, their ability to call in the Air Force. He had become acquainted with CIA agents, too, who gave him cash in exchange for vehicle rental contracts. The American officials had introduced him to Blackwater agents, who trained and armed his policemen.[9] In terms of a relationship, Raziq had a lot to gain and little to lose from the early American presence. They were his cash cow but were few enough in number to stay out of his way and steer clear of collateral damage. Now, Bill Clark had shown up with a squadron of 500 troopers behind him. These new forces threatened to play bull in a china shop.

His new American partner, when they met, placed a loaded pistol on the table pointed in his direction. Didn't Clark know that the Border Police suffered in much greater numbers than the Americans in their Strykers? How much would their presence disrupt operations in his home district? Raziq sighed. Maybe he could find a way to work with these cavalrymen, too.

A Brief History of Drugs in Afghanistan

How had Raziq's Kandahar become awash with narcotics in the first place? Though most histories of drugs in Afghanistan highlight the effects of the Soviet war, the region had long been known for a thriving culture of intoxicants. The Second World War caused an abrupt change to United States trade policy, as moral concerns about drugs suddenly took a back seat to national security. To ensure a supply of morphine for its military, the US stepped into the Afghan opium market. The first deal, negotiated in secret weeks after the Pearl Harbor attack, sent half a million dollars to the Afghans for thirty tons of opium. The drugs ended up in the vaults of the US Treasury and served as the nation's strategic reserve for morphine production. As the need for morphine decreased at the end of the war, and as trade routes across the Atlantic and Pacific became safe again, Americans returned to their traditional supplies of medical-grade opium from Iran, Turkey, and South-Eastern Europe. The royal Afghan state banned opium in 1945 to curry favor with the Americans. If agents in Kabul could not secure international funding through the opium trade, they would attempt to frame their government as a deserving case for Cold War development.[10]

Meanwhile, through the middle decades of the twentieth century, thousands of young Europeans and North Americans trekked from Istanbul eastward on rattling trains, battered buses, and corroded cars, stopping at outposts in Iran before skirting south of the Hindu Kush to Kandahar on the way to Kabul, and from there to India, Nepal, or South-East Asia on the celebrated tendrils of the Hippie Trail.[11] Along the route, Kandahar became notorious for its entrepreneurial attitude toward hashish. On the dusty street out of town where the hostels sat, small retail shops featured clothing, trinkets, and furniture in front window displays. In back rooms, proprietors sold opium and cannabis. Some vendors sewed half-kilo sheets into traditional Afghan vests; smaller amounts could be fitted between jock straps.[12]

Over time, the grassroots locals who catered to travelers began to attract the attention of more resourceful businessmen. In the 1960s, Afghanistan had been a destination for small-time users. But in the next decade, 'entrepreneurial drug traffickers' introduced Central Asia to networks of global narcotics distribution. A select few of the surfers, drifters, and eccentrics who connected tourists to hash dealers learned to expand and develop international shipping capabilities. Hashish bricks, cannabis oil, and morphine base could be packed into automobile compartments.[13] Car dealing was already big business on the Afghan-Pakistan frontier.

A flurry of issues beyond the demand of recreational drug users led more Afghan farmers to turn to opium. Drought in the early 1970s forced a production downturn in South-East Asia, which had been Central Asia's biggest competitor. The lack of cultivation during the drought years drove drug prices up. President Richard Nixon's administration declared a war on drugs and disrupted more established crime syndicates operating in the Mediterranean and Mexico, which reinforced trends of lower global supply and higher prices for narcotics.[14] The Soviet invasion at the end of the 1970s was only the latest event in a decades-long chain that tethered Afghans ever tighter to the drug industry.

Though the Taliban flirted with prohibition when it came to power in the 1990s, poppy cultivation increased steadily throughout the decade. Throughout his time in power, Mullah Omar turned his blind eye to those opium farmers with close connections to the government. Though Taliban leaders issued proclamations throughout their reign that banned opium, bazaars in Helmand and Kandahar continued openly to offer poppy and its derivatives, close to highways and Taliban government headquarters. Indeed, one of the results of the student movement takeover was to remove many of the checkpoints that local strongmen had established throughout the country after the withdrawal of the Soviet Union. The improvement to transit once more facilitated drug trafficking.[15]

Critics of the Taliban have been quick to point out the movement's connections to narcotics. The Taliban imposed taxes on farmers and traffickers that netted millions of dollars each year, comparable to revenues from duties on legal goods such as timber, minerals, automobiles, and electronics. For example, in 1997 the regime drew over $75 million in trade with Pakistan, whereas it made roughly $30 million from taxing opium traders, plus another $15 million from a tithe on farmers.[16] But the Taliban allowed opium more out of deference to small farmers than to produce revenue. The regime had almost no budgetary requirements due to its decentralized structure and unambitious public services program. The head of the regime's narcotics regulation in Kandahar reported in the late 1990s: 'Everyone is growing poppy. If we try to stop this immediately, the people will be against us.'[17] Leaders installed patronage networks to provide security on the route from Kandahar to Pakistan, where cartels processed the crops and distributed them worldwide.[18]

The Taliban did ban poppy cultivation in 2000, though their motivation was debatable. Officially the regime justified its measure, like many other prohibitions, by interpretation of *sharia* law, which banned intoxicants of all kinds, along with playing music, dancing, and kite-flying. On the other hand, outside observers suggested that the opium ban was a calculated scheme to drive up prices, to increase the value of harvested stockpiles. Several members of the regime's leadership stood to profit from such a move.

The most pressing reason for the Taliban prohibition was to improve their image in the court of public opinion. The UN began to impose sanctions on the Afghan government in November 1999 due to the support it offered to Osama bin Laden. The Taliban, due in large part to this developing image problem, had just lost out on a lucrative deal to allow the Union Oil Company of California (UNOCAL) to build a pipeline from Central Asia to a port in Pakistan. Taliban leaders thus sought to replace income from the drug trade, which was dispersed and difficult to regulate, with income from international businesses and humanitarian donors, which would flow into the country via the central government.[19]

The ban seemed to be effective, whatever the reasons for its implementation. Land used for opium poppy fell from 82,000 hectares to less than 10 per cent of that area by the time of the US invasion in 2001. Yet the Taliban's reduction of opium came at a steep cost, especially for small farmers. The Taliban compensated key growers from powerful families for their projected losses, but they could not satisfy the hundreds of thousands of landless or indebted workers of the South who depended on the crop for survival wages. For the impoverished masses, aid dollars could be years away, if not an empty promise.

After Mullah Omar's proclamation of 27 July 2000 that banned cultivation of poppy, armed rebellions against his regime broke out in Kandahar and Helmand. The plight of opium farmers drove many Afghans into the arms of the American invaders when they arrived in October 2001.[20] Most of the territory where opium grew that season was on ground held by UN-supported rebels in the north, which made the anti-drug rhetoric of foreign advisers appear foolish. During the Global War on Terrorism, Taliban leaders could no longer collect taxes or foreign duties. As a result, they turned to illegal activities – kidnapping, extortion, theft, and drug trafficking – to raise money for weapons and fighters.

Though policymakers focused on opium, cannabis had a longer history in Afghanistan. Legend holds that an ancient mystic healer introduced the plant to the region, where it thrived on the sunny mountainsides. In the sixteenth century, Mughal Emperor Babur encouraged the cultivation and use of cannabis in all its forms. Throughout the country, and especially in areas where opium had been banned, cannabis remained a popular crop. In some places, farmers planted a ring of corn or wheat around illicit cash crops.[21] Foreign newcomers to Kandahar could not help but marvel at the prevalence of the cannabinoid plants and their derivatives. Soldiers and linguists reported regular hashish use by the Afghan Border Police. Often Raziq's men invited linguists who worked for the US to smoke hash with them, and some happily accepted.[22] During the surge, soldiers recalled smelling the distinctive odor wafting in the breeze. As one lieutenant rode in his 9ft-high Stryker, he poked his head 'outside the air guard hatch and there's weed, eye-level with me.' He led a patrol to a Border Police checkpoint close to FOB Spin Boldak and found that the commander had grown cannabis plants to form an enormous fence around a courtyard used for meals and leisure. When US soldiers took pictures in front of the peculiar green fence, their Squadron leadership complained to Raziq. The next time the Americans visited, the checkpoint commander had cut down the plants.[23]

Another American, Lieutenant Anthony Formica, regularly encountered cannabis while patrolling south of Kandahar City. 'I can't tell you how many marijuana fields I walked through,' he recalled. Some officers in his infantry battalion reported on the weight of 'marijuana seized' in their daily briefings, which Formica found to be a form of showboating. 'That's not what we're really here for . . . Did you report it to your ANP [Afghan National Police]? OK, let the ANP handle it.' Sometimes, however, drug confiscation did accompany broader counter-insurgent efforts. One day, the Lieutenant led a patrol that discovered bomb-making materials in a mud hut; radio transmissions had been sent from the village to a suspicious location in Pakistan. 'Oh, by the way,' Formica mentioned in his radio report from the scene, 'there's a bunch of marijuana.' The response from higher headquarters was: 'Burn it down.'[24] Policy took on a host of local justifications in the name of military necessity.

Though the US devoted significant funds to fighting drugs, official efforts proved inconsistent. The Bush and Obama administrations developed different visions for counter-narcotics operations. President Bush urged his closest ally, the British, to adopt an aggressive policy as the 'lead nation' for NATO on the issue. The British attempted a 'two-pronged' strategy: interdiction of drug traffickers and compensated eradication for farmers. Interdiction was difficult; officials likened the practice to finding needles in the haystack of Afghan commercial traffic. The UK received new support at the end of 2004 in the form of Plan Afghanistan, a framework modeled on Plan Colombia, which substituted compensation of farmers for forced eradication. The Afghan government rebuffed calls for aerial eradication, the spraying of toxic chemicals to kill the harvest, which Karzai argued would evoke memory of the Soviet policy of rural destruction. The Bush administration quietly dropped the plan on its way out of office.[25]

US officials, instead of spraying from the sky, landed on a ground strategy to be pursued by new agents. American officials sidelined both the British and Afghan governments when they gave a $50 million contract to DynCorp, a corporation tasked to form a 'Central Poppy Eradication Force,' four Afghan teams of 150 men each. One former employee of the program conveyed its ineffectiveness: the Afghan workers were lightly armed, they 'eradicated' fields by knocking over the plants with sticks, and they were easily persuaded by locals to abandon their efforts. More effective operations threatened to provoke a popular backlash. When the CPEF destroyed 217 hectares of poppy in the Arghandab Valley in 2005, it sparked violent protests.[26]

Despite resistance in rural Afghanistan, anti-narcotics became a point of cross-aisle political cooperation in the United States. Congresswoman Nancy Pelosi, in a show of support for President Bush's war, visited Kabul in 2007 to urge Hamid Karzai to clean up the drug-running in his government. Despite the Democratic-Republican handshake on limiting Afghan narcotics, officials with distinct mandates clashed over what was to be done in a practical way. The Pentagon's Counter-Narcotics chief found that operational leaders were 'not interested' in her office's mission, since it stood to expose and embarrass allies that Special Forces and CIA agents had cultivated in the early years of the war. Rather than admit this, defense and intelligence agents claimed that anti-drug policies represented 'mission creep' that would divert resources from the primary goal: to prevent the return of a regime that sponsored terrorists.[27]

The added attention to counter-narcotics during the second term of the Bush administration arrived as Afghan production reached record levels. Greater numbers of troops on the ground, now able to leave cities and FOBs to patrol the countryside, forced cultivation from its peak in 2007 down 16 per cent by 2009. Whereas there were only 25,000 US troops in the country in 2007, that figure more than doubled two years later, even before Obama's announcement of the surge that followed.[28]

But the national decline of narcotics crops belied striking regional differences. In 2002, the UN identified 22,000 hectares of land under cultivation in the east, compared to 39,000 hectares in the south. Seven years later, the east had fewer than 1,000 hectares under cultivation, while southern opium farmland had ballooned to over 100,000 hectares.[29] Moreover, eradication efforts often proved counterproductive. Those with close connections to government bribed officials to leave their fields alone. Isolated farmers bore the brunt of the foreign initiative, while those under Taliban control remained invulnerable to republican decrees.

British and Canadians troops who arrived in the south came under attack for previous anti-opium operations. They had difficulty convincing Afghans that their crops would remain safe after the early American efforts. Major Slade Lerch, a Canadian adviser, had to reassure elders many times throughout 2008 in Panjwai district. When he tried to ask about intelligence, all he heard in reply were pleas to leave their crops alone. 'We're not going to touch your poppy,' Lerch replied. The translated response usually came back as a more emphatic 'Don't burn our poppy.' The adviser, frustrated by the repetition, responded, 'We're not gonna; we're good . . . just like when we were here last week, we didn't touch it.'[30] Officers on the ground refrained from targeting drugs when they found it interfered with local partnerships on security.

When the Obama administration inherited the war in 2009, the President tapped veteran diplomat Richard Holbrooke as his Afghanistan czar. Holbrooke turned against eradication efforts in favor of encouraging 'alternative livelihoods' for Afghan farmers. Instead of targeting the crops themselves, Americans now sought to apprehend key traffickers. A US DEA cell compiled a list of over 300 suspects, of whom fifty were 'nexus targets,' to be killed or captured on sight. The Bush-era Central Poppy Eradication Force was disbanded, and in its place a new Governor-Led Eradication Program forced Afghan leaders to develop their own counter-narcotics strategies based on local conditions. From 2010 to 2011, the proportion of arable land growing poppy dropped from over 50 per cent to less than 5 per cent.[31] The number of missions dedicated to drug seizures grew from 204 in 2010 to over 500 in 2011, enabled by the surge of troops now able to establish a presence in the rural parts of Afghanistan's South.

But the rosy interdiction numbers during the surge years belied another problem, which was prosecution of offenders. When US forces arrested one of Karzai's aides in mid-2010, it set off a dispute that ended the possibility of cooperation on the matter.[32] In the end, Karzai was able to shield his client from the charges. The interests of Afghan sovereignty won out over anti-narcotics. Despite some scares, Raziq too would be free to continue to build his security empire with the aid of drug money.

Lieutenant Colonel Clark was not thinking about drug policy in November 2009 when he ordered Navy jets to bomb the facility in his area of operations. He was using the official stance on drugs to put pressure on Raziq, in the hope of persuading his Afghan partner to release more intelligence about IEDs. It became a creative means to make a personal power play.

The F-18 bombing of the hashish processing plant, though significant for American relationships with Raziq, was but a drop in the bucket of the Afghan narcotics industry. The November bombing destroyed 15 tons of drugs, but this cache paled in comparison to a bust executed by the US DEA with the aid of British and Afghan partners the year before. On 9 June 2008, British Harrier jets had 'cracked open' two cavernous bunkers that contained 262 tons of cannabis, the largest police confiscation of intoxicants in world history. The bunkers had been discovered in what reporters called 'Taliban-controlled areas of the region,' but the location was close to the Pakistan border in Spin Boldak, where Raziq claimed responsibility. Rumors circulated that the Border Police commander was somehow involved in this record-breaking stash, either by facilitating its movement and storage or in looking the other way for those who did.[33]

Even these massive confiscations of drugs could not long put a dent in the production and consumption of cannabis in Kandahar. A new crop was always just weeks away. Hash was so prevalent as to be available to US soldiers through interpreters and their contacts in village bazaars. Its availability resulted in a problem for Clark's superior officer in the 5/2 SBCT chain of command. One of the brigade's other subordinate units experienced a scandal that linked drug use to murder and mutilation.

Chapter 10

TRIALS (2009–10)

Colonel Harry D. Tunnell had faced his trials head-on since his undergraduate days at West Point. Both he and his 1984 classmate H.R. McMaster played on the academy's rugby squad, where they honed traits of mobility and violence. The cadets found the offensive spirit of the pitch reinforced by lectures on the military art. They studied Frederick the Great and Napoleon, Grant and Lee, as they cultivated an admiration for boldness in command. Both men accumulated accolades when they joined the army. McMaster gained fame as a tanker in the Gulf War's Battle of 73rd Easting, while Tunnell commanded in the elite 75th Ranger Regiment.[1]

The US invasion of Iraq in 2003 was a boon for the careers of officers such as Tunnell and McMaster. But their paths through Iraq pushed them to opposing views on counter-insurgency. Tunnell, as commander of the 1-508th Parachute Infantry Regiment, jumped into northern Iraq in 2003. After six months of patrolling with little enemy contact, the regiment received orders to Kirkuk, where they began reconstruction efforts. It was in this phase of civil-military operations that an insurgent shot Tunnell in the leg. The wound was so serious that he had to be evacuated, first to Germany and then to Washington DC. Tunnell saw his wound as painful proof that the army's embrace of counter-insurgency exposed soldiers to needless danger on misguided missions.

McMaster, on the other hand, survived Iraq with his body intact and his faith reinforced.[2] In part, the difference between the two men was temperamental. One had to be an open and patient thinker to accept the more nebulous, less 'kinetic' approach to counter-insurgency operations. The conclusion Tunnell drew, based on his Iraq experience and his interpretation of 'successful' historical campaigns against Native Americans and Filipinos, was that 'oppressive measures' were necessary to defeat insurgencies. Militaries were suited to control populations by force, not win them over by hearts and minds. The prevailing culture of political correctness in America, Tunnell lamented, prevented a frank discussion of the means required.[3]

Change in Mission

As Bill Clark's squadron settled into Spin Boldak and began to partner with Raziq's border police, the rest of the brigade began a desperate fight to the west of Kandahar City. The initial mission of 5/2 SBCT was to support the Afghan national elections that took place in the fall of 2009. But the unit found itself dodging IEDs and complex ambushes rather than delivering ballots. Some polling locations in remote stretches of the Arghandab valley remained off limits to the Americans throughout the election period, the first in the country since the seminal 2004 contest had confirmed Karzai's leadership.

In one sense, Tunnell was right to have prepared his brigade for a lethal mission. Armed resistance emerged as more foreign troops ventured farther from the highway, into the Afghan countryside. But in another sense, the type of threats that the brigade encountered, IED cells and machine-gun teams, proved unsatisfying targets for American firepower. The US forces lunged about in a reactive and frustrated manner, like the proverbial lion pestered by insects.

Moreover, Tunnell's unit was unable to translate armed presence into political stability. The US had dramatically increased the coalition's combat power in Kandahar Province. The Stryker brigade's 1-17 infantry battalion, more than 700 men, replaced a 72-man Canadian reconnaissance troop in Arghandab District. Nevertheless, the presidential election was a flop. Voter turnout was less than 5 per cent in Kandahar Province. Across Afghanistan, only half as many ballots were cast as in 2004. Journalists reported on widespread fraud, including by the Border Police on behalf of Raziq's patron Hamid Karzai.[4]

Taliban violence disrupted preparations for the voting. Days before the election on 18 August, complex IED attacks killed two US soldiers on a dismounted patrol. A week later, an IED exploded under one of the brigade's Stryker vehicles, blew a hole in its bottom, and set off secondary explosions inside. The resulting turmoil flipped the truck upside down and started a fire inside. Rounds stored within the vehicle began to 'cook off' and fly around the chaotic interior. Four Americans perished, including a company commander and a battalion physician's assistant. It was the first instance of soldiers dying inside one of the new vehicles during this first deployment of a large formation of Strykers to Afghanistan. By the end of 2009, thirty-two 5/2 SBCT soldiers had been killed, the highest brigade total throughout the American war.[5]

In November, Tunnell's unit received a change to its mission. A new RC South commander, British Major General Nick Carter, wanted to stop the brigade's bleeding and rotate fresh soldiers into the Arghandab river valley. He tapped an infantry unit from the incoming 82nd Airborne Division. The light brigade made more sense on this mountainous terrain, and the Strykers could pull back from the countryside onto highways. The soldiers of Tunnell's unit were unhappy with the new orders; the troopers could no longer hunt down the Taliban on foot, yet they remained in danger within their vehicles, now evidently vulnerable to Taliban IEDs.

One platoon, originally from 2-1 IN but now attached to 8-1 CAV, suffered the loss of a popular squad leader. He was injured by an IED blast just after the change in mission to focus on the roads. The platoon had shuffled between commands to balance the proportion of infantrymen to cavalrymen at the smallest possible echelon. In theory, this personnel arrangement created hybrid units that combined the speed and firepower of the Strykers with the agility and precision of dismounted troops. The downside to this shuffling was that human ties were broken right at the moment their units deployed overseas. Leaders met their subordinates for the first time on remote FOBs, so they lost the ability to forge connections and develop the trust needed for camaraderie and effective command.

Some within 5/2 SBCT believed this was a problem that Tunnell was especially unable to recognize. He was an engineer and a 'self-proclaimed asocial individual.' He thought in systems to such a degree that organizing men as if they were functions, or lines of code, seemed more natural to him than to the average brigade commander.[6] As a result, Alpha Troop from 8-1 CAV found itself attached to 2-1 IN, stationed at FOB Ramrod, west of Kandahar City, at the mouth of the Arghandab valley. Platoons from Alpha Troop in turn swapped out with those from other companies in 2-1 IN. Even before the IED blast that disrupted squad level leadership, the command relationships between platoon leader, company commander, and battalion commander had been severed and transplanted. The arbitrary decisions regarding unit placement had momentous effects: the difference between the relative safety of Raziq's protection in Spin Boldak and the danger of the Western Kandahar valleys. Personalities, along with unit policies, came to the forefront.

When the injured squad leader from 2-1 IN left Afghanistan for Germany to recuperate, his replacement was Staff Sergeant Calvin Gibbs, who had served on Colonel Tunnell's personal security detail. As one who worked alongside the brigade commander for the first months of the deployment, Gibbs heard an aggressive message reinforced with consistency. While 5/2 SBCT prepared at the National Training Center, staff overhead Tunnell counsel, 'The locals want water? Give 'em Gatorade, because war is a contact sport.'[7] He gave his units 'counter-guerrilla' streamers, to distinguish them from the army's shift toward counter-insurgency. Several sources summarized Tunnell's message as 'Let's kill these motherfuckers,' though the commander's supporters within the brigade argued this was an uncharitable description.[8] Tunnell wanted his men to be aggressive, but he expected them to behave in a professional and discerning manner. Some could not appreciate this distinction.

Murder in Kandahar

Corporal Jeremy Morlock of 2-1 IN was one of those soldiers unable to translate Tunnell's guidance into productive action. He recalled that though the brigade had trained in high tempo 'counter-guerrilla stuff,' after November 2009 they found themselves shuttling senior leaders to talk with Afghan elders and waiting to be blown up on the roads. According to one soldier, Kandahar 'didn't live up to the hype' of what their brigade commander called a 'warrior's paradise.' The soldiers became frustrated with what they considered restrictive rules of engagement. Staff Sergeant Gibbs began to talk about getting revenge for the injured comrade he had replaced, their former squad leader.[9]

As time went on, and boredom and anxiety festered, the squad counseling took darker turns. Gibbs began to suggest that Afghan villagers knew more about the Taliban than they admitted to the Americans on patrol. He told his squad-mates that on a previous deployment to Iraq he had gotten away with shooting civilians at checkpoints. Discussions continued over the next two months until Gibbs, Morlock, and a handful of others developed a plan to 'drop' captured enemy weapons on unsuspecting villagers as justification for killing them.

The attacks followed a pattern. An American soldier would lead a friendly Kandahari to a mud wall, then ask him to raise his *shalwar khameez*, ostensibly to show he was not hiding weapons or wearing an IED vest. With the victim exposed, the soldier threw a live grenade at him and then opened fire. The resulting confusion made it impossible for fellow soldiers to tell whether the Afghan had thrown the grenade or the American had planted it on him. Between January and May, they killed at least three defenseless people for sport. One victim was an elderly religious leader, another a middle-aged farmer, the third a 15-year-old boy.

The plot came to light at the end of the deployment, and only because one soldier threatened to expose his squad's smoking of hashish in their living quarters. Private First Class Stoner, perhaps conscious of his suggestive surname, was wary about the smell of cannabis in his room and did not want to be blamed. When his squad-mates warned the would-be snitch by showing him the severed fingers of their victims, Stoner realized he could now inform on them with impunity. Army investigators would be much more interested in fingers than hash. Once authorities learned about these gruesome trophies, the floodgates were opened to extensive legal trials.

A question remained. Had the brutality been systemic, motivated by the command philosophy, or was Gibbs simply a bad apple who had infected the platoon? Media reports on the incident branded the perpetrators 'thrill' killers, implying that they had no motive besides boredom. The trials that resulted offer more clues. Morlock testified that his comrades had been forced to 'operate in such bad places and not being able to do anything about it. I guess that's why we started taking things into our own hands.' Gibbs claimed the killings had been 'legitimate,' due to a unit culture, or perhaps an infantry-wide culture that glorified killing and rewarded emotional detachment. 'I think I was trying to be hard, a hard individual, and not let it affect me,' Gibbs claimed in reference to the stress of highway patrols in Kandahar.[10]

An army investigation decided that there was indeed a problem with Colonel Tunnell's leadership. The report concluded that the brigade commander's 'inattentiveness to administrative matters' had encouraged the misconduct and created an atmosphere in which indiscipline could occur.[11] It was a condemnation of the minute task organization that sent so many soldiers into new command relationships, a policy that handicapped the junior leaders tasked with supervision of their platoons. Tunnell's push to mix infantry and cavalry elements had turned each unit into 'a shell of its former self,' according to one staff officer.[12] Still, this kind of reproof was muted, less direct than an attack on Tunnell's military ethos or his character would have been. Nor did the army issue its critique of its own initiative through a public forum. A German publication, *Der Spiegel*, leaked the army-internal report along with the trophy images of American soldiers posing next to Afghan corpses.

The army did submit its enlisted soldiers to public trial, and the government confined them in physical captivity. Gibbs received a life sentence. Morlock got twenty-four years in exchange for a guilty plea and testimony against his former squad leader. Five more soldiers from 2-1 IN received between one- and seven-year prison terms for their roles in the killings and the cover-up.[13] For the officers in charge of the rogue squad, the trials did not endanger their physical freedom, but instead the liberty to pursue their profession.

Rather than risk further censure, Colonel Tunnell retired soon after redeployment to the States. It was an abrupt end to a career that many believed would end with general's stars. His supporters believed he had been railroaded out of the army due to the inherent racism of some of his subordinates. Tunnell declined to comment. He retreated from the messiness of people under the strain of combat to the familiarity of systems engineering. 5/2 SBCT retired as a unit and 'reflagged' under a new name. The 'Search and Destroy' brigade emerged phoenix-like from the ashes of the scandal as 2/2 SBCT, the 'Lancer Brigade,' shorn of its association with Tunnell and the hellish Kandahar deployment.[14]

Halfway into the 'thrill killings,' but before Tunnell knew of the atrocities, he had weighed in on Raziq. The brigade commander remained suspicious of the Border Police commander, despite the commendations of his American partner at the battalion level. The Afghan leader's recent good behavior, according to Tunnell, had been mere posturing. He believed that even Raziq's honor pact against the Taliban for killing members of his family could be countered by material suasion from the insurgents. The Colonel cited his logic that Border Policemen had not had any 'major successes against the Taliban' in Spin Boldak district in recent months, because the fighting factions had made some unauthorized local arrangements among themselves. It was evidence of a typical American mindset, in which only offensive operations indicated progress or merit. To accept the status quo reeked of corrupt bargains to create a 'permissive environment' for smugglers and enemy fighters. The US commander advised his subordinates to approach their partner 'carefully,' because of 'the possibility of empowering him due to his reported corruption related activities.'[15] It was this kind of arms-length, transactional partnership that alienated Afghans across the country. Whereas most of Raziq's growing chorus of critics feared his potential brutality, Tunnell criticized his local national partner for not being aggressive enough.

The episode of the rogue US soldiers suggested a broader problem of command authority. Though Tunnell's case differed from Raziq's in significant ways, both leaders came under censure for their aggressive philosophies. The violence that US soldiers wrought against Afghans had been indiscriminate, as it served emotional, identity-based urges. Raziq's violence was more discriminate against those suspected of threatening his security forces. Though they made mistakes, and though some personal grudges were settled in the name of official police work, Raziq's forces based their attitudes on the enemy threats they encountered. Raziq explained to an American journalist, 'We don't take prisoners. If they are trying to kill me, I will try to kill them. That's how I order my men.' Yet Raziq could also demonstrate restraint, as he elaborated, 'If [suspected enemy] submit and say they made a mistake, then yes, we will take them prisoner.'[16] But how important were a commander's words to the conduct of his subordinates? Were they more likely to pick up on the message of aggression or of restraint?

The case of the Stryker brigade in Kandahar revealed the interaction between trends at distinct echelons of leadership. The brigade commander's emphasis on killing rather than nation-building met with negligent leadership in the middle ranks, due to the shuffling of units during the deployment. A squad leader who boasted about his killing of noncombatants in Iraq found a willing disciple in an overeager team leader. To blame the atrocities on the policies of either leader, Colonel Harry Tunnell in one case, or Colonel Abdul Raziq in the other, is an oversimplification that obscures more than it explains.

Instead, the incidents of violence or abuse followed from complex decision-making that played out over cultural landscapes, American and Afghan, tribal and military. It may have been appropriate at times for both Tunnell and Raziq to adopt a bellicose posture as a way to motivate their soldiers, who were exposed to a dangerous insurgency. It may have been more appropriate for Raziq to do so, given that his authority spread across both formal-legitimate and informal-referent bases of power. Tunnell's authority, on the other hand, was restricted to his legal authority as a military commander. Raziq's leadership had more to do with his abilities to inspire loyalty through graft, fear through the threat of violence, or motivation to fight through personal acts of physical bravery.

Tunnell's leadership was circumscribed by his formalized roles: to reward meritorious performance and punish misdeeds according to the Uniform Code of Military Justice. In this confused atmosphere, in which forms of power overlapped, the US military maintained a tenuous hold on its soldiers, while Raziq's reputation continued to grow.

Hashish had been at the center of Tunnell's undoing, the weak link in Gibbs's team. But cannabis, while taboo for the American military in 2009, was a normal part of life in Kandahar. The substance was merely the more socially acceptable cousin of the opium poppy. Americans in Afghanistan were more comfortable with other types of drugs – painkillers, sleeping pills, and steroids – which occupied a central place in the story of yet another atrocity during the American surge.

The kill team's massacre was not an isolated occurrence in Kandahar. In March 2011, Staff Sergeant Robert Bales snuck off his base in Panjwai District and murdered sixteen civilians in two nearby villages. Bales claimed to be under tremendous stress, partly due to a previous operation in which he had seen a close comrade injured. Moreover, he felt besieged by marital issues on the home front and dismissed by the Special Forces team that ran his outpost. To deal with this stress, Bales admitted to drinking alcohol and taking sleeping pills the night of the massacre. Subsequent trial defenses attributed the sergeant's rampage to other drugs: mefloquine, supplied by the army to prevent malaria, or stanozolol, an anabolic steroid that Bales acquired in hopes of becoming, as he testified, 'huge and jacked.'[17]

The centrality of drugs in all of these stories indicated that military authorities viewed the incidents as resulting from the interaction of personalities rather than as the predictable outcome of systems. Each US atrocity seemed to reveal psychological, rather than systemic, explanations for the abuses. After Bales wrought his violence, Raziq stepped in to stanch the suffering. The border police leader provided housing and supplies to family members of the two villages who had survived the horrific night of violence.[18]

Building

The American surge resulted in tremendous construction of infrastructure. US troops and contractors set up hundreds of Forward Operating Bases, the largest of which became sprawling cities that housed tens of thousands. The concept of the Wild West underlay these construction efforts. American newcomers projected a frontier mindset onto Afghanistan, one which suggested that loyalties were uncertain, and that lawlessness reigned. Abundant threats rendered violence a default response. The Americans in Kandahar, like the sheriffs of the Wild West, developed mandates to stand their ground at newly built outposts.

Soldiers used a Wild West lexicon in different contexts. The phrase could suggest 'austere' bases located in areas where fighting was common, but 'wild' also denoted the boomtown atmosphere of Kandahar Airfield. In the imaginations of the NATO personnel who flocked there, the airfield recalled scenes from *Indiana Jones* or *Star Wars* films, dimly-lit cantinas populated with a crowd pulled together from distant lands.[19] The economic opportunities drew diverse and desperate characters together, and the setting evoked the historical American West and its amalgamation of black and white people, Chinese railroad workers, and locals of French, Spanish, and Native American ancestry.

At Kandahar Airfield, this boomtown version of the Wild West manifested in the form of aid workers, journalists, intelligence agents, defense contractors, and military officers from across the region. They joined civilian workers from neighboring states, contracted security guards from Africa, and displaced Afghan people – Pashtun, Tajik, Uzbek, and Hazara – from remote provinces. All sought a steady paycheck and some measure of security. The British maintained a large contingent in neighboring Helmand Province, as Australian and Dutch officers monitored and supported their elements in Uruzgan. Then there were small collections of others: officer augmentees, special forces contingents, military police, engineer units, and civilian contractors from Spain and France, Romania and Bulgaria, Poland, Japan, and South Korea. The biggest foreign population, until the Americans surged in, had been the Canadians, whose presence lingered after the nation's soldiers left in 2011, due to their construction of a Tim Horton's restaurant and a cement street hockey rink known as 'Maple Leaf Gardens.'[20]

Newcomers adopted the language of the American Old West to describe their surroundings. Outposts at the 'end of the line' for logistics trains were called 'Alamos,' organized with conscious thought so as not to be similarly overrun.[21] Opening the flap of a dining facility tent in Afghanistan felt like swinging the hinged gates of a western saloon, especially for soldiers who carried pistols in hip holsters. The DFAC at Spin Boldak was called 'Old Bill's,' and its exterior sign featured the outlined image of a lone, Stetson-wearing horseman. Soldiers referred to leaving their bases as going 'outside the wire,' into 'Indian Country.'[22] Americans touched down on hostile terrain from helicopters named for Native Americans: Chinooks and Blackhawks. Other choppers, Apaches and Kiowas, provided fire support.

This new American frontier, a series of enclaves across Afghanistan's mountainous terrain, had a temporary appearance. Electrical generators were ever-present, humming, stinking of diesel fuel, and a reminder that power was tenuous and easily lost. Building materials were lightweight: plastic tents and plywood buildings. There were few below-ground foundations to be found. The advantages of building in this style were obvious: the material was cheap, and construction was fast.

The temporary appearance also sent a message, underlined by President Obama's speech, that the presence of American surge troops would be limited to some eighteen months, before numbers began to draw down again.[23] One Marine officer cited an Afghan contractor who warned, 'Wars are not won with plywood.'[24] But would sturdier building have sent a better message? The contractor, of course, had a personal motive to suggest more expensive materials. Rather than a sign of foreign commitment, more permanent construction might have exacerbated Afghan fears of an imperial occupation, already a mainstay of Taliban warnings about the danger of allowing infidels to remain in the country.

As a result of the limited US commitment, those who built in Afghanistan during the surge did so by leveraging existing infrastructure. Kandahar Airfield had long been the region's functional air hub. Since the 1960s it had featured a lone dusty air strip and a few flights per day to Kabul, occasionally one to Iran, Pakistan, India, or the USSR. The Soviets had expanded the old airfield during their occupation, and they added residential towers that US soldiers continued to call the 'Russian flats.'[25] Under the American regime, the little-used runways expanded into a bustling city of tens of thousands, complete with a 'Boardwalk' that featured multiple corporate coffeehouses and a TGI Friday's.[26] The name derived from the raised wooden paths that connected the shipping container shops, but it also called to mind Boardwalk Avenue in the board game Monopoly. For Kandaharis, this part of the airfield represented the greatest concentration of American dollars in the South.

Soldiers and military operations brought a constant flow of dollars into Kandahar, but they produced a constant flow of waste as well. Bottled water arrived wrapped in clear plastic, on top of wooden pallets, which accumulated in mounds around the living spaces. Food came in cardboard boxes, with brown and green sheets of plastic that sealed the edible contents inside. Soldiers carried meals on top of cardboard trays or inside Styrofoam boxes. Bodily waste collected in plastic porta-johns. Afghan contractors rolled in on vehicles equipped with tanks and hoses to suck up fluids and solids cast off by the inhabitants of the multinational bases.

KAF exhibited some of the vice-related aspects of a Wild West boomtown. A few shops offered black market goods; their merchants were linked to criminal or Taliban networks. Employees who had been fired often remained on the base and became potential spies. The airfield had unique elements, too. One landmark was a waste treatment facility known as the 'poo pond.' During one college football season, a mischievous soldier erected a sign in the characteristic purple and gold colors of Louisiana State that read, 'LS Poo.' In addition to a source of comedy, the waste treatment plant became a symbol for the spreading discontents and refuse of the commerce, another kind of 'ink blot' that the foreign coalition generated.[27]

FOB Spin Boldak, far from this emerging metropolis, was in the borderlands of Kandahar Province. There had been an Afghan fort on the site of the coalition's base since at least the late nineteenth century. A single tower a few stories high provided a vista into Pakistan, a few kilometers to the south. Spin Boldak itself had scant infrastructure to justify the brigade-sized base that emerged during the surge period; proximity to the frontier was the determining factor.

While most of 5/2 Stryker brigade struggled to the west of Kandahar City in the summer of 2009, Lieutenant Colonel Bill Clark's squadron built partnerships with Raziq and his forces to the south-east. Building of the FOB proceeded apace. When 8-1 CAV showed up in the area, the existing facility had housed a handful of CIA agents, guarded by rotating teams of US and French Special Forces. For a brief period, the outpost had been home to a Canadian platoon of thirty soldiers. The few stone and cinder-block buildings standing reminded the first American troopers of prison cells. From a lone lookout tower in the middle of the FOB, the Americans quickly established an expanded security footprint.[28] Clark recalled thinking, 'I'm in the middle of nowhere.' The prospect was at once chilling and well suited to the weapons of his Strykers: high-powered 40mm grenade launchers and .50 caliber machine guns that could reliably hit targets over a mile away if the line of sight was clear.

Around these vehicles, 8-1 CAV built a massive system of defense and life support. They surrounded themselves with an earthen berm and set up guard towers along the perimeter. 'We had to do a lot of construction. HESCO barriers, putting in CHUs,' Clark recalled, with reference to the Containerized Housing Units, shipping-container dwellings that were considered plush compared to the typical plywood or tent barracks found on most military bases. The upgrading process lasted throughout the year-long deployment.[29] By the time that replacements from 4-2 CAV showed up in the summer of 2010, the FOB boasted a spacious gymnasium and a twenty-four-hour dining facility, with a rotating hot bar and daily dessert specials. The MWR facility contained a dozen phones in banked rows, a large screen TV with DVD rentals, ping-pong, billiards, and foosball. The FOB had its own post office, as well as a laundry facility that featured a dozen washers and dryers. The machines hummed at all hours, in order to deliver 48-hour turnaround service. With these amenities in place, most soldiers preferred the quiet and space along the border at this newly built base to the bustle of the airfield.

Cemetery of the Englanders

Raziq made additions to his own infrastructure while the Americans built up FOB Spin Boldak a few kilometers to the west. He was in the process of building a new council (*shura*) room for hosting guests on the highest point of the hills that poked up from inside his fortress. Clark and Raziq, along with Clark's interpreter Najib Fazel, entered a recently constructed room. Raziq pointed out a window.

'Come here, I want to show you something,' he said to Clark.

Raziq pointed down to a field about a kilometer from the fortress walls, marked by tattered blue and white flags that fluttered in front of small, worn headstones.

He told his American partner, 'Down there is the cemetery of the Englanders. You see the British soldiers? This is their grave down there.'[30]

Raziq was aware of his historical role as a defender of Afghanistan. The fortress on which the men stood had the appearance of a great ruin, ironic because the stone edifice was known as *Qala-i-Jadid*, the New Fort. The structure had still been new when its defenders, outnumbered ten to one, fell victim to the British and their Punjabi allies during the Third Anglo-Afghan War. A prominent Afghan historian has called this action the 'Alamo of Afghanistan,' as folk songs emerged in memory of the defenders and their sacrifice. One song features the lyrics: '*Qala-i-Jadid*, the honorable site; it is the resting place of the martyrs blessed by the lights from heaven.'[31] Afghans continue to celebrate their Independence Day on 19 August, the date that their final war against the British ended. Raziq knew that the British were currently surging into nearby Helmand Province. He knew that Clark's boss two levels up, RC South commander Major General Nick Carter, was a British officer.

At one meeting toward the end of 2009, Carter revealed a cultural blind spot that threatened to disrupt the relationship with his Afghan partner. The British commander visited FOB Spin Boldak to meet with Raziq, Clark, and his interpreter. Najib understood the potential pitfalls in conversations between Afghans and Westerners, since he had a foot in each world. He had left his homeland during the Soviet period and settled in Germany. In 2002, he moved to California, where he was recruited in 2006 to return to Afghanistan as a cultural adviser.

The men sat down cross-legged in a meeting room. Enlisted soldiers doled out hot tea and dried fruit. As Carter was getting to know his new Afghan partner, he asked an indelicate question. Somehow the conversation had touched on the topic of education. Raziq, like most Afghans his age, had no formal schooling. Carter, on the other hand, had graduated from the prestigious Royal Military College at Sandhurst.

Perhaps to assert his formal authority, Carter asked Raziq, 'Where did you go to school?'

Najib, thinking on his feet, gave Raziq a different question: 'What have you done to improve schools here in Spin Boldak?'

The interpreter understood that a correct translation would have embarrassed Raziq, whereas the adapted one flattered him. If the Afghan leader had to admit his lack of schooling in the mixed company of British and American soldiers, even the lowliest among them with some high school education, it might have soured his relationships with Carter and Clark. So Najib intervened and allowed the police commander to discuss how many new schools he had built, how many teachers he had hired, how many children still needed books or uniforms, and so on.

When the answers came back to Carter in English, the British general glanced at his own interpreter in puzzlement. But rather than persist in his problematic line of questioning, the General wisely moved on to another topic. Najib had narrowly averted an unfortunate revival of imperious British attitudes toward their Afghan hosts.[32]

Investigations and Inspections

In October 2009, a Border Police Zone commander who served as Raziq's nominal boss was arrested for pension embezzlement. Questions emerged in coalition headquarters across Kandahar and Kabul. Did this detention signal the fall of Raziq, too? One intelligence report gives some clues as to the deliberations on Raziq at a key moment of the US surge.

The document discussed potential outcomes if the foreign coalition decided to arrest Raziq as a 'malign actor' in Afghan politics. The most likely course was that Raziq would continue to pull strings from prison through his associates, and that an 'erosion in the cooperation' between foreign troops and the Afghan Border Police would ensue. The most dangerous course was a 'combative reaction' from Raziq, which could result in 'minor riots, a wave of desertions,' attacks on the rival National Police, or even violence against the Americans themselves. All of this would disrupt the movement of supplies across the Pakistan border.

The report then specified distinct downsides to acting against Raziq. First, detaining him would 'remove the only major tribal figure in Kandahar' with a base of power separate from the Karzai and the Sherzai families. The Americans wanted to be able to keep Karzai honest, so they could not remove all of potential checks on his power. Second, Raziq had 'no clear potential successor.' Any potential replacement pulled from obscurity was almost certain to continue to 'leverage the force to manage Achakzai narco-smuggling,' albeit less effectively than Raziq. This degradation in Border Police operations might allow for more influence over transit routes by the Noorzai, the Taliban, and other criminal smuggling organizations.

Finally, with some speculation about the ripple effects of American intervention, the report considered Kandahar politics. Raziq's 'arrest would reinforce a perception of Achakzai targeting,' since his uncle, a National Police Chief in a neighboring district, had been arrested in July. Raziq's boss, another fellow tribesman, went down in October. 'Politically engaged Kandaharis,' the report claimed, would see the arrest of Raziq in one of two ways: as evidence of the foreign coalition eliminating a Karzai rival to power, or as Karzai caving to the demands of the American anticorruption campaign. Either interpretation was likely to 'enflame' tribal relations in Kandahar, the report concluded in dejection.

In Raziq's absence, the Border Police's prestige might have suffered, to the benefit of the newly-created Afghan Highway Police (AHP) now led by Hajji Lal Jan of the Noorzai tribe. The Highway Police had checkpoints along the highway, like the Border Police, but their mandate covered the few kilometers around Takteh-Pol; the ABP watched over the majority of the route from the border to Kandahar City. Because the Achakzai formed most of the district's population, their tribe's predominant political opinions mattered to American decision-makers seeking to encourage democratic governance. And because Achakzai villages were closer to the highway than those of the Noorzai, their support for the government was paramount.

Moreover, the Americans on the ground who worked with Raziq could not point to a reliable replacement for him in the Afghan security forces. The intelligence report therefore concluded that over the next six to twelve months, the coalition should begin to look for another Achakzai leader to groom.[33] In the meantime, Raziq could help address some of the American missteps across southern Afghanistan.

On 16 December 2009, the Headquarters Troop from 8-1 CAV conducted a health and welfare inspection on FOB Spin Boldak. Narcotics had turned up in the Border Police barracks during a previous search, so the command urged a more thorough scan this time. After combing through living spaces, an Air Force dog-handler walked through the Spin Boldak mosque. Afghan witnesses protested that not only had a dog entered the holy space, but it had been led by this particular sergeant, an American woman. Offended parties threatened to take to the streets of Spin Boldak, so Clark called Raziq to enlist his support. Raziq stood by his American partner's side and apologized to local leaders. On Afghan recommendations, 8-1 CAV purchased a cow for sacrifice to purify the mosque. All members of the Headquarters Troop underwent cultural sensitivity training over the next three days.[34]

Farewell Gift

By the spring of 2010, Clark's deployment was approaching its end. Unlike sister battalions under Colonel Tunnell to the west of Kandahar City, which had waged a series of kinetic operations, 8-1 CAV had built a FOB and patrolled the highway without much resistance. After the initial month of IED explosions on the outer limits of their area of operations, the deployment had settled down to a relative predictability, alongside Raziq and his policemen.

Clark's power play with the F-18 bombing of the drug facility seemed to impress Raziq. From the American's perspective, the relationship throughout that year grew stronger after the early point of tension. Over time, it became cordial. Raziq appeared to respect the cavalry commander for his boldness, and he became more enthusiastic about sharing intelligence after the airstrike. Raziq was savvy enough to maintain his relationships with the Americans and keep their dollars flowing in his direction. But there were signs of a closer personal connection, as well. At the end of the squadron's year-long stay in Spin Boldak, Raziq invited Clark to visit his home, the only such invitation extended to a conventional army officer.

Raziq's residence was a massive structure, two stories with twelve-foot ceilings, and dozens of rooms. The front of the building featured solid stone steps, which conveyed visitors to an entrance of pillars that supported a rooftop balcony. Sleek glass windows lined the walls and made Raziq's home shimmer in the glare of the Kandahar sun. It was one of the most impressive of the 'poppy palaces' that began to dot the landscape of Southern Afghanistan during the US surge.[35] When Raziq heard that his American partner had been looking for an authentic Afghan rug to present to his wife as a souvenir, the border police leader provided a beautiful navy and maroon specimen, one that continued to grace the Clark family den many years later.[36] No other American commander got such a gift upon his farewell from Spin Boldak.

CAB Rides

In May, when the advance party of 4-2 CAV touched down at KAF, they met the grizzled veterans of 8-1, coated in the reddish dust found down the highway to the south-east of the city. The ways the 8-1 troopers donned their kit signaled their experience in theater; they had customized gear layouts for their individual roles on patrol. They took the new replacements from 4-2 CAV in and showed them marked-up maps and radio techniques. Some of the veterans pointed to places on the maps off the highway, where they told the new arrivals they could go for 'CAB rides.'

The CAB was the combat action badge, issued for engaging or being engaged by the enemy. Its award was a kind of legitimizing stamp on a deployment. There had been scant opportunities for the troopers of 8-1 CAV to earn awards in Spin Boldak district. Raziq had preserved a bubble of security around the border for his American guests. The older members of 4-2 CAV, who already had combat badges from Iraq, shook their heads. You didn't want to go looking for that – bad juju.[37]

The changing of the American guard at Spin Boldak brought a sea change in command philosophy. In place of 5/2 SBCT's 'let's kill' mentality preached by Harry Tunnell, the troopers of the 2nd Cavalry Regiment heard about a 'love bank' in Kandahar, and about the need to make deposits rather than withdrawals. Could Raziq use the resources at his command, thanks to his growing cohort of more willing American partners, to extend the benefits of security beyond the highway, into the villages?

Chapter 11

PEAK OF THE SURGE (2010–11)

Lieutenant Colonel Andy Green arrived in Vilseck, Germany to take command of 4-2 Cavalry Squadron only a few months before the unit's deployment to Kandahar. His previous assignment had been at a NATO command, as executive officer to a Dutch major general, so he was at home in Europe by this point. But Green was not supposed to have command of this squadron on its deployment to Afghanistan. He was a fill-in for the previous commander, who had been a well-liked and spirited leader scratched from the deployable list when army doctors discovered lymphoma at a unit-wide medical screening. The shuffle at the top of the squadron's hierarchy was an extra obstacle for 4-2 CAV as the unit prepared for its year in Kandahar.

Green glanced around his new headquarters. Large placards announced the space as belonging to the Saber Squadron. The unit was the Reconnaissance, Surveillance, and Target Acquisition (RSTA) element for the regiment. It was a set of tasks that seemed well suited for hunting insurgents across an open plain. This was perhaps the purest mission for the cavalryman, to ride out in advance of the main body of troops, in order to collect intelligence and screen for signs of the enemy. The squadron's soldiers thought of themselves, within the Cavalry regiment, as the 'real Cav.'[1]

Green's position as the replacement, the 'alternate command list' choice, would have been difficult for many leaders to handle. But Green had the appropriate attitude for this kind of combat deployment. Though the army tended to select commanders for their aggression, what was needed most in Kandahar as the American surge rolled in was humility. Green's credentials did not suggest the modest mien he displayed before his men. He had earned the coveted Ranger tab, and he had deployed to Iraq in 2004, when the conflict turned into a bloody guerrilla fight. But Green was not a West Pointer; he was an ROTC product of Seattle University. He was neither loud nor square-jawed, but well-read and reserved, more comfortable in the quiet of a hunter's tree stand than politicking in dress uniform with fellow officers and their wives. Perhaps this was why he had been left off the primary list for command in the first place.

As he took on leadership of his squadron, the main message Green received from his regimental commander, Colonel Robin Blackburn, was to bring a lighter touch to counter-insurgency operations. No longer would the counter-guerrilla 'let's kill' philosophy issue from higher command. Instead, Blackburn championed the concept of 'the love bank.' Troopers should think about their actions in Afghanistan, Blackburn counseled, as making either deposits to or withdrawals from the love bank. Too many withdrawals could result in a dangerous situation for the Americans, far from home and surrounded by Raziq's 4,000-strong force.[2]

Andy Green, the untraditional hero squadron commander, led a subtle shift in his unit's culture that put partnership first. Instead of a heroic, Custer-esque 'we're *the* cavalry' approach, Green told Raziq, 'We're *your* cavalry.' In the American Western imagery, Raziq had been promoted from Tonto to the Lone Ranger. The Americans under Green no longer played a lead role like Custer, arrogant yet overwhelmed. Instead, Green reimagined his unit as a faceless auxiliary force, hidden behind helmets and dark goggles, riding 'hell bent for leather,' as the 2nd Cavalry regiment's song declared, to the aid of Raziq's policemen and Afghan villagers under duress from the Taliban.[3]

A central tenet of counter-insurgency doctrine is to put an indigenous face on all operations. Raziq provided that face. His image began to grace billboards, Humvee windows, and the patches of his border policemen around Kandahar Province. In part, the shift of the Americans to a supporting role resulted from Green's recognition of conditions in Kandahar Province. But mostly it had to do with Raziq's own growth in resources and prestige over the past twelve months. Whereas Raziq had played second fiddle in the early years of the American war to more established Governors Sherzai and Khalid, now he was better able to dictate the terms of his security to the new technocratic appointee, Governor Tooryalai Wesa.

Raziq's growing prominence in Kandahar politics came at a cost. The more he accumulated power and resources, the more he came to the attention of the US intelligence community, which saw its role, along with the journalists and human rights activists of the country, as the morality police of the American-Afghan partnership. Most of Raziq's critics framed their actions as anti-corruption, rather than anti-torture or anti-summary execution. It was perhaps an understandable objection. If the Americans went after Raziq's executions, he could always feign ignorance or bad intelligence. The Americans mixed up their targets, too, after all. But the Americans at least had their paperwork straight. Their mistakes were all above board, in terms of bureaucratic legality, appropriately documented and sometimes condemned.

The Anti-Corruption Crusade

In early 2010, ISAF commanding general Stanley McChrystal launched Afghanistan's biggest operation to date, as 15,000 combined NATO and Afghan forces occupied Marjah, a Taliban stronghold in Helmand Province, west of Kandahar. McChrystal sought to add 'building' to the end of this massive operation to 'clear' and 'hold' territory contested by the insurgency. In a publicized effort to wage a new kind of war, the command proposed to roll in a 'government in a box,' pre-packaged and ready to operate in the wake of the fighting.[4] To do so required not only bravery, but competent officials, who would spend American dollars on development rather than their cronies, or worse still, Taliban protection rackets. The emphasis of operations had shifted to good governance, and some in the American camp saw Raziq as incompatible with the new guidance. One report assessed him as 'an effective combat commander, but [he] does not perform his police role as well. He is good at the "sweep" phase of operations but is not as good at the "hold" phase.'[5]

When McChrystal and his intelligence deputy Major General Michael Flynn arrived for a meeting in Kandahar in mid-January 2010, Raziq came under the microscope. ISAF leadership faced questions from journalists on their partner's alleged links to criminal activity. The Border Police commander had risen to regional prominence over the past few years, and the attention he received from the Western press threatened to diminish support for the American surge. Raziq now faced allegations of election-tampering and skimming border customs, in addition to the well-known Shin Noorzai massacre of 2006.

Major General Flynn found an unlikely ally during his effort to remove Raziq in former NPR reporter Sarah Chayes, who had been hired to the top-level ISAF staff as a cultural expert in the late aughts. The pair could not have been more different in terms of personality. Flynn, like many US generals, was a 'cowboy,' rough and boisterous. Chayes, by contrast, was cautious and thoughtful, ready to respond to any military officer's testosterone-fueled claim with a studied, 'Well, actually . . .' She recalled that Flynn, who later became a Donald Trump acolyte and conspiracy theorist, was not 'nakedly partisan' at the time.

One thing that Chayes and Flynn agreed upon was corruption. In particular, the odd couple believed that the most significant threat to the government of Afghanistan was not the Taliban, but the venality of the Karzai regime itself. The poster child for corrupt practices appeared to be Raziq, who made his money skimming off the top of drug rackets and border customs revenues, but who was isolated from repercussions because of his military alliance with the Karzai brothers.

Locals told Chayes they were 'horrified' by Raziq's rise. Even members of his own tribe, the Achakzai, Chayes recalled as being 'revolted at the corruption of how he was running the show.' She brought out a salient point about tribal politics. Many Americans simplified Raziq's patronage network as being run by and for his own tribe. In fact, the network included many Achazkai tribal leaders, but not all of them, and it extended to members of other Pashtun groups and Afghanistan's minority ethnicities. Karzai's network functioned in much the same way on the national level, heavy on Popalzai and Pashtun men, but including a sprinkling of key allies from other bases of power.

Chayes, Flynn, and others in American government used corruption as a wedge issue to pressure the Karzai government to adapt to Western political culture. The anti-corruption crusade also paved the way for American excuses, a way to shift blame and salvage careers as the surge ended and the drawdown began amid ambiguous results.[6]

Chayes was one of the few American women who had been in Afghanistan regularly since 2001. She was the author of *The Punishment of Virtue* (2006), a probing account of recent Afghan history. After publication of this comprehensive and multifaceted book, Chayes began to distill its message, focusing on corruption as the explanatory factor that doomed American efforts in Central Asia. Her message emerged from study as well as from deep-seated emotion. Chayes, before she began to advise general officers, had run non-profit organizations in Afghanistan. From this perspective, she witnessed heartbreaking incidents of ordinary Afghans being victimized by callous and predatory officials.

Debates on the ISAF staff took shape as some analysts sought to separate and prioritize different types of venality. For example, Special Forces Lieutenant Colonel Chris Kolenda compared corruption to a disease, more or less harmful depending on the type. Kolenda used cancer as an analogy: the petty shakedowns that occurred at the border or at checkpoints were like skin cancer, something to address perhaps, but far from life-threatening. On the other hand, the purchase of high offices in the Afghan government, the system of patronage that allowed Karzai to consolidate power, was a fatal 'brain cancer,' because it resulted in a chain of predation by which the purchasers of office retained power not through merit, but by leaning on subordinates to make good on their spending for the official title. This was the top-down version of vertical integration. The high office-holders were the most significant because the money tended to accumulate with them. Cut off the head of corruption, and the tail would wither.

Chayes saw the problem in a different way. Vertical integration could be bottom-up as well. There was no telling whether getting rid of corrupt leaders would make subordinate commanders behave. There was little to prevent the petty offenders from developing their own venal schemes after the ouster of a former boss. Moreover, Chayes claimed it was the 'street level corruption' that had a 'disproportionate psychological effect' in making local Kandaharis 'furious.' In this line of logic, violence and humiliation drove common people into the arms of the Taliban. The counter-insurgents could not afford to parcel out corruption into separate 'flavors,' which diffused accountability across organizations: not the army but the police, or the State Department, or the Afghan Ministry of Interior. Corruption became a hot potato to pass around. Chayes lectured commanders that they had to combat corruption at all levels at once, or else corrupt actors would simply shape-shift and redesign their rackets.[7]

Major General Mike Flynn, too, became interested in preventing corruption, though he was more interested in Raziq's connections out of the country than his network's abuse of Kandaharis on the domestic front. Flynn wanted to connect Afghan corruption to global networks. He sought to encourage the Treasury Department to act on the illicit flows of money across Afghanistan's national borders. Treasury, however, had little interest in pursuing this. With his international angle frustrated, Flynn turned to General McChrystal to stop Raziq's alleged fraud. Would McChrystal listen to his intelligence chief and remove the young police commander?

Colonel Steve Beckman Sr., an intelligence officer at Regional Command (RC) South, had a front row seat to the dispute. The RCs had been established in 2004, as part of Lieutenant General David Barno's policy of battlefield 'ownership' by various echelons of military units.[8] The ISAF headquarters in Kabul, staffed by the top general in command, organized operations and resources through the RCs, which in turn issued guidance and tools to the divisions and brigades under them. Early in 2010, Flynn at the top ISAF level developed 'a wild hair' about wanting to remove Raziq, part of what Beckman characterized as anti-corruption talk 'boiling in Kabul' at the time. When Beckman heard that Flynn wanted to remove his regional commander's most important military partner, he realized he could not accommodate the effort without top-cover.

'I work for General Carter. You need to tell him that,' Beckman protested to Flynn.

But before Flynn got the chance, Carter decided to head off the effort.

'Tell you what, Steve,' Carter told his intel chief, 'just sit off camera here for my Tandberg,' – an early video conferencing platform.

When Carter had Flynn on the line, he said, 'I understand that you want to want to come down here and fire Raziq.' Flynn began to explain himself, but Carter cut him off. The British general was not in the mood to debate the finer points of governance with his American partner that day. Carter didn't talk about Raziq after this initial mention.

Instead, he made two points: 'A. I'm the commander of RC South. B. You can fly into Kandahar anytime you want. But no helicopter is going to fly you down to Spin Boldak.'

Flynn's plan had been blocked.

The exchange highlighted two trends in the Afghan surge. Resources were divided among the various Western military leaders, who could be as tribal in their jealousies as the Afghans. Secondly, commanders were the decision-makers. Staff officers, especially intelligence sections, might have had more insight into what was going on, but the maneuver officers held the commands. Thus, they could embrace or ignore the guidance of their staffs as they deemed fit. In effect, Carter favored the input of his subordinate combat commanders, whose operations depended on Raziq, over a staff and its theories about good governance.

Colonel Beckman, for his part, agreed with Carter's decision. He acknowledged it was almost certain that Raziq was 'dirty,' connected to illegal rackets. And yet, unsavory as his behavior was, he had found a way to provide a level of stability to Kandahar that had been missing for years. Sarah Chayes and Mike Flynn wanted a more ambitious 'Jeffersonian democracy' in Afghanistan. Beckman saw the potential for such political reforms to work at 'cross purposes' with tribal leaders, who dealt more in respect and power than republican ideals, especially as they related to cultural questions of women's rights, justice, and education.[9]

Moreover, though corrupt practices were widespread in both Raziq's Kandahar and Karzai's Kabul, it was difficult for Americans to prove specific acts of wrongdoing. About the best they could do was to create 'link diagrams,' with known associations generated by witnessed meetings or cell phone calls. When US intelligence analysts created a link diagram for corrupt agents in Spin Boldak in September 2010, they put Raziq in the middle, along with Afghan Highway Police (AHP) leader and Noorzai elder Sahib Lal Jan. Both government officials had associations with known criminal smugglers. Lal Jan had contact with on a robust narcotics ring and Taliban cell that operated in the desert area south of the main border crossings. Raziq's links to smuggling comprised two separate networks, one run by Border Police (ABP) officials and the other by National Police (ANP) leadership. Raziq had been connected to one of Ahmed Wali Karzai's illicit shipments of explosives. The diagrams gave a sense of corruption at every turn in these organizations; it was unlikely that swapping out any one individual would yield positive results, since more corrupt actors crowded into the diagram from all angles. The potential replacements for Raziq, Achakzai tribal elders or the Border Police commanders from neighboring units, would likely engage in the same behaviors, albeit with less competence and greater risk of Taliban infiltration.[10]

After the 17 January 2010 meeting, at which journalists laid out their case to ISAF brass about corruption, Raziq began a public relations campaign. He protested to American officers that the media had spread false statements about him. He accused *Washington Post* reporter Joshua Partlow of libel, and he told military partners he was considering legal action. The Border Police leader then dictated a letter to President Karzai to request an Anti-Corruption Task Force to be run by Kabul's Ministry of the Interior. Raziq reasoned that the new government entity would allow others to do the monitoring and leave him to focus on police work. In an effort to clean up his own organization in the interim, Raziq arrested the Spin Boldak Finance Minister in late February on charges of skimming $250,000 per month in customs payments. US officials noted these steps with tepid approval, as they remarked that at the beginning of the month, ISAF truck drivers continued to be charged unauthorized staging fees at Border Police checkpoints.[11]

Despite the growing attention to corruption in Kabul, Carter decided to protect Raziq. To keep his Afghan partner in power, to tolerate some graft in hopes of preserving security, had been the most reasonable, least dangerous course of action. It was also in accordance with the guidance of CENTCOM commander General David Petraeus, to work with who we have, not who we want. If one wanted to privilege stability, Raziq was the clear choice. If one wanted to prioritize Afghan sovereignty, again Raziq seemed to be the best option. Not only did he work well with both the Sherzai and the Karzai families, but as an Achakzai he had a tribal base of power independent from these elites. He was a charismatic 'rising star,' an authentic Kandahari 'diamond in the rough,' who had demonstrated he could run a large-scale military operation alongside a multinational smuggling ring. According to Beckman, Raziq 'didn't have that Western taint to him.' He was not part of the crowd of Afghan republican officials who had expatriated to Europe or North America for the past two decades.[12]

American commanders opted to mentor Raziq rather than remove him. They reasoned that since he was a young man, he would be 'impressed and impressionable' at American expertise. Intelligence analysts, perhaps themselves enamored with their boss's cult of personality, noted Raziq had an 'extremely favorable impression' of General McChrystal, calling him a 'thoughtful leader,' and more 'diplomat than military commander.' Many remained hopeful that with greater counseling and oversight, Raziq could be slowly cultivated into a more acceptable partner.[13] For the disappointed Flynn and Chayes, only time would tell if this were possible, but they were not optimistic.

Raziq acquired another partner, in addition to Andy Green, who had replaced Bill Clark as the cavalry squadron commander in Spin Boldak. This new mentor came straight from General McChrystal's hip pocket. The ISAF commander tapped an old buddy, a fellow Special Forces officer he had known for decades, to coach Raziq's professional development. The Green Beret liaison, who preferred to remain anonymous, brought new energy to the moribund Joint Border Coordination Center (JBCC) established to monitor the border. Not only would Raziq's methods have more oversight, but the dormant tripartite agreement between the U.S., Afghanistan, and Pakistan could restart from a new institutional angle. McChrystal's man on the inside counseled Raziq that if he wanted to stay in America's good graces he would have to refrain from closing the border at will, work to legitimize his business interests, and confine his operations to Spin Boldak, as the Border Police were supposed to do.[14]

Another Special Forces initiative that arrived with the surge was the 'augmentation team,' deployed at provincial and district levels. This new institution recruited officers to become 'AfPak Hands,' modeled on the concept of the Second World War 'China Hands' community of long-serving regional experts. General Scott Miller developed the program in 2010, which included fourteen weeks of language training and a commitment of two year-long tours in Afghanistan. But the local Hand at Spin Boldak, rather than mentor Raziq, became more of a coordinator of intelligence. His Pashto skills were insufficient to counsel Afghans, but they helped him to listen in on their conversations and interject familiar phrases that built rapport.[15]

Another scheme was intended to reduce Raziq's power through the use of border 'zones.' The Afghan government created a new echelon of responsibility between the provinces and Kabul. RC South leadership arrived at FOB Spin Boldak with an Afghan general and announced to Raziq, 'This is your new boss.' The meeting thereby got off to a rocky start, with this public affront to Raziq's authority. The Achakzai leader's 'wealth was his reputation,' so he would not acquiesce in sharing power with this new zone commander along the southern border. As a carrot for good behavior, Raziq's mentors proposed English language courses. The move, though well-intentioned, was 'right out of the imperial age,' in the opinion of one journalist. Raziq ignored the offer and went on with his affairs much as before.[16]

After a few months, with the arrival of a new Full Bird Colonel on FOB Spin Boldak, the Special Forces officer stepped down from partnership with Raziq to focus on the organizational processes of the JBCC. The new organization was fraught with the difficulty of creating working relationships between Afghan and Pakistani military officers. Over time, the Americans learned that many of the Pakistani officers sent to coordinate at the JBCC were in fact ISI spies. Institution-building came with its own set of risks, and American officials had to weigh the benefits of dealing with the devil they knew against unknown or unvetted entities being invited to participate in new ventures.[17]

An Afghan Robin Hood

Lieutenant Colonel Green was willing to tolerate Raziq's rackets if he could provide stability. As one of his lieutenants serving in Spin Boldak put it, 'It was probably the right move to try not to rock the boat.'[18] First, there was the risk that Raziq might stop sharing intelligence about the Taliban. In a worst-case scenario, Raziq might even use his loyal force of nearly 4,000 men to confront the outnumbered Americans. Even a slight disruption of Green's partnership with Raziq threatened to endanger the lives of 4-2 CAV troopers and upset the freedom of movement of goods along the highway to Kandahar City.

Furthermore, Green was attuned to the positive elements of Raziq's grip on Spin Boldak, especially in terms of economics. He referred to Raziq as a 'Robin Hood' figure, who was better than most Afghan leaders at sharing resources with the district's general populace.[19] Raziq was robbing the rich, American contractors and international border customs payers, to give to the poor who made up the various contingents of his supporters.

Green was on the mark in a particular way with his comparison of Raziq to Robin Hood. In recent popular versions, the mythical English archer has been depicted as a pure outlaw, an anti-authoritarian as much as a re-distributor of resources. But the origins of the myth in fifteenth-century England point to the messiness of state-making and the fluid lines between organized crime and the consolidation of royal power. In the earliest versions of the Robin Hood story, the outlaw from local government at Nottingham became part of the King's force of royal archers. After he later fell out of favor with the monarch and returned to the woods, he was 'treacherously slain.'[20] Raziq's story followed similar lines, as his close relationship with central power in the Karzai regime did not survive the change of administration under Ashraf Ghani.

During his years in power, Raziq gave first and foremost to his own gang of merry men, his security forces and the network of associates dominated by Achakzai contacts. He also spent money on those displaced people from throughout Afghanistan who had come to settle in the New Village (*New-e Kalay*) that sprang up between the border crossing at Wesh and Spin Boldak city. As violence pushed waves of refugees out of Helmand and Uruzgan, many settled close to the Pakistan border along Highway 4, around the checkpoints of the ABP. Raziq dispensed patronage and protection to this community that mushroomed to 80,000 people, who in turn provided rents, sons for the police force, and sources of local intelligence. One police official pointed to the New Village as 'evidence that all Pashtuns can live peacefully together' without traditional tribal allegiances. The safety that Raziq provided, free from the predation of previous government officials, attracted refugees from elsewhere in Afghanistan and allowed businesses to function throughout the district.[21]

Without security, commerce was impossible. And without commerce, the populace was vulnerable to recruitment by anti-government forces. Green explained that the local people in his AO were 'all about making money. It's the border, it's smuggling. It's people who go down there to make it rich. This is like San Francisco in the 1840s.'[22] Instead of precious metals as in the Gold Rush, those who flocked to Spin Boldak came for government contracts and the markets that foreigners provided. Over the course of a year, 4-2 CAV allocated $74 million through more than one hundred projects in Spin Boldak and its neighboring districts.[23] Green elaborated on the historical comparison with the United States in terms of irregular security forces. 'The Texas Rangers . . . [and] some other groups in the Wild West were part-time militia, part-time police, part-time business agent. Even the Earp brothers were running gambling and other things.'[24] Green was on firm footing regarding the acceptance of graft throughout America's history. Corruption had not impeded development so long as a rising tide of economic opportunities lifted all boats.

Those who worked with Raziq pointed to more recent examples of Americans backing questionable allies abroad. Around the world, Cold War politics drove US agents to support dictators who claimed anti-communist credentials. In Afghanistan, the preferred warlord for Western intelligence agents was Ahmed Shah Massoud, styled by British MI6 as the 'Afghan Napoleon.' Massoud's resistance movement based in the Panjshir valley was rife with brutality and corruption, but there were bright spots as well. Massoud led from the front, he was charismatic, and he displayed genuine care for his subordinates. Raziq, who had fought briefly in anti-Taliban militias while Massoud was Minister of Defense in Kabul, kept a painting of the legendary freedom fighter on proud display in his office.[25]

Both men inspired a cult of personality. The streets of Kabul and Kandahar filled up with murals of each man's face, first Massoud and later Raziq. Some said that when Raziq enlisted as a teenager in Gul Agha Sherzai's militia, he used the surname 'Panjshiri,' as a homage to Massoud's home valley.[26] From here, however, the similarities dissipated. The older man was a member of the Tajik minority from the north, unlike Raziq the southern Pashtun. Massoud, whose father was a colonel in the Royal Afghan Army, had learned French at the prestigious *Lycée Esteqlal* (Independence High School) before taking engineering courses at Kabul Polytechnic University.[27] Raziq, on the other hand, cultivated his image as a humble village boy, without formal education uneducated but schooled in oral tradition, common-sense Koranic interpretation, and harsh experience in the Afghan countryside.

The Owl

Regardless of who was in charge, the different cultures of each force in Spin Boldak, American and Afghan, ensured there would be some friction in the partnership. Staff Sergeant Dustin Carroll, a platoon sergeant in Maddog Troop, was a seasoned soldier by 2010, having experienced what he referred to as a 'barbaric' deployment to Iraq. As a result, he had become an advocate of leniency toward host nation soldiers and civilians. However, achieving this on the ground remained a challenge at times.

On one patrol, the Americans noticed a large owl tied up outside a police checkpoint. Maddog troop's platoons were there to augment security during the parliamentary (*Wolesi Jirga*) elections. One of Carroll's squad leaders notified him that a group of Raziq's 'Border Police guys were just kicking the shit out of this owl.' He told his subordinate, Staff Sergeant Wilson, to grab his concertina-wire gloves – not the Nomex ones, because he'd get his hands cut – and remove the bird from its Afghan tormentors. The NCOs sheltered the battered owl in their Stryker for the day. The platoon doc donated a medicine dropper to give it water, and other soldiers chipped in sunflower seeds and jerky to help resuscitate the injured bird.

The NCOs brought the owl back to the TOC, where it soon became a distraction to the daily battle rhythm. Its body was over two feet in length, and its wingspan more than double that. It was too weak to fly, but it flapped and shuffled about, hooting and shedding ragged feathers. It was missing an eye, and it seemed to be malnourished. Several of the American NCOs took turns nursing it back to health.

After about a week, the owl seemed to have regained some strength. Its movements around the room began to resemble flight, and it had exhausted the patience of most of the staff officers. The Americans took the bird to a nearby police station to set it free. On a bright, clear morning, Wilson threw the owl into the air, and it gained some upward momentum. But after a few seconds, perhaps impaired in its navigation by the missing eye, the owl swerved into a line of concertina wire that topped the base's stone walls. It fell to the ground and then hopped back up onto its feet. Wilson took the bird up once more and tossed it up again. This time, the owl hit the wall itself and fell down, whereupon an Afghan policeman pulled his pistol and shot it.

Maddog troopers stood back, aghast. They were unprepared for the callous attitudes that pervaded the Afghan security forces. The rumor that the Afghans had gouged out the bird's eye in the first place to keep it as a pet underscored their apparent cruelty. The incident, recalled one lieutenant, caused 'quite a lot of consternation.' Some soldiers became 'frustrated and angry' about having to work with their host nation counterparts. The revelation of different values caused American soldiers 'even more stress' in their daily lives than IED-related incidents, according to one officer.[28]

Carroll was upset, too. But he thought of the incident in terms of its potential effects on discipline. He could not let himself or his subordinate troopers allow emotion to affect the working relationship with their Afghan partners, distasteful as their actions might be at times. The Afghans, of course, must have wondered at the folly of the Americans trying to resuscitate a one-eyed bird, among the other unfeasible projects they attempted.

Then again, there were times when Raziq's forces had to step in and bail out their American counterparts. A Ranger Task Force stationed at Kandahar Airfield conducted raids on high value targets across RC-South. Since Afghan dwellings often looked similar, it was easy to get confused in the dark and hit the wrong house. Carroll paid close attention when Special Operators carried out raids along his patrol routes. Often, his platoon had to perform 'IO [information operations] mitigation' to calm the local populace afterward. The American

NCO rushed to one scene, a few blocks from the border, with a handful of American soldiers and an equal number of Afghan Border Policemen piled into two small Ford pickups. On arrival, Carroll noticed that the Task Force soldiers had broken the door of a house and damaged a car parked in front. One of the Rangers had drawn a dripping penis in the dust that coated the car. The people of Wesh village were furious.

A crowd formed around Carroll and his men, who began to fear for their safety. The American platoon sergeant placed a call to one of Raziq's lieutenants, Aktar Mohammad, who arrived in minutes in his Toyota Corolla. The large Afghan man, sporting a thick black beard and a turban, stood side by side with Carroll and crossed his arms. Carroll was relieved; he did not have to say anything more to the crowd.

Aktar explained to his countrymen that these Americans were not the ones who had attacked the house, nor had they drawn the offensive symbol. They were there to help investigate what had happened and to compensate the owners of the home. Then Aktar made sure that everyone watched as he led his American partner, arm in arm, to the vehicles and opened a passenger door for him. He didn't have to do that, Carroll recalled. But the Afghan commander 'legitimately trusted us and looked at us like comrades.' Carroll described his partner as 'great,' an 'amazing man.' In this case, the respect flowed both ways, an atypical arrangement for partnerships during the American surge years.[29]

Chapter 12

HOW SPIN BOLDAK WORKS (2010–11)

Lieutenant Colonel Andy Green decided early in the deployment to leverage the human capital of his subordinate troops. He had an abundance of junior officers, but not enough soldiers for them to lead in platoons. One of the additional duties that fell to First Lieutenant Thaddeus Fox, an artillery officer, was to manage the Troop Intelligence Support Team (TIST). Because FOB Spin Boldak was so close to the Pakistan border, 4-2 CAV squadron was restricted in its use of artillery. As a result, soldiers who had fired howitzers at targets now shifted to a different kind of targeting: information about high-value individuals (HVI) and the networks that connected them.[1]

Green ordered Fox's team to accompany patrols on the ground, unlike most intelligence analysts, who stayed sequestered on FOBs. Discussions with ordinary Afghans during their daily routines became grassroots intelligence for higher-level analysts to dissect. The information uncovered in patrol reports drove planning for the next cycle of operations. Green wanted to understand the totality of his unit's area of operations – both the physical space and the human element. He wanted to understand, in his words, 'how Spin Boldak works.'[2]

The resulting report, first issued in November 2010, became a resource for Green's unit and those that arrived later in the district. Discussions with locals contained repeated mentions of 'mafia,' secret relationships between four major powers in the borderlands: Raziq's Afghan Border Police, the Pakistani truckers, Pakistani intelligence (ISI), and the Taliban. The system boiled down to a series of exchanges between the various power brokers: truckers allowed the Taliban to infiltrate on their vehicles, and the Taliban agreed not to disrupt the trucking business along Highway 4. The Taliban arranged not to attack the ABP in exchange for assistance (or salutary neglect) in moving drugs, weapons, and fighters. The ISI provided funding and safe havens for the Taliban in Chaman, but they also bribed insurgents not to attack the Border Police. The ABP allowed those who played along to avoid tolls, while they punished those who attempted to subvert the system.

The benefit to all parties, when the border was safe, was the money made from customs and the delivery of foreign goods. The only losers in the scenario were the Afghan government in Kabul, which missed out on customs revenue and oversight of the border, and the people of Kandahar City, exposed to the brunt of Taliban fighters, who without this system of peaceful graft might have had to fight their way through the border.

The historical cooperation between Pakistani intelligence, business interests, and the Taliban that originated in the 1990s now enveloped the new republican security forces of the post-9/11 environment. There was simply too much money provided by the American surge to spoil the arrangement, at least in this one location on the border. The district became an oasis from violence.

The Border Police demonstrated that they would fight away from the frontier. But they tolerated low-level Taliban presence in their home district, so long as insurgents did not commit overt acts of violence. A November 2010 report found that Raziq maintained contact with a Hizb-I Islami commander and coordinated with him to protect insurgents from arrest when it suited him. US Army Human Terrain study in April 2010 estimated that each truck that crossed from Pakistan to Afghanistan paid three times the official toll ($600 vs. $200), which meant the ABP could collect and distribute potential profits of hundreds of thousands of dollars per month. Another study estimated that Raziq took in a total of $5–6 million per month in bribes.[3] On the other hand, Pakistani intelligence officers saw Raziq as a means to keep their own Taliban contacts under control. These handlers could use the Border Police like an attack dog to sic on wayward insurgent commanders.

Opportunities for double dealing and secret arrangements abounded. Almost every Afghan Border Police 'discovery' of weapons or bomb-making materials came from one official, Sadullah Khan, Raziq's childhood friend. Sadullah's role within the organization was to monitor the customs and serve as intelligence chief at the border. He had a staff of half a dozen Border Policemen, including a driver-secretary, plus a rotating crew of 'cooks.' The most important employee was his 'son,' a twenty-year-old businessman who appeared regularly in civilian clothes and often slept in the police official's headquarters. It was unclear to Americans whether Sadullah was in fact his biological father, or rather an avuncular mentor. Sadullah was unmarried due to his 'notorious' reputation; he often entertained US troops with photos of his many girlfriends. Local rumors supported the intelligence chief's unscrupulous bachelor status; some said his mother could be found wandering the streets of Quetta, crying at passers-by to bring her son home.[4]

Sadullah had deep connections in Pakistan. He spoke fluent Urdu and, when away from his office dorm at the border crossing point, lived in a large Quetta

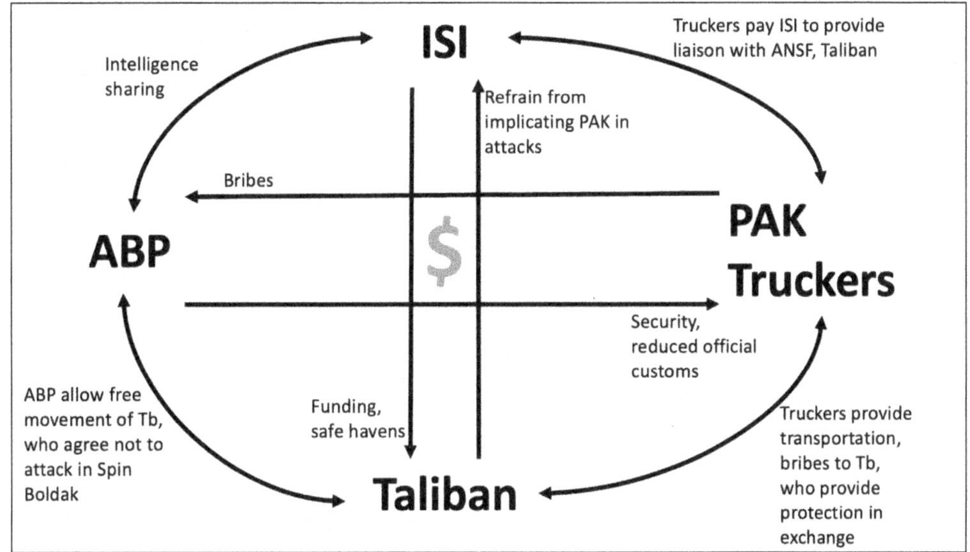

Diagram based on reports from M/4-2 CAV troop intelligence support team (TIST), November 2010.

residence in a neighborhood dominated by ISI officers. He bragged of spending over $5,000 per month, when his Border Police salary was only $210. Moreover, he claimed that his 'son' spent over $15,000 per month, more than 150 times the salary of an average local worker, though he never identified the nature of his business. In late October 2010, Maddog troop soldiers discovered a parking pass for the ISI Headquarters in Chaman that had fallen out of Sadullah's vehicle.[5]

Another example of graft comprised the fertilizer smuggling ring run by Wesh Customs Yard official Haza Regi. He split about a third of his daily income from selling ammonium nitrate on the black market – 600,000 Afghanis ($10,000) per day – between a Pakistani Frontier Corps colonel and one of Raziq's brothers, as bribes to protect the scheme.[6] The complexity of the situation made partnership a difficult proposition, despite the shift in American command emphasis from 'let's kill' to the 'love bank.'

Cavalry Screens on the Border

Though the surge brought large conventional units to Spin Boldak, the cavalry troopers who patrolled the border still faced a daunting task. Both 8-1 and then 4-2 CAV had an entire maneuver troop – effectively one-third of their forces – stripped from their tactical control to perform duty in more 'kinetic' areas of RC South, outside their home district. This meant that only one troop, about a hundred soldiers, was responsible for hundreds of kilometers of the border.

The remaining troop had to patrol the highways and villages to the north and west of the American FOB to ensure the outpost's security. One lieutenant broke down the units by the predominant tribes of the region: Maddog was the Achakzai troop at the border crossing; Lightning was the Noorzai troop in the hinterland.[7]

Maddog troop's daily battle rhythm comprised a rotation by platoon. One group of troopers was at the Wesh-Chaman border crossing point (BCP) every day, but they switched between this duty, refitting at the FOB, and patrols elsewhere along the border. First Lieutenant Jim Fortune recalled that the soldiers tended to prefer the latter duty. Standing at the border for hours on end was monotonous and soul-crushing. There was a great deal of political oversight at the BCP. On the other hand, riding the Strykers through the Afghan countryside was liberating, 'more fun.' Fortune explained, 'You get to be on your own and felt like you were in the Wild West out there.' The young lieutenant recalled finding an old British fort with stone towers to occupy to the north of Spin Boldak city. He based his platoon there whenever he could, for its picturesque setting as well as for its defensibility.

Sometimes these patrols through the countryside (*atraf*) took on higher stakes. Fortune recalled one night spent observing a man who crossed the border from a Pakistani fort. The Americans watched through the infrared sights on their Stryker vehicles as the individual – it was unclear if he was in the Pakistani military or only abetted by them – crossed into Afghan territory to place an IED in the road about a kilometer away from the American position. Fortune's unit called explosive ordnance disposal (EOD) the following day to dig out the bomb that had been laid on their path back to the base.[8]

When the platoons of Maddog troop rotated down to the border crossing point, rather than screening the less-traveled border points used for infiltration, it was difficult to assess whether their presence was making much difference. Troop commander Captain Matt Kelley eventually established an outpost in the courtyard of the ABP station in Wesh. Kelley wanted to keep a better eye on Raziq's lieutenant Sadullah Khan, in addition to the crowds of people and the lines of trucks that crossed the international boundary every day. The company's move ensured continuous American operations at the border and allowed more flexibility for commutes through Spin Boldak city, the thickly-settled, threat-rich environment that separated the FOB from the border.

The American presence at the border crossing point was mostly symbolic, though it may have had a deterrent effect. There was no way to keep the traffic flowing and to maintain effective surveillance of people and goods at the same time. Maddog troopers and their ABP partners required just one or two out of hundreds of vehicles to pull over and download their contents for inspection each day. It was simply too hot, and there were not enough soldiers to go around, for more thorough searches.[9] They looked mostly for weapons; drugs were a secondary concern to machine guns, rockets, and IED components. The

Americans had some limited success convincing Raziq and Sadullah to bring them ammonium nitrate, but sketchy details surrounding the 'seizures' left 4-2 CAV officers with more questions than answers.[10]

The ammonium nitrate issue illustrated the complexity of border control operations. Fertilizer was an important aspect of agricultural extension, a key part of the strategy to provide 'alternative livelihoods' for the narcotics farmers of Southern Afghanistan. But certain types of fertilizer with high concentrations of ammonium nitrate provided the primary explosive content for IEDs. Lieutenant Fortune recalled that the Americans had difficulty distinguishing between 'good' and 'bad' fertilizer. His platoon received test kits to swab suspected materials, which often arrived in great heaps that filled the backs of pickup trucks and shipping containers. One day, the Americans and their Border Police partners downloaded a pile of fertilizer in the customs courtyard and swabbed the contents. The test came back positive, and the Maddog soldiers rejoiced. 'Oh, we just found the motherlode of fertilizer for a bomb,' the lieutenant recalled. Upon further examination at FOB Spin Boldak, however, the soldiers realized that the tests had a high false-positive rate. The seizure, upon further investigation, proved to have been unnecessary. In the meantime, the soldiers had disrupted the work of the unlucky farmer who expected a delivery that day.[11]

The Americans took steps to address the lack of government oversight at the border. During 4-2 CAV's time as the sole conventional unit in the region, the main goal was to get the Border Police to adopt ASYCUDA, a digitized ledger that would have allowed the government to track vehicles and the payment of tolls from a centralized system. This would have made it more difficult for Raziq's policemen to collect unauthorized tolls, and they resisted the new technology at every turn of its implementation.

For people, rather than vehicles, the Americans used a biometric system known as BATS/HIIDES, a handheld device that scanned fingerprints and irises. The information went to an electronic database that would alert scanners if the individual had been apprehended before.[12] But again, there was no way to scan everyone who crossed the border. More regulation would have interrupted the local economy, which required laborers unencumbered by international politics.

The Americans depended on their Afghan counterparts to help screen for likely insurgents. One of the Border Policemen, Daoud or David, became famous in American circles as 'Super Dave,' an 'Afghan Captain America,' because unlike most of his peers he was motivated and equipped with 'tacti-cool' gear he had picked up from foreign friends over the past few rotations.[13] Super Dave and his police compatriots stood guard at the border, on a thin asphalt road that banked around the Friendship Gate. Out of the thousands who passed by, Border Policemen picked out individuals from the crowds, perhaps as many as one hundred per day. A team of American soldiers operated the electronic devices from inside the police station. Maddog troopers noted that the ABP assumed darker-skinned men to be Punjabi and therefore ISI agents. 'Anybody they didn't like, they'd always call them a Punjab,' Fortune recalled. Indeed, Raziq commented at a border security meeting that Punjabis represented a 'major source of trouble' in Spin Boldak, ignoring the near-total Pashtun leadership of the Quetta Shura Taliban. The police commander claimed that all suicide bombers in the area were Pakistani.[14] Raziq was still more emphatic in an interview with *Vice News*:

> I have been targeted by suicide attackers many times. But I am telling you now, I could be attacked one hundred more times, but as long as I am alive, I will be the enemy of Punjab [Pakistani Taliban]. As long as I am alive, I have to let Afghans know that these Punjabis won't let our country be safe. And Punjab is our enemy. If they attack me one thousand times, as long as I am alive, I will say that Punjab is our enemy.[15]

As such, even the most advanced technology continued to rely on rudimentary decision-making and crude biases.

Kirby's Shura

At the same time that he coordinated military operations against the insurgency, Raziq participated in the broadening of political representation. On 11 October, Spin Boldak district held its first council (*shura*) in months. It would have been an auspicious occasion for local governance even if the meeting had simply replicated the pre-existing institution. Even a return to previous levels of inclusion would have indicated a return to normalcy and a sign that politicians were unafraid of becoming Taliban targets. But there were new additions to the gathering. In addition to twenty Achakzai and twenty Noorzai members, the *shura* welcomed ten representatives from the New Village (*New-e Kalay*). The community was not affiliated with any one tribe, but included displaced people from all over Afghanistan. On 24 November, a director of local governance arrived in Spin Boldak from Kabul to validate the council.[16]

The new *shura* was an important development for Owen Kirby, the local State Department representative. By the end of 2010, Kirby had deployed to Afghanistan for extended periods from 2002 through 2004 under the auspices of the International Republican Institute. For most of the next five years, he worked at the Bureau of Near Eastern Affairs, which like most of the US government, focused on Iraq. But in 2009, Kirby returned to Afghanistan, where he became the senior governance adviser to Spin Boldak district. Now, over a year later, the resumption of the district *shura* was his crowning achievement.

In short, Kirby was invested. When he looked over to Raziq, present at these meetings, Kirby lamented that the Afghan leader did not share his values-based conviction. Political institutions seemed to be 'a joke' to Raziq, who believed he alone had the power to get things done in the district. By this point, Kirby had grown cynical about the political process, which he characterized as a 'dirty' game of 'carving up the pie' offered by foreign aid agencies. Representation for the displaced people had been contentious for this reason. Noorzai leaders were wary of giving up some of the scant power they had mustered under Raziq's regime to newcomers without any tribal claims to the region. At one point, the Noorzai co-chair of the meeting left in protest to take up residence in Pakistan. Raziq remained, but he mentioned to the district governor, 'This is Kirby's *shura*,' with a wink and a nod in the American's direction.

Kirby interpreted the remark to mean the district *shura* had become an inauthentic political body, which Raziq allowed only 'for the sake of the outsiders,' who funded his operation and provided him with auxiliary combat power. 'He was willing to go along with it. But to him, it was just all a game,' Kirby recalled.[17] One might say in Raziq's defense that at least he was willing to play this game. Others in Afghanistan might have made more deliberate efforts to obstruct the new *shura* than letting slip an occasional snide comment.

Raziq, indeed, had reason to include internally displaced people in the governance and spoils of Spin Boldak. He recruited in New-e Kalay. To those who said that his Afghan Border Police was a mere tribal militia in official uniforms, Raziq had a ready response. He employed many policemen who had been recent refugees from other parts of the country. The Tajik interpreters who worked with the Americans confirmed Raziq's inclusivity. In the words of one of them, 'He was not a racist,' since he was enthusiastic about working with anyone who would help him combat the Taliban insurgency.[18] Some Pashtuns were intolerant of Persian-speaking (*Farsiwan*) northerners in meetings, but Raziq acquiesced in their presence. His leniency, however, may have been more pragmatic than idealistic. In addition to recruiting policemen from the impoverished displaced communities, Raziq found many willing informants who, due to their migratory status, could slip in and out of Spin Boldak's businesses and alleyways without notice. Inclusiveness made up part of a strategy for information dominance at the border.

Americans disagreed about the context of Raziq's actions in New-e Kalay. Some believed that if he had a master plan, this was it: to gather unaffiliated Afghans around him in a nationalistic ploy for power, apart from the tribal leaders of Kandahar. Others thought that Raziq was not a planner, but had fallen into the position by chance. Either way, Raziq's presence at Kirby's *shura* boded well for the fortunes of those seeking resources and representation outside of established family power structures.

Chapter 13

SURVEILLANCE BRIGADE (2010–11)

The troopers of 4-2 CAV, after a summer to themselves, began to have company on FOB Spin Boldak toward the end of 2010. Theater-level Army leaders at the peak of the surge designated the base as a brigade-sized headquarters due to its strategic location. They deployed a new type of unit, the Battlefield Surveillance Brigade (BfSB), to take on the sensitive mission at the Pakistan border.

The BfSB was the brainchild of then Lieutenant General David Petraeus from his time at the Combined Arms Center at Fort Leavenworth in 2007. The unit was a hybrid intelligence-cavalry brigade – two intelligence battalions, one cavalry squadron, plus support troops – designed to tackle the specific challenges of counter-insurgency. Petraeus harped on the maxim that intelligence had to drive operations, because the most difficult task was to find the insurgents, rather than to fight them. Intelligence in the chaotic environment of the Afghan borderlands was only valuable for a short duration, so the intel unit needed an integrated cavalry 'tail' that could swat emergent threats on the move or fix high-value targets in place. At the same time, the army streamlined its heavy armored footprint, as armored cavalry regiments and Military Intelligence Brigades downsized into the smaller Brigade Combat Team structure.

Colonel Jim Edwards, a Gulf War veteran who had commanded the Abu Ghraib prison in Iraq, led the 525th Battlefield Surveillance Brigade on its first overseas deployment to Kandahar in 2010. In the end, Edwards admitted, the combined unit was like the proverbial camel, 'a horse built by committee,' and it pleased neither intelligence officers nor cavalrymen, who each thrived in different cultures.[1]

The arrival of the new intelligence-heavy unit brought about a shift in operational concept. Whereas the cavalry squadrons had been limited to bottom-up intelligence collection from patrols, the BfSB favored a top-down approach that relied on new technological tools and greater analytical capability. Perhaps the most significant change involved the use of a backscatter X-ray machine, which scanned the radiation emitted from passing vehicles, removing the need to unload trucks and search their contents. The machine had arrived at the border before the soldiers of the BfSB, but 4-2 CAV was under-equipped to analyze the tremendous amount of information that the machine produced.[2] The main difference between the cavalry squadron and the surveillance brigade was that the latter unit comprised a preponderance of intelligence soldiers trained to exploit available data.

Edwards and his unit brought more pieces of advanced technology, as well. The newcomers boasted an ability to track insurgent cell phones in real time, through a portable device that remains classified. 4-2 CAV had some limited drone capacity with the hand-launched Raven, but Edwards acquired an attached US Navy team that operated a larger TigerShark Unmanned Aerial Vehicle (UAV). After the brigade built a UAV runway on the FOB in the summer of 2011, the drone linked real-time video of the borderlands to the headquarters at FOB Spin Boldak. The RC South commander told Edwards at the end of his tour that the TigerShark had been the most effective asset in the area of operations.[3] Prior to this development, 4-2 CAV had relied on JSTARs flights to capture a wide-angle view of movement in the area, without the ability to control the flight pattern, as one could with a drone.

The two units disagreed about the effectiveness of the new technological regime. Edwards claimed that his predecessors in the 4-2 CAV had formed merely a 'pebble in the stream,' due to their lack of signals awareness. The placement of one troop at the border crossing point still left much surrounding terrain open for infiltration. Edwards touted the statistics that his unit compiled: his soldiers interdicted 145,000kg of 'chemical weapons' (to include ammonium nitrate), 1,360kg of narcotics, eleven suicide vests, and nine vehicle-borne IEDs.[4] 4-2 CAV officers countered that this kind of score-keeping missed the point of cooperation with Afghan partners and development of their capabilities. Afghans could not replicate the technology of the BfSB. Moreover, some of the outgoing unit's leadership questioned the concept that more data provided a better picture of what was happening on the ground. Most of what the electronic 'signals intelligence' (SIGINT) provided was noise, rather than quality information. In this environment, technology could be a distracting liability rather than an asset.

One of the 525 BfSB intelligence analysts assessed the pitfalls of his unit's policy. The soldier claimed that all the data in the world could not substitute for the qualitative details that came from accompanying patrols in person, 'out the wire,' and seeing for oneself the mannerisms and context from which the reports came. Only by getting on the ground and talking to locals could analysts develop the proper 'fidelity' to their assessments. In combat situations, seeing was believing, especially in the personality-based oral culture of Central Asia. Early in the deployment, 4-2 CAV provided the command authority for the BfSB analysts to accompany patrols. It was Lieutenant Colonel Green's squadron that emphasized the TIST concept of bottom-up human intelligence gathering (HUMINT). When 4-2 CAV rotated out, and the 525 BfSB intelligence companies changed leadership, the new commander pulled all 'non-combat' troops from patrols through the district.[5]

This small unit personnel policy shift was connected to a higher-level debate in the military about collecting intelligence during an insurgency, as opposed to a conventional conflict. Months before the BfSB found itself in Spin Boldak, then Major General Mike Flynn co-authored an article on 'Fixing Intel,' in which he argued that 'sweeping changes' were necessary in order for the Americans to eliminate the Taliban threat to the Afghan government.

Experience in Iraq had led army leaders to create 'Fusion Centers' that compiled data from human and signals sources, and then linked reports to real-time video surveillance. In Iraq, the focus had been on enemy combatants, Flynn opined, 'with good reason and some great results.' But Americans had become too focused on collecting information about prospective enemies, and not enough effort had gone to understanding the populace. Battalion intelligence officers were well versed in HUMINT and SIGINT data, but they spent little time analyzing censuses, radio broadcasts, or minutes of meetings with farmers and elders. As a result, Flynn concluded, the intelligence community was 'reacting to enemy tactics at the expense of finding ways to strike at the very heart of the insurgency,' that is, ordinary Afghan people.

The article posited that the solution to intelligence problems in Afghanistan was twofold. First, Americans had to recognize the distinct roles of information in regular versus irregular wars. In conventional combat, information flowed from the top, where large organizations had the resources to launch spy planes and direct satellites. Higher headquarters fed information to subordinate units about where the enemy was and what weapons he had. In counter-insurgency, however, intelligence had to originate from human sources on the ground, because only by 'thick' description could analysts understand the networks they discovered through signals technology. Due to the complexity of counter-insurgency, commanders had to step away from simplistic PowerPoint storyboards, which the article denigrated as 'slides with little more text than a comic strip.' Instead, they had to take the time to read and digest 'substantive' multi-page reports. 'There are no shortcuts,' Flynn counseled.[6]

Yet army leadership did not apply Flynn's guidance to policy in this case. The BfSB focused on mass data capture with technology controlled by the upper echelons of command. The 'Wild West' days of the cavalry patrol gave way to machine surveillance in the short span of US surge unit rotations.

Lieutenant Colonel Andy Green and his squadron's staff had little chance of winning any arguments against Colonel Jim Edwards and his brigade. The latter's rank and resources all but ensured he would get his way in the end.

The two units attempted to split responsibilities in Spin Boldak district, but Raziq only had time to partner with one conventional officer in addition to his links to the Special Forces and other Government Agencies. Unofficially, Raziq continued to meet with Green. He often stopped by for a cigarette and a gripe session on his way out of more formal meetings. But Edwards became the de facto authority for coordination with the Afghan Border Police. The two Americans brought different personal styles to the partnership. Whereas Green had taken a self-effacing 'we're *your* CAV' approach with Raziq, Edwards often felt miffed by what he considered a lack of professionalism in his Afghan partner. Edwards attended one meeting that he hoped would build the relationship with his Afghan counterpart, only to find that Raziq was using him as a 'prop' to impress local elders.[7]

The Dog

A stray dog at the border crossing point illustrated the difficult working relationship between 4-2 CAV and newcomers to Spin Boldak from the 525th Battlefield Surveillance Brigade (BfSB). The incoming unit's own subordinate 1-38 Cavalry Squadron had already been in country for several months by the time it arrived at the border area. But even veterans of Afghanistan could feel out of place in these new surroundings. Soldiers became unnerved by the chaotic crowds moving around at random. The 4-2 CAV soldiers, who had built up some measure of goodwill with the locals, took the 1-38 CAV troopers to the border as part of their 'right seat, left seat' ride, to expose them to the environment on a joint patrol with soldiers familiar with the area.

On one of these training patrols, a local dog blocked the road in front of a 1-38 CAV trooper and began to bark in a threatening manner. A crowd of Afghans formed to see what was going on. The new trooper shot the dog, and the rounds ricocheted off the ground and hit an Afghan civilian in the buttocks. Rumors then came back to the soldiers that the injured Afghan was somehow related to General Raziq. The incident soured relations between the incoming unit and the Border Police, and it created more friction among the Americans themselves. Though the military often hammers home the message that all its members are part of one team, tense operations at the border strained this innate camaraderie, at times to breaking point.[8]

Cooperation

By this time, the Border Police had many other sources of support besides their partners in the surveillance brigade. In mid-2010, Raziq became an integral part of Operation *Hamkari*, a joint Afghan-NATO series of maneuvers that addressed the lingering Taliban threat west of Kandahar City. *Hamkari* means 'cooperation' in Pashto, but in practice the action revealed deep fissures between the Border Police commander and some of his foreign allies.

One operation under the umbrella of *Hamkari* was the brainchild of Ahmed Wali Karzai. The President's half brother had suffered the loss of the Daman District Chief of Police, one of his close associates. The Daman leader had been unpopular with locals, tarred as one of the primary 'land grabbers' who used his position in government to sell public lands for his private benefit. The Taliban claimed his assassination, but the Karzai associate had made plentiful enemies throughout the province with his shady business deals and arbitrary arrests.[9] AWK called on his brother in Kabul, who then ordered Governor Wesa to form a 'military *shura*' (council) to deal with the ongoing violence around Kandahar City. Together, the power brokers turned to the rising star of the Achakzai tribe for military manpower.

On 28 August, Raziq departed from Spin Boldak without informing Colonel Edwards, who was thus unable to support or track his partner's movement. With the cooperation of three US military police companies stationed in Kandahar City, Raziq and his forces rolled out to meet the Taliban fighters to the west. The insurgents had grown so brazen as to use the town square in Malajat for the public hanging of collaborators with the twin Satans of the Karzai government and their foreign backers.

Ahead of his Border Police, Raziq sent informants out of uniform, in ordinary *shalwar kameez*, to seek information about Taliban fighting positions and IED emplacements. One of Raziq's Special Forces mentors assessed that Raziq had more than enough money to sway people to his side. 'He just hired local boys to mark these IEDs,' they recalled. With the path to Malajat cleared of danger, Raziq's forces went on a 'thunder run' through the district. The highlight of the run, which suggested the often slapstick nature of operations in Kandahar, occurred when a order Policeman fired an RPG at a pickup truck loaded with bombs. The RPG missed the target high and hit the top of a nearby tree. It turned out to be a lucky miss, which ejected a Taliban fighter from his hidden perch in the branches. The insurgent's armaments then detonated on impact with the ground and ignited the explosive cargo of the pickup truck.[10]

Though the international security forces saw the Malajat campaign as a positive sign that their partners could take aggressive action against the Taliban, some Kandahar locals learned a different lesson. Those who were 'politically aware,' who knew the operation addressed the killing of the corrupt Daman Police Chief, saw that 'AWK and Raziq still controlled the province, had ISAF's support, and would not tolerate interference in their interests' from anyone, Taliban or otherwise.[11] Many Kandaharis saw foreigners propping up only those Afghan elites who were best positioned by education, wealth, or family history to become preferred partners.

Nevertheless, some villagers west of Kandahar City embraced Raziq and implored him to rid their communities of insurgents. In September 2010, over one hundred Alokozai elders lobbied the governor to ask his young Achakzai security chief for assistance. Raziq led the charge in person, as 400 hand-picked Border Policemen and a team of US Special Forces dug up over one hundred bombs and rounded up thirty Taliban suspects in one day.[12] About a month later, toward the end of October, Raziq once again left his base without consulting Edwards to ambush a suspected Taliban location. Raziq 'unexpectedly accelerate[d] the operation by 24 hours,' without reporting his intentions to his partners at the surveillance brigade.[13]

The Kabul government celebrated the *Hamkari* operations as evidence that Raziq was an effective military leader. Whereas in 2006 the Border Police had to retreat in advance of Operation Medusa, by the summer of 2010 their clearing operations had become an efficient means of fighting Taliban insurgents. In all three operations, Raziq collaborated well with coalition Special Forces teams. One report noted that he was not only competent but 'virtually fearless when leading his men.'[14] This reputation had earned Raziq other sources of support, so he could ignore the recalcitrant Colonel Edwards with impunity.

Uncle Ramazan, October 2010

Raziq's headquarters, co-located with the 4th Border Police *Kandak* (Battalion), dominated the city of Spin Boldak from the north-east. The compound commanded views in all directions from three hills that emerged out of the surrounding desert plateau. Raziq had left the junk of ruined military vehicles on the pathway up to his fortress. The rusted 23mm anti-aircraft guns and charred hulks of Border Police pickup trucks were mechanical martyrs to the homeland. In a practical sense, the remains justified Raziq's frequent requests to the Americans for sturdier US Humvees to outfit his quick reaction force (QRF). More symbolically, the wrecked machines served to remind all who dared to approach about Raziq's persistence through such hostility.[15]

The walls of the headquarters stretched 10m above the ridge line. Some Americans believed the structure was a relic from the era of Alexander the Great, but the weathered compound had been known as the 'New Fort' when the British and their Punjabi allies stormed it during the Third Anglo-Afghan War in 1919. An observer prior to the war described the imposing defenses as such:

> The fort is situated at the foot of the western spur of the Spin Baldak hill [*sic*] . . . [comprised of a] double line of walls about 20 yards apart . . . Both the outer and inner walls have bastions with embrasures and gun emplacements at each of the four corners,

> and in the center of each face . . . From 1500 to 2000 men could
> be accommodated in the fort, and the round towers on the hill.[16]

Inside the stone walls, less sturdy buildings had been constructed of plaster and plywood. Blackwater contractors set up metal shipping containers equipped with plumbing and air conditioning in one corner of the enclosed courtyard. Elsewhere within the walls were pomegranate trees, and manicured grass and flowers stood out from the surrounding pale dust of Spin Boldak.

Within the main headquarters building, Raziq had made comfortable rooms for his frequent guests. Chairs abounded, their backs to the wall and interspersed with customary pillows, propped so that men could lean against them as they sat on the floor with crossed legs. Heavy, colorful rugs lined the floors. In Raziq's meeting (*shura*) room, the carpet had a dark maroon background, with pink and golden flowers bursting from the center in concentric patterns. The room was air-conditioned, and it featured a slick, two-tiered glass coffee table. To one side, a television set was switched off. Its darkened screen reflected the shoulders and profiles of the men seated around the transparent table.[17]

Raziq called for a routine meeting of his inner circle, composed of relatives and fellow Achakzai tribesmen. Today, his closest adviser was missing. Ramazan Agha was the father-in-law of Raziq's brother, so he was known as 'uncle.' He had been a *mujahidin* fighter during the Soviet era. Now, in addition to his leadership of a smuggling racket, he served as Raziq's most trusted deputy.

Ramazan Agha took care of problems, in particular the troublesome prisoners that found their way into police custody. Raziq knew enough about the Americans by now to try to keep his uncle in the background, behind the scenes. The foreigners didn't seem to appreciate his methods: the deep holes in the middle of the desert, with ladders leading down into blackness, where Taliban captives were sent. Sometimes they returned to the light of the world missing a finger or an eye. Sometimes they never returned.[18]

Raziq sat to meet with his closest subordinates, Hajji Janan and Sadullah Khan. Both Border Police officials had been Raziq's friends since childhood. Janan was a hulking man, nearly six feet tall and burly; he had served as a policeman since the days of the Taliban regime. Sadullah was smaller and softer. He had a trimmed mustache, and short hair combed to the side. Unlike Janan, who was a battlefield commander and Raziq's direct tactical subordinate, Sadullah was Raziq's money man and intelligence chief. He had a desk job, and the long office hours were steadily adding a paunch to his slight frame.[19]

'Peace unto you (*Salaam, alaikum*),' Raziq began. He dispensed with the customary small talk and asked, 'What has happened to my uncle, Ramazan? He was supposed to be here.'

'It was the Special Forces, Raziq *sahib*,' Sadullah explained, 'They heard him talking with some friends in Pakistan on their target list. They picked him up in their helicopter.'

Sadullah had to hide his satisfaction. He was one of Ramazan's rivals for power, which ebbed and flowed through the police organization depending on one's closeness to Raziq.[20]

The young commander scowled in frustration. 'Don't these Americans understand? We are always communicating with Taliban. Talking and fighting go hand in hand. How do they think we get such good intelligence?'

'The soldiers who took your uncle are not from Spin Boldak. They came in a few weeks ago from Kandahar Airfield. They didn't know who he was.'

The thought that Ramazan might stay imprisoned filled Sadullah with a glee he could hardly contain.

But Raziq was concerned. 'My uncle is not going to be happy about this. Get me on the phone with the Special Forces commander.'

Indeed, Ramazan Agha was not happy as he rode with the Green Berets back to his residence after a brief captivity. He had already heard chatter on the radio from the very mid-level Taliban connections who had landed him in the sights of US Special Forces in the first place. The Taliban fighters taunted, 'Hey Ramazan, how was prison? Did you have a good time with those American dogs? While you were away, we saw the Americans go to your house and fuck your wives. Then we went over, and we fucked your daughters.'[21]

Raziq's uncle could barely contain his rage as he switched off his ICOM radio and threw it to an aide. 'Keep this thing away from me,' he snarled, as the convoy of American trucks pulled up to the gates of Hajji Janan's compound, where Ramazan Agha lived.[22]

The Special Forces Captain who escorted Ramazan Agha back home tried to make amends as best he could. The mission had gone awry somewhere along the way, although the tone of the conversation between this purported American ally and known Taliban operatives had seemed to suggest a relationship a bit too close for comfort. Maybe Ramazan should have remained in the captivity of his SF team, regardless of Raziq's protests. Then again, even elite American units made mistakes. The Captain had heard the dark jokes about the Green Berets that the conventional officers whispered: 'What's so "Special" about those guys? They roll in, make a mess, and leave us to clean it up.' The Captain stepped out of his vehicle, strode up to Lieutenant Jordan Bass of 4-2 CAV, and pulled the younger officer around the side of the Stryker, out of view from the growing crowd of locals.

Bass was one of the conventional army officers stationed on the international border crossing at Wesh. His soldiers conducted multiple patrols every week to stay attuned to local conditions. Bass himself was new to the position of platoon leader. For the first months of the deployment, he had been a staff officer assigned to governance, reconstruction, and development (GRD) projects. The young lieutenant could see that Ramazan Agha had half a dozen bodyguards, members of Raziq's Border Police, waiting for the converging American convoys outside his gates. The guards had their weapons drawn, safeties off, at the low-ready. It was a tense standoff for Bass, who could still count his patrols outside the wire on one hand. Now he would do his best to soothe Ramazan Agha, to smooth relations between Raziq's organization and the unruly Americans.

The SF Captain introduced himself and then quickly counseled Bass:

> This is a tricky one, Lieutenant. Here's how we need to finesse this. I'll walk up to your guys and hand off the local national. You get in my face a little bit. Say something like, 'What do you think you're doing? Don't you know who this guy is?' Really sell it to the locals; sell it to this elder. Let him save some face. Once the Afghans get the picture, you make a show of getting us to leave. Like you're kicking us out of here.

The Green Beret officer paused to check the developing situation. 'Looks like they're getting out of the trucks now, so get back to your convoy before they see us talking.'[23]

Despite Bass's inexperience, the show went off without a hitch. Uncle Ramazan returned home with a bit of dignity still intact. As a result of the incident, Raziq finally agreed to host a liaison officer from 525 BfSB inside his Kandak Ridge headquarters. The Afghan commander was wary of what the Americans might find if they got too close to his business, but he was willing to accept the intrusion to protect his associates from being arrested.[24]

Promotion

Raziq had been calling himself a general for at least two years by the time of his official promotion at the end of December 2010. In the hours prior to the ceremony, Colonel Jim Edwards had been with his partner at a weekly security meeting held at the governor's compound. They traveled through the city in a convoy to Mandigak Palace, the symbolic seat of power in Kandahar. Raziq sat next to his nominal boss, the commander of the 3rd Border Police Zone, but everyone knew who was really in charge. Raziq waited as several Afghan politicians made speeches, and then he took the stage. He explained to the audience the benefits of his rise to power. He mentioned the improved security in Spin Boldak and the opportunities for business. He mentioned his distinction from the Taliban: 'This is why I do what I do. I want our women to be able to walk down the streets.' Raziq heaped praise on himself, yet he still postured as a 'servant of the people.' It was, according to Edwards, 'classic Raziq.' He knew what would please his audience, and he had developed an expertise in delivering rousing speeches.

When the ceremony ended, Raziq's lieutenants rushed onto the stage to congratulate him. Unlike the subdued receiving lines for US military promotions, this one was raucous. The revelers grabbed large potted plants that were scattered around the palace. Greenery was prized in Kandahar, since the arid climate of the region made growing difficult. Raziq instructed his men to 'take those plants back with us to Spin Boldak,' and they obeyed.[25]

One week after the ceremony, an incident in Loy Karez highlighted the limits of the Afghan government's reach. Loy Karez was a Noorzai village about 30km north-east of Spin Boldak city, connected to the main artery of commerce on Highway 4 by a gravel road called Route Fern. The road was an IED hotbed, so much so that American patrols almost never used the route, itself. One lieutenant recalled, 'We always hand-railed it in some way,' either over the packed desert sand or along dry canal beds that ran parallel to the road. 8-1 CAV had suffered casualties along this route at the beginning of its deployment in the summer of 2009, and by the end of the year the unit had sworn off patrolling in the area. Nevertheless, 4-2 CAV troopers determined to spread the inkblot of security and building projects farther than their predecessors.[26]

Loy Karez became a kind of white whale for the American units of the surge. One of the early joint patrols between 4-2 CAV and the Surveillance Brigade was to escort the latter's leadership and Raziq's team around the Noorzai town, a way for Raziq to demonstrate that 'he could go anywhere.' He sought to cut a striking figure in his light *shalwar kameez*, as he strutted through the town square alongside Americans who dared not remove their armored plate-carrier vests.

Lieutenant Bass recalled discussions about the problem parts of the district, those still untouched by American development dollars. When the 4-2 CAV staff asked about the possibility of using military funds to woo the people of Loy Karez, the deputy governor of Spin Boldak district counseled them to start small. A plethora of micro-grants had already been approved in $5,000 increments. Why not use one to build a clinic in the Noorzai town? The Americans found an acceptable contractor and began construction. On 29 December, just as the project was about to wrap up, a mysterious explosion destroyed the building. For 4-2 CAV, as for their predecessors, connecting Loy Karez to the Afghan government became a 'Sisyphean effort,' in the phrase of one officer.[27]

Uncle Ramazan, 7 January 2011

Raziq summoned his inner circle of advisers to his meeting room. Once again, his Uncle Ramazan was missing. It had been four months since his abduction. Maybe there was a new Special Forces group at Kandahar Airfield that had not yet learned from the mistakes of the previous rotation. Suddenly Raziq's subordinate commander Hajji Janan walked into the *shura* room. The men had been friends since childhood. Raziq could tell by his downcast gaze and hunched shoulders that he was bearing bad news about their colleague.

Ramazan Agha had gone to his favorite barber, as he did every week on Friday. The shop was a stucco building located on the main traffic circle in the center of Spin Boldak. The building had a front room with chairs and a back-room bathhouse containing showers for ritual cleansing on the holy day. Raziq had warned his uncle that he shouldn't be so predictable in his habits. To visit this same spot in Spin Boldak so regularly was an invitation to the Taliban.

The assassin hoped he would catch Raziq himself at the barbershop. Where Ramazan Agha was, the Taliban knew, his boss and kinsman was likely to be nearby. He watched as the Pashtun elder entered the shop, accompanied by several of his aides and bodyguards from the Border Police. He checked the explosives strapped under his clothes one last time and slunk into the building.

The resulting blast killed twenty people, local Afghans and Pakistani workers who had packed into the establishment along with Raziq's uncle.[28] The Americans who went to document the attack recalled a gruesome scene. Chunks of flesh were stuck to the walls of the concrete shower room, which acted as a ricochet chamber for the thousands of steel ball bearings that had filled the suicide vest. Blood flowed out of the building and trickled into the dusty street. The American soldiers sent to collect intelligence on the event could not help but step through dark red puddles that stained their tan boots. One soldier recalled taking pictures of Ramazan Agha's remains. There were only 'bits and pieces of him,' left scattered among the other fragments of bodies inside the bathhouse.[29]

For a few days, Raziq was inconsolable. He did not speak of the killing for upward of a week, for fear that its mention could unleash feelings that would prevent him from working.[30] Colonel Edwards arranged a meeting with his grieving partner at which he and several US generals urged Raziq not to exact retribution. Edwards recalled advising Raziq not to 'go out and whack a bunch of people. I know you're hurting right now, but don't do it.'[31] The Afghan commander abided by his partner's counsel at that time.

Ramazan Agha's murder was part of a Taliban campaign. Targeted killings of government officials dissuaded people from participating in the Karzai regime. The tactic alienated the government from the people, as officials had to take isolating security measures. Moreover, civilians did not want to associate with those who had targets on their backs.

One effect of the bombing was to deprive Raziq of a trusted and loyal subordinate. In some ways, he could not replace his uncle. However, the assassination allowed Raziq to branch out and promote other subordinates, in order to expand his base of power to new networks. Within a few years, Raziq's inner circle would no longer be formed of his own Achakzai tribesmen. His best-connected aides came to him from Barakzai and Afridi backgrounds, rather than from his own family.[32]

Another effect of the Taliban's spate of killings was to propel Raziq up the hierarchy of Kandahari politics. As an Achakzai outsider and a competent military commander, he benefited from the vacancies provided by the assassinations of previous Kandahar Chief of Police Khan Mohammad Mujahid (April 2011) and Ahmed Wali Karzai (July 2011). The official title, as well as connections with elite tribal elders, fell to Raziq in the macabre tontine of governance in Afghanistan.

Some observers connected the two assassinations and suspected Raziq had a role in the latter. Once Raziq received the appointment as provincial Chief of Police, he began to consolidate funding authority and thus the allegiance of the militias of the region, including that of Karzai insider and Popalzai tribesman Sardar Mohammad. After much negotiation, Raziq convinced Sardar to release his militia to join the national police (ANP). Just one week after relinquishing his authority, Sardar killed his former patron Ahmed Wali Karzai. It is easy to imagine this attack as revenge for the dishonor that state forces had wrought upon this proud tribesman. Other explanations, however, suspected more personal dynamics at play: one held that the two men were in competition over a potential bride, another that AWK was about to fire Sardar for alleged abuses of village boys, and still another that a dissident Karzai cousin had hired Sardar for the purpose. In any case, Ahmed Wali Karzai's murder resulted in a major political void into which Raziq stepped, with the acquiescence of the President and over objections from his Ministry of the Interior.[33]

A former Afghan mentor described the devolution of power to Raziq after AWK's assassination in effusive terms. He claimed, 'Raziq is the god, the prophet, the governor, and the president here in Kandahar. He's the king.'[34] One American adviser in later years described Raziq more modestly as the foremost of the 'two kings of Kandahar,' the other of whom commanded the Army 205th Corps.[35] Despite the tightening of the noose around his own inner circle, Taliban violence cleared a path for Raziq to become the most powerful leader of Afghan security forces in the South.

Yet at first, he resisted the call from his President to accept the position of Provincial Chief of Police. Raziq did not want to lose his valuable position on the border, and he knew that he would be even more vulnerable to Taliban attacks in Kandahar City than he was in his home district of Spin Boldak. The previous provincial chief had been a powerful and well-respected Alokozai tribesman who had experience as the police boss in Ghazni Province before his assassination at the Kandahar post.[36] To persuade Raziq to take on the dangerous responsibility, Karzai made a key concession. The Achazkai leader could retain a position with the Border Police as the 3rd Zone executive officer, so his links to loyal policemen and valuable territory at the border remained intact. Raziq's family friend and lieutenant, Hajji Janan, would run Spin Boldak in his absence. But the new provincial Police Chief found ample opportunities to check up on his original seat of power.

In addition to his usual visits to family and business associates, Raziq found himself caught up in a United Nations mission against torture that singled out his facilities in Kandahar for the 'systematic' abuse of detainees. The UN highlighted the Sarhadari facility, a Border Police checkpoint in Spin Boldak city, where prisoners reported beatings, whipping of the feet with cables, and prolonged suspension from ceilings and trees. Policemen claimed they used these techniques in a pragmatic rather than a sadistic way, in order to obtain intelligence. One Afghan interpreter noted that suspending individuals off the ground was also practiced at a drug rehabilitation clinic that Raziq funded in New-e Kalay, where staff hanged addicts upside down as a way to encourage them to sober up. The technique's application in such distinct settings suggests the possibility of confusion about what constituted torture. Cultural attitudes to crime and punishment diverged sharply between Kandaharis and the newcomers to their region.[37]

Though the majority of prisoners reported torture in facilities across Afghanistan, the practice seemed to occur more often in Kandahar, in particular after Raziq's appointment as chief of police. When the ISAF command learned the contents of the UN team's impending report in July, they halted detainee transfers from NATO forces to Afghans in the Southern regional command. The human rights community considered this step of distance from Raziq to be perhaps the first in a process that would eventually acknowledge him as a war criminal. Laws passed in the late 1990s at the instigation of Vermont Senator Patrick Leahy forbade the United States government from providing funds to foreign units that had 'committed a gross violation of human rights.'[38] But military support to Raziq by this point seemed to be inextricable from fighting the Taliban.

Moreover, military prospects had become tenuous. The arrival of American resources in Afghanistan had now peaked, with only diminishing amounts promised for the future. The Leahy Law contained the caveat that if the host government reformed itself through 'effective remedial measures,' then support could continue.[39] But who was to decide if Raziq was making effective reforms? Amid the continuing relationship between Raziq and the Americans at the end of their surge period, eighty-one reports of missing persons emerged after their arrests by government forces in Kandahar. As more and more Americans prepared to leave Afghanistan, dozens of unidentified bodies, all with gunshot wounds to the head or chest, some with broken bones and holes drilled in their skulls, appeared at Kandahar's Mirwais Hospital.[40]

Green on Blue

As the last full year of the American surge dawned in 2011, 4-2 CAV was on its way out of Spin Boldak. The uneasy relationship between the Surveillance Brigade and the Cavalry Squadron had devolved into a series of arguments between officers and pranks by soldiers. At one point, the BfSB guidon ended

Raziq (second from right) poses with other Afghan leaders of the Spin Boldak Joint District Coordination Centre (JDCC), circa 2006. (Author's collection, confidential source)

A U.S. soldier makes a "sand angel" in the Registan desert, 2010. (Ronald Savage)

Raziq poses with LTC William Clark of 8-1 CAV and linguist Najibullah Fazel in front of his home in Spin Boldak, 2009. (Najibullah Fazel)

Headquarters of Afghan Border Police in Spin Boldak, with Blackwater barracks in the foreground. (Andrew Green)

Raziq (second from left) meets with Sadullah Khan (right). (Author's collection, confidential source)

Raziq leads LTC Andrew Green of 4-2 CAV by the hand during a tour of his home district, 2010. (Andrea Bruce)

Raziq, back center, conducts a meeting with elders from the rival Noorzai tribe after a U.S. raid killed local civilians, 2010. (Andrew Green)

COL James Edwards (left), Raziq (second from left), and LTC Andrew Green (third from left) eat pomegranates during a meeting, 2010. (James Edwards)

COL James Edwards meets with Raziq, who uses the American officer to impress local elders, 2010. (James Edwards)

GEN David Petraeus, Raziq, and MG Mike Flynn at the Friendship Gate on the Pakistan border. (Author's collection, confidential source)

Raziq shares a laugh with GEN Stanley McChrystal. (Author's collection, confidential source)

The pet owl briefly adopted by 4-2 CAV squadron, September 2010. (Ronald Savage)

Troopers from 4-2 CAV squadron input the biometric data for an Afghan man, September 2010. (Ronald Savage)

Headquarters building at the Kandahar Airport (KDH) with Raziq's image above the door. (Kincy Clark)

up flag-side-down in a latrine.[41] 4-2 CAV moved first to FOB Lindsey, a base on the outskirts of Kandahar Airfield. The unit relocated again in March to FOB Frontenac, on the route north from Kandahar City to Uruzgan Province. It was there, away from the security oasis that Raziq provided in Spin Boldak, that the squadron suffered its first deaths of the deployment.

On 20 March, Lieutenant Colonel Green's security detail was cleaning weapons outside their new tactical operations center. They were vulnerable at that moment, since they had all their heavy weapons broken down from the vehicles. One of the Afghans employed by a private security company chose this moment to approach the group of soldiers as they sat outside the TOC. He looked like he wanted to ask a question. Some of the Afghans liked to practice their English. But instead of speaking to them, this Afghan raised his AK-47 and began firing into the cluster of soldiers.

Green was inside the operations center at the time. He recalled hearing a noise he believed to be an air-powered nail gun. His unit was continuously building, always improving their positions. But that 'whack-whack-whack' did sound suspiciously loud. As Green considered, one of his soldiers ran into the building, with a notch the size of an axe-wound in his shoulder. 'Hey boss, they're shooting us,' he managed to report, and then passed out in a heap. The commander and his staff grabbed their carbines and ran out of the TOC looking for the assailant, who had begun to dash around the FOB in search of more targets. He had already killed two troopers. Green's driver, Private First Class Arocha, met the gunman as they both ran around the corner of a HESCO barrier wall. From fewer than 20m, the American shot the Afghan twice in the chest. But instead of seeing blood spurt, he observed only 'little white puffs,' from a bulletproof vest. Arocha ducked behind HESCO barriers as the insurgent fired back. The US trooper then rolled to his left, shot the insurgent twice in the knees, and saw him go down. By this point, the Squadron's Fire Support Officer, Major Art Stringer, emerged from the TOC and covered Arocha's movement toward the Afghan. Both Americans fired rounds as their opponent reached for his fallen rifle. The fatally wounded insurgent continued to writhe on the ground for a few seconds, perhaps invigorated by a dose of amphetamines.

The officers of 4-2 CAV conducted an immediate stand-down on FOB Frontenac. The Afghan security guards, from whom the attacker had come, were quarantined inside their barracks. Green held a meeting to calm the collective nerves. 'Everybody was amped,' the American recalled.

His message to the Afghans was simple in this trying time: 'Nobody in my battalion is blaming you. We had one person do something awful today. We need to be very careful. But I've never had a problem with any of you people here, and I want to make sure that we are all taking care of each other.'

The leader of the Afghans responded, 'We love working for you guys. We don't know that attacker. He was never one of us. Do not judge us by him.'

The subsequent investigation found that the attacker had volunteered as a security guard at FOB Spin Boldak, but had been turned away on suspicion of Taliban connections. He had changed his name and reapplied at FOB Frontenac.

It was not lost on the American squadron that none of their troopers had been killed in action while stationed alongside the ABP. The attacker had been properly deterred when he confronted Raziq's forces and had only succeeded in gaining access to FOB Frontenac, where a private Canadian contractor ran base security. Yet Green did not blame the contractors, as it was next to impossible 'to vet Afghans with no written records.'[42] The tactic of the insider threat, the 'Green on Blue' attack, emerged toward the end of the American surge, and it continued to drive wedges between the Americans and their purported allies for the rest of the war.

PART III

THE FALL OF PARTNERSHIP

Wherever ye are, death will find you out, even if ye are in towers built up strong and high!

Quran, Sura 4, verse 78

Chapter 14

DRAWDOWN (2012–13)

Reform was dangerous in Afghanistan. For over a century, young people in the region have struggled to reconcile aspects of modernity – secularism, feminism, and representative government – with the traditions of homeland and religion. For Raziq, reform operated in two ways. His American advisers attempted to change some of the ways that he operated, to make him acceptable to those who funded his security empire. In turn, they expected Raziq to reform the way that governance functioned in Kandahar. One goal for a counter-insurgency campaign was to reduce the sources of grievance that pushed people to support the insurgents. Ordinary people had to believe they were better off under Raziq's system than under the Taliban's. How much could Raziq change conditions in Kandahar to make its young immune to the longstanding calls of anti-imperial *jihad*? At the end of his life, Raziq sought to lead Kandaharis down a path of reform. Perhaps it was not the American path, but it was an adjacent one, translated for local conditions.

Meanwhile, the US military continued to reform its own efforts in Kandahar. At the beginning of the surge, the US sent cavalry units to augment the existing Special Forces and CIA agents along the border. By the surge's end, a large conventional intelligence unit had expanded the cavalry squadron's presence at the border crossing point to construct a systematic Gorgon's Eye made up of advanced technological systems and bureaucratic watchdogs.[1]

Still, questions remained. After more than a decade of American occupation, had the foreigners helped to create a sustainable and representative government? Or had the US and its NATO partners reinforced a new generation of regional warlords, such as Raziq, at the expense of the national government? As the Americans withdrew forces, starting in 2012, they could not help but hand over more power to those still willing to fight for the republic against persistent Taliban threats. Partnership became a way to offload more responsibility onto their Afghan hosts.

Raziq appeared ready for this role, as he took steps to professionalize his forces. While critics credited the arrival of peace in Kandahar to the brutality of Raziq's men, others pointed to the efficiency and enthusiasm in enforcement that he brought to the republican forces. He sent key police leaders to train in academies. He hired 145 new technicians to help keep the streets clear of explosive devices. The institutional moves seemed to pay off. A group of Kandahar teachers claimed that since Raziq took charge, 'parents no longer keep their children locked up at home, off the streets.' The number of Taliban attacks in Kandahar City dipped from 150 in 2011 to just 60 in 2012, Raziq's first full year as provincial Chief of Police.[2] As the province stabilized, the Americans prepared their exits.

The US withdrawal was visible in the units assigned to partner with Raziq. Though the Afghan leader was now a lieutenant general, the American units deployed with his forces fell from a brigade to a battalion as 2012 turned into 2013. Raziq retained his own personal mentors, independent of the conventional units, taken from Security Forces Assistance Teams (SFATs) based in Kandahar City. But these advisers also illustrated the diminished priorities of the US in Afghanistan. At the end of the surge, Raziq's liaison was an active-duty 'full bird' colonel. By 2016, he was a Lieutenant Colonel from the National Guard.

Changes to the infrastructure signaled withdrawal, as well. The site of the SFAT's headquarters moved from Camp Nathan Smith, a tiny footprint built up vertically through an old fruit cannery in the heart of Kandahar City, to FOB Walton on the periphery. The logic for the move was force protection, to shift 'away from clear lines of approach' by Taliban forces to the west.[3] Units in Kandahar after the surge focused more on closing American bases and repatriating equipment than fighting the Taliban. One battalion commander shut down seventeen FOBs and COPs in the province, a little over half of the total in his area of operations, within a nine-month span.[4] In this environment, Raziq's reforming forces became vulnerable targets.

Lieutenant Colonel Terry Nihart and Command Sergeant Major Billy Counts formed the leadership team of the 503rd Military Police battalion that arrived in Kandahar at the beginning of the drawdown in spring 2012. They had planned to split responsibilities for security of Kandahar City with 8-1 CAV, Bill Clark's old unit that had returned under a new commander, then Lieutenant Colonel Patrick Michaelis. After arrival in country, the battalions coordinated to reshuffle their responsibilities. 8-1 CAV became the 'battlespace owner,' since they were a maneuver unit equipped with the artillery and engineer assets that helped exert control over terrain. The MPs focused on their expertise: training the Afghan police. Nihart had plentiful experience with the foreign training mission thanks to a fifteen-month deployment to Northern Iraq. In Afghanistan, his unit fell in on efforts initiated by their predecessors, who had established a police academy and worked out relationships with various police substations (PSS) throughout the city.

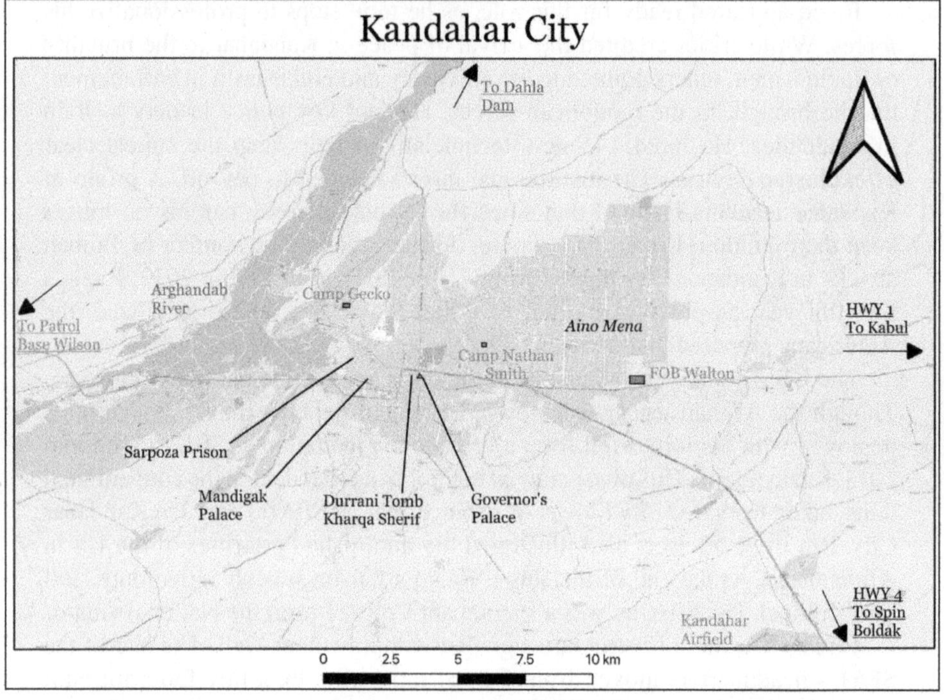

Nihart's everyday partners were Raziq's direct subordinates. Together with his Chief of Security (CoSEC), Raziq managed sixteen police substations (PSS). Each one had its own commander, whose skills and experiences varied. Two of the most effective, in Nihart's consideration, demonstrated a willingness to risk their lives for the Afghan government. Major Fareed was a Karzai appointee from an inner branch of the sprawling Popalzai network. Fareed was not in the position long; it was a stepping stone to political office in Kabul. He was, Nihart remembered, 'kind of smooth with his interaction with people.' His English was good, which was of particular importance to the Americans. While he remained at PSS 9, Fareed was effective. His partner recalled him as a 'fierce' fighter and a 'patriot,' someone who 'was definitely not running from trouble,' as some commanders tended to do.

Then there was Nihart's favorite, Major Qayum, of PSS 2. He was new to the job; the man he replaced had been an old *mujahidin* fighter. Like Raziq, Qayum was unpolished, disorganized, and 'sort of goofy.' Nihart recalled, 'Half his people wanted to beat him up half the time,' due to Qayum's tendency to commit administrative gaffes. He was also known to indulge in whiskey and cigarettes during Ramadan. Still, in terms of their combat operations against insurgents, the effectiveness of Substation 2 was undeniable. Qayum was a 'poster child' for the Americans when visiting dignitaries came to see well-drilled Afghan policemen in proper uniforms, with working weapons.

By this point, Nihart assessed that Raziq had a 'deity-like status' among the Afghans. The police chief had survived four assassination attempts in the nine months that the MP battalion had occupied Kandahar City. His ability to remain a step ahead of his attackers gave him an aura of invincibility and resulting celebrity. Nihart quipped, 'It was like watching Brad Pitt walk down the street,' as crowds swarmed around his small entourage of aides and guards. Another adviser around the same time compared Raziq's popularity to Elvis Presley's, while a third later compared his celebrity to Lady Gaga's. The common thread: they were all 'rock stars.'[5]

What set Raziq apart from other effective operational leaders, besides his cult status, was his ability to think strategically about the effects of prospective operations on Afghan politics. He listened to American plans and then pointed out the negative results they might incur, from the level of the national government down to that of local families. After putting down the ideas of the Americans, Raziq often proposed one of his own. 'It was five or six waves ahead of anything we were thinking of,' Nihart recalled.

As insider attacks picked up in frequency in 2012, changes to US force protection made partnership with Afghan leaders more difficult. The Americans instituted a 'Guardian Angel program,' which posted two guards at the door of every meeting. Coalition partners had to be 'very hesitant about who can be in a meeting and who can't.' For Afghans who had grown used to easy access to offices and bases that the Americans occupied, this new treatment often came as an affront. In the early months of the 503rd MP battalion's deployment, conditions went from a 'comfortable and relaxed environment' to the Americans showing up to meetings 'completely kitted up.' Senior officers might remove their helmets as they sat down to discuss business, but often continued to wear their armor in plate carriers, sometimes augmented with various bulky protective gear: high collars, crotch guards, and the like. Nihart admitted the policy did not 'send the same message in cooperation' to Afghans wearing linen *shalwar kameez*.[6]

The Americans decided to protect themselves from an environment that seemed to be teeming with threats. When danger emerged unannounced from the ranks of their purported partners, Americans began to suspect that foul play lurked behind every misunderstanding. Anyone could be a silent enemy. Even those not actively engaged in the insurgency might be passing information to those outside the FOB. For example, the massive attack on Raziq's headquarters in July 2012 had likely been coordinated by an insider.

9 July 2012

The Provincial Police Headquarters was a football-field-sized compound surrounded by 5m walls, located in a residential neighborhood of Kandahar City. An adjacent three-story school provided a view into the courtyard of the headquarters. Nihart and Raziq stood there discussing logistics with their staff officers. That day's talk focused on 'tracking equipment and supply chain,' which was a chronic concern for the Afghan police. Fraud was rampant in the impoverished environment as the Americans planned their withdrawal. After a few minutes, Raziq parted from Nihart to return to his office on the other side of the compound.

While the leadership talked logistics, Nihart's subordinates participated in another kind of reform. The first course to train women as police officers was underway. It was a 'big initiative,' Nihart recalled, because Afghan security forces needed to be able to search and interrogate women; in Pashtun culture men were not supposed to perform these tasks. The idea had come from Nihart's predecessors, but at the end of their rotation the concept still had to gain traction with Americans and Afghans alike. Nihart recalled Raziq as a proponent of the new project. Like most senior leaders, he 'saw the value in it and appreciated it.' Resistance came more from Afghan subordinates, who undermined their women colleagues at every turn in an effort to discourage their participation in the male-dominated field.

On one occasion, an Afghan policeman made lewd sexual comments and gestured toward an American soldier. Command Sergeant Major Billy Counts recalled, 'By the time I got there, [the Afghan leader] had stripped the badge and gun off this kid, beat the shit out of him all the way up to the front gate, opened the door. Told him, you got an hour to get out of Kandahar. If I ever catch you again, I'm gonna shoot you on sight.' The incident brought in line with official policy many of those recalcitrant about working with women, though it may have bred resentment along the way. Afghans knew that Americans were the ones pushing the operations that featured women. But they also knew that the Americans provided their salaries and the bulk of their supplies.[7]

Under Nihart's tenure in Afghanistan, several women MP officers joined Captain Erin Barrett and her Female Engagement Team (FET) to train the first fifty-five Afghan women to enlist in Kandahar's force. Nihart credited the presence of his female soldiers with a shift in opinion among their Afghan partners. But the presence of armed, professional women also presented enticing targets to the Taliban, and perhaps to insiders who wanted to see the program fail.[8] On 9 July, complex attacks erupted all over Kandahar City, but the brunt of the violence was borne by Raziq's police headquarters.

In the early afternoon, the scene of partnership erupted in chaos. Over the past weeks, teams of laborers had buried thousands of kilograms of explosives beneath the walls of the compound. The sheer weight of the load suggested that someone inside the base had been involved in the planning. Having executed the headmaster and killed the children who were too slow to escape, the attackers occupied the schoolhouse that overlooked the compound. When the insurgents were in place with machine guns and rocket-propelled grenades, they blew the dug-in explosives. The blast knocked out every window from the police headquarters and many houses in the surrounding blocks. Nearby observers claimed that the mushroom cloud from the explosion reached dozens of stories into the air.

Nihart had been standing in a second-floor office, about 25m from the explosion's epicenter, chatting with the Afghan supply officer over a large ledger used to track logistics. The blast blew shattered glass at the men and tossed them across the room, over a row of couches and against the adjacent wall. The American battalion commander was knocked out for a few minutes. When he regained consciousness he was already crouched behind a desk with his pistol in hand and a round chambered. 'There's training for you,' Nihart chuckled later.

He could see through the broken windows that a team of insurgents had stormed through the hole blown in the compound wall. They carried satchels filled with grenades, which they tossed into buildings as they jogged along. The enemy fighters had gotten between the Americans and their protective armor, which they had dropped at the entrance of this 'secure' area. Nihart, his security detail, and their Afghan partners hunkered down behind the rubble of a ruined wall, trapped by two attackers with rifles who hemmed them in while their counterparts launched grenades into the compound from the roof of the schoolhouse. 'We were waiting to die,' Nihart remembered. Raziq was across the compound in a separate office at the time. His SFAT mentor had to physically hold him back from charging out of the room. The American officer could not risk his partner's engagement in the developing nightmarish scene.

For the next ninety minutes, chaos reigned at the police headquarters. According to Nihart, it was similar to 'a paintball park, but with real guns. Just craziness.' Though there were perhaps only four insurgents inside the compound, it was difficult to distinguish them from the Afghan policemen in various uniforms who turned their AK-47s in on the courtyard. The battalion's sergeant major, taking reports in the operations center, recalled the Afghan police were 'just spraying and praying.' Dozens of rifle barrels melted during the firefight, bent out of shape from overuse.[9]

Major Qayum and his 2nd Police *Kandak* were the first to respond to the incident. They established a cordon to ensure that more insurgents could not enter the compound. Close on their heels, 8-1 CAV sent a company that had been in wait as a quick reaction force (QRF). Their commander, Lieutenant Colonel Michaelis, offered his unit to the MP battalion's XO at Camp Nathan Smith. The incoming units guided air assets to provide fire support. Raziq's mentor finally allowed him out of his office once the relief force cleared the compound. As the Americans prepared to use close air support to level the school, still teeming with insurgent fighters, Raziq led a charge up the three-story structure and routed its defenders.

After five hours of fighting, Nihart surveyed the damage. He counted twenty-two insurgents killed, but more fighters had doubtless been involved. Some had fled. Others perhaps never revealed themselves, but blended back into the crowd thanks to uniforms used as cover. Six Afghan partners had perished, while five Americans suffered serious injuries. Nihart was able to walk away from the scene, albeit with glass shrapnel protruding from his face and neck. He and many other Americans had suffered concussion from the initial blast. Once the dust settled, the Afghan survivors lit up celebratory hashish. Smoke wafted up from each guard tower into the stifling evening air. 'It was like a Cheech and Chong show,' Nihart smiled.[10]

End of the Surge

President Obama had limited his troop surge to Afghanistan from the start. When he announced the policy in a speech at West Point in December 2009, he indicated that US force levels would begin to drop again after eighteen months of the heightened deployment posture. From a peak of just under 100,000 troops at the beginning of 2012, the total dipped to 76,500 by the end of that year, and fewer than 56,000 by the end of 2013.[11]

Obama emphasized three 'core elements' of his plan for Afghanistan. As well as additional troops, and re-engagement with Pakistan, the Commander-in-Chief counseled surge personnel to build relationships with Afghan partners. He elaborated that partnerships should be 'grounded in mutual respect – to isolate those who destroy; to strengthen those who build; to hasten the day when our troops will leave; and to forge a lasting friendship in which America is your partner, and never your patron.' These were noble sentiments. But the signals Obama sent to loyal Afghans – we are coming with a diverse coalition of foreigners, and we will soon leave – resonated with another audience as well. The Taliban learned that December evening they could simply wait out the surge troops, whose multinational composition of infidels would be a liability rather than a strength in much of rural Afghanistan.[12] The reason the President gave for his self-imposed deadline was to give 'urgency' to the Americans, and to force the Afghans opposed to the Taliban to 'take responsibility' for their own security.

The speech closed on a moral note. The true source of US authority was not military, Obama argued, but ethical. He promised those who lived 'under the dark cloud of tyranny, that America will speak out on behalf of their human rights, and tend to the light of freedom, and justice, and opportunity, and respect for the dignity of all peoples.'[13] As the Americans surged, observers began to question whether the additional troops were in fact defenders of human rights. Had they instead enabled Afghan leaders such as Raziq to trample upon them?

The surge policy, President Obama's compromise with General Petraeus for more resources in Central Asia, demonstrated a repudiation of the 'blank check' mentality that the Bush administration had brought to the Global War on

Terrorism. When Obama inherited those conflicts, he sought to distance himself and extract Americans from places of questionable strategic value compared to typical American foreign policy concerns: Israel in the Middle East, and Pakistan, India, Russia, and China in Central Asia. Iraq and Afghanistan, which had swallowed vast sums of US dollars, returned to their former positions as peripheral places of interest. For Kandaharis, the policy had predictable and disastrous results.

The Kandahar Provincial Reconstruction Team (PRT) employed 250 military personnel and forty-seven civilians at its peak strength during the surge. In 2010, total foreign aid to Kandahar approached $325 million, or $625 per capita, three times the average annual income earned in the domestic economy. Afghans had long relied on foreign aid, which tended to increase in dramatic fashion during times of war. Government contracts filtered down from the top to the Popalzai and Barakzai networks in Kabul. Raziq, on the other hand, controlled the other source of external funding: import duties on cars and electronics, to include Roshan mobile phones. Sources of funding dwindled by the end of 2012 as the PRT shut down and opportunities for contracts dried up. The effect on Afghanistan was like pulling the rug out from under its 'extreme rentier' economy.[14]

Perhaps the biggest foreign contract scheme involved Hamid Karzai's family and the construction that took place at Aino Mena, also known as Little Canada or Little America. Aino Mena was a luxury community for Afghan politicians and their international friends that had sprung up in the city on land owned by the Afghan government before the Americans arrived. Two Karzai brothers and their 'land-grabber' associates claimed the real estate and sold it to developers for a fraction of its market value, allowing the speculators to divide their holdings into smaller plots and flip them for huge profits. Contractors in Kabul sold their rights to build to subcontractors and pocketed the surplus. The process sometimes took place three or four times, until the money left to build was less than half of the original foreign contract.[15]

In addition to the rich contracts that arrived with foreign military forces, soldiers themselves provided opportunities for local entrepreneurs to sell food, cold drinks, Afghan clothing and trinkets, provide haircuts, clean and repair uniforms, and so on. The average income for street vendors in Kandahar City was anywhere from $4 to $20 per day, depending on the goods sold. Tarpaulin and clothing salesmen were on the low end of that range; electronics vendors made more.

In Kandahar City's largest bazaar, an estimated 250 vendors sold cell phones. Devices arrived at the market through two sets of wholesalers, one in Pakistan that imported phones from South Korea and India, and another in Afghanistan that distributed to local retailers. A smaller third group smuggled the phones across the border. One vendor said that his business peaked with the American surge in 2011, when he averaged seven phone sales per day for a profit of $20. By 2015, sales plummeted to one per day. Raziq was the hero of these vendors. His police provided the security they needed and kept thieves at bay. Though some substation commanders were known to run limited extortion rackets, even those victimized tended to distance Raziq from predation by his subordinates. The vendors in turn became a major source of informants for the government against the Taliban.[16]

Senior military commanders increasingly saw their mission as handing over responsibility to the Afghans. Since 2014, Raziq's regular army partners had left Kandahar. The officers who remained to link Raziq with the American government were adviser teams from the National Guard. Though some active-duty officers denigrated the Guard as part-time soldiers, others saw them as more natural partners for Raziq. Conventional military officers, this logic went, are formed in federal institutions, where they receive the benefits of an abundant defense budget, and where they may learn the best textbook ways to do things. But their training regime makes regulars competent yet 'cookie-cutter' in their approach.[17] These regular officers do not necessarily learn the skills that one develops by being integrated into a community, as National Guard officers tend to be. In addition to their military roles, Guard leaders serve as teachers, police officers, and in other roles integral to their neighborhoods.

The Global War on Terrorism reduced the distinction between the Guard and the army in terms of overseas deployments. As a result of the Vietnam War, the US ended its military draft. Rather than rely on teenage recruits, the regular military establishment would lean on its reserve component. National Guard units developed formal training relationships with active-duty counterparts. Federal reserve units adopted specialized administrative and logistical tasks necessary for deployment. Military planners used a twofold rationale. First, they sought to leverage the experience of volunteers rather than take in untrained draftees. Moreover, the model sought to limit the use of these reserve troops to overseas missions that were broadly acceptable to the public. By the morning of the 11 September attacks, more than 12,000 reservists were already in Europe to support the Bosnian peacekeeping effort, while a similar number had been deployed to Central America for hurricane relief. The Global War on Terrorism, during which the reserve component made up 45 per cent of all US forces, only accelerated a well established trend to send this category of volunteer soldier beyond the national frontiers.[18]

Raziq throughout his career had been closest with partners who did have a traditional overseas mandate: the US Special Forces. Like National Guardsmen, SF officers tended to believe that regular active-duty army officers struggled with foreign partnerships because of the rigidness of their training and collective mindset. One veteran officer described the difference as 'transactional' versus 'transformational' leadership. The former, employed by conventional types, was to ensure good behavior by the use of both carrots and sticks. The latter approach, which SF officers favored, was to bond with partners on a fundamental level, to share as much as possible of their living conditions and the dangers of combat in proximity. Green Berets trained above all to think outside the box.

Within the Special Forces community, however, distinct approaches emerged. From an institutional standpoint, 3rd SF Group rotated in and out of Afghanistan with 7th Group, which in peacetime had focused on South America. 3rd Group had more of a reputation for 'killing bad guys,' whereas 7th Group was more engaged in building partnerships. Raziq developed deep friendships with men from both organizations. In 2015, he ditched a meeting with a US four-star general to reconnect with an old friend, a mere Colonel from 7th Group.[19] As the US drew down its conventional forces, Raziq reinforced his existing relationships at the same time that he branched out into new, political roles.

Chapter 15

Chapter 15
ADVISERS (2013–18)

General Raziq sat at the head of a table for a 2013 gathering at FOB Walton. He was first among equals in the Afghan branches represented at the weekly security meeting, along with the National Police, 205th Army Corps, and Afghan intelligence service. The Afghans in the room all deferred to him. They knew that if they needed something done in Kandahar or its neighboring provinces, they would need at least his tacit support, if not active cooperation.

FOB Walton, a sprawling headquarters on the eastern edge of Kandahar City, was representative of the American surge, fluid and transitory as a rolling storm wave. The American base surrounded an existing Afghan Police Headquarters, where Raziq maintained one of his offices. In 2011, the Americans began to supply electrical power and set up a few buildings. Then came the barracks for American advisers and their supporting staffs, the logistics to keep their vehicles and computers running, and the dining facility to keep them fed. Now, Raziq heard new plans: Walton was going to be closed down next year, in a matter of months, some said by July 2014. Were the Americans really going to withdraw? They had started to pack up some of their equipment already.[1]

These days, when he was in Kandahar City, Raziq spent less time at FOB Walton and the Police Headquarters than at Mandigak Palace. His third wife and her children lived in a house that shared a wall with the imposing workspace.[2] Raziq's weekly schedule took him throughout the province, and he made regular trips to Kabul. Of course, he liked to visit his old stomping ground in Spin Boldak when he could. Raziq, in absentia, had his brother Tadin keeping an eye on family businesses, while Hajji Janan, Raziq's former Quick Reaction Force (QRF) commander, had taken charge of military operations.

As the security meeting was set to begin, Raziq stood joking outside. The Americans began to fill up the conference room. First came the general's aides and the Afghan advisers with their interpreters. Then members of the staff shuffled into the room. Finally, the US commander arrived. Major General

Robert 'Abe' Abrams was the son of Creighton Abrams, who had shepherded the US out of Vietnam by engaging his indigenous allies to shoulder more and more of the load on their own. Now, his son had a similar mission in Kandahar Province. The end of Abrams the younger's command of RC South corresponded with the end of the surge and the beginning of the drawdown.

As they thought about the future, the Americans considered what handing over more power to Raziq might look like. By this point, doubts about the young Afghan's character had been subsumed by larger doubts about systemic incompetence in the Afghan Security Forces. Raziq's domain had become a bright spot on a map of Afghanistan that was dark with Taliban infiltration and growing darker. Abrams assigned some of his highest performing colonels to partner one-on-one with Raziq. The commanding general pulled each one aside upon taking the role. The mission was simple: 'Don't let this guy die.' He warned they were certain to be shot at and blown up on this assignment.

Abrams also happened to be on a health kick. In addition to the dangers of Taliban violence, there were unseen, internal threats. He counseled his partner: 'Raziq, you need to stop smoking cigarettes, and quit drinking those energy drinks. Those things are going to give you cancer.'

Raziq waited for the translation, smirked at the American, and exhaled smoke. He had been thinking about the cigarettes. They had been a comfort on so many hard days. Sometimes, he wished he could find another way to calm his nerves. He had begun to ask his interpreters to buy him nicotine patches when they went abroad on leave.

Abrams went on nagging. He was on a tear today: 'You want a heart attack, Raziq? If you don't start taking care of yourself, this stuff is going to kill you.'

Raziq stared down his counterpart as he took a long, last drag from a Dunhill cigarette, a luxury brand he had picked up on his last trip to Dubai, then stubbed the butt out in an empty can of RipIts. Sometimes the Americans gave Raziq good advice. Sometimes they were off the mark, but still it was better to agree and nod along with them. Raziq blew final wisps of smoke with a toothy smile toward General Abrams. He wagged his head in his characteristic manner: not quite defiant, but sly, and replied through his translator: 'Let's start the meeting. Where are we fighting today?'[3]

A few days later, back at Mandigak Palace, Raziq heard a different kind of advice. His primary American partner, a Colonel in the Texas National Guard, opened up a laptop. The screen showed the video feed from a PTIDs surveillance balloon located on an American FOB. The Colonel showed Raziq the footage: members of the police force in Panjwai district had unloaded a handful of prisoners from the back of a pickup truck, stood them up against a wall with their hands tied behind their backs, and shot them at close range.[4]

'You have to do something about this,' the Texas Guardsman said. 'You know that we are not going to be here forever. Every NATO military force and every civilian aid agency is looking around right now and asking themselves, how can we get out of Kandahar? What excuse can we give to pull our people and pull our funding? This is going to give them that excuse.'

Raziq knew his adviser was right this time. He called the Panjwai District police chief and asked for a report. The district leader replied, 'Those men were Taliban; they were killed in a firefight.'

Raziq told his subordinate about the video footage and began to deliver a verbal reprimand. 'We need to find out who was responsible for this. We can't allow a few bad policemen to get in the way of reform. We will hold whoever shot those prisoners responsible for their actions.'

'Yes, honored leader (*rais sahib*).'

Raziq hung up the phone. He would see to it that the policemen who had gotten out of line would be fired. Was his American adviser satisfied now?

'By the way,' Raziq said as the Texan got up to leave, 'look at this.'

Raziq walked over to the side of his bedroom office that used to feature stacks of boxes filled with uniforms and old radio equipment. In their place, he had installed a new treadmill. Raziq lit up a cigarette and began a leisurely stroll on it.

'Now,' he laughed, 'you can tell General Abrams you saw me exercising.'[5]

Raziq was in a bind. He knew the Americans shuddered at the methods of his policemen. But he believed that it was better for them to err on the side of aggression, to kill captives in some cases, rather than let them languish in prison for a short term, only to be released again to resume their violent opposition to the republic. It is important to consider the context in which these executions or disappearances took place. During the Achakzai term leading security forces in Kandahar, from 2011 to 2021, a recent *New York Times* exposé uncovered 2,200 complaints of missing persons following their incarceration by the government. People were difficult to track in wartime Afghanistan, however, so only 368 individuals across the decade could be confirmed by two witnesses as victims of police 'disappearance.'[6]

Though this statistic presents a troubling picture, the numbers were dwarfed by the campaign of violence that Taliban insurgents waged at the same time. In 2010, Kandahar Province suffered 288 civilians killed as bystanders to IEDs alone. Dozens more became targeted victims of Taliban assassinations and suicide attacks. In 2011, the first year of Raziq's appointment as Chief of Police, the Taliban caused 2,332 civilian casualties across the country. Their violence focused on the South: in the second half of that year, they killed 290 noncombatants in Kandahar and Helmand Provinces alone. The insurgency's toll only increased throughout the years of the US drawdown: in just three years between 2012 and 2014, anti-government forces killed more than 7,000 civilians. About 40 per cent of the victims were from Raziq's southern region.[7] It was against this backdrop that Raziq reiterated his aggressive policy to a reporter in the summer of 2014. He claimed that he 'ordered his forces to execute militants on the spot, rather than take them prisoner.' The Police Chief, who later retracted his comments, argued these methods prevented fighters from returning to the struggle. Authorities in Kabul, he claimed, were more likely to 'demand a bribe' than to prosecute suspected insurgents.[8]

While violence perpetrated by local government forces and by foreigners stoked more emotion in Afghanistan, Taliban violence without question posed the greatest threat to ordinary noncombatants. The tactics of Raziq's ABP – abduction, torture, and sometimes execution – proved offensive to Western sensibilities, but they were more discriminate means than either Taliban bombs or attacks by foreign aircraft. Raziq and his brother-successor, even at the high estimate of 2,200 forced disappearances, killed as many Kandaharis in ten years as the Taliban did every two or three years over the same period. This is not to excuse the abuses that Afghan security forces committed against local nationals, nor to minimize Raziq's role in their frequent occurrence, but only to place sensational media stories about Kandahar in context.

Eco-terrorism in Shorabak District

Back in Spin Boldak, Hajji Janan carried on using the Raziq playbook. The subordinate commander aimed to distribute the wealth that foreigners brought, to 'take care of the folks,' as one of his advisers, put it, and to 'hold court' when people of the region had disputes. Janan at the district level, like Raziq at the regional, served as a middleman between the people willing to approach him with problems and the US-sponsored government with the resources to address some of those issues. These exchanges allowed Janan to maintain the robust network of intelligence that Raziq had cultivated prior to his move to Kandahar City. He had further inherited his chief's role as military 'troubleshooter.' Whereas most commanders oversaw static checkpoints, Janan retained personal control of the QRF role he had developed under Raziq's leadership. As a result of the unit's frequent deployments to the various border districts, Janan gained a reputation as dynamic and offensive-minded.

Ken Scheidt, an AfPak hand assigned to Spin Boldak, was a seasoned infantry officer by 2013. His career had commenced three decades earlier as an enlisted soldier in the Ranger Regiment. Lieutenant Colonel Scheidt characterized Hajji Janan as effective on operations, but a 'diva' in meetings. The American liaison found himself in a difficult position, as he tried to support his partner and to encourage his independence. The Afghan commander used dramatic emotional outbursts to emphasize his importance and extract more resources from his foreign colleagues. For example, Janan often requested US air support for his forces. When Scheidt counseled his partner to find another way to conduct operations that did not rely on American assets, Janan instead complained to Raziq. The Kandahar Police Chief then informed his high-ranking partners at RC South of his subordinate's needs in Spin Boldak district, which the local conventional unit was then tasked to provide.

One ploy that Janan devised late in 2013 was a model of leveraging American resources, though results of the scheme were dubious. He convinced his foreign patrons that insurgents were using vegetation as cover in the vicinity of a remote village close to the Pakistan border, on the edge of the Reg desert. Janan proposed to deploy bulldozers to raze the great areas of concealment, in order to eliminate this route of infiltration south of the official border crossing point. Scheidt summed up the operational concept as 'ecological terrorism.'[9] During the convoy to the operation, as Scheidt rode in a Stryker and the Border Police flanked them in their Ford Ranger pickup trucks, Janan sped past with a small group of luxury SUVs. Scheidt recalled that the vehicles seemed out of place in the rustic desert setting. The cars were so new that a protective film still stuck to the windows.[10] American officials at the time sought 'Afghan sustainable' operations, which could be replicated once the Americans sped up their drawdown of troops and resources. But what Scheidt's partner seemed to want was unsustainable, in both technological and ecological terms. Janan asked for American assets to help him destroy a fragile vegetated area and extend the desert further eastward.

One of the last conventional units to be based in Spin Boldak, 2-23 Infantry Battalion, helped to coordinate the operation. The focus of regular units in the province had shifted from fighting to advising. The battalion's mission was to provide security for the 'main effort' of the region, six Security Forces Advisor Teams (SFATs) that had been culled from the Texas National Guard.[11] Many of the team members had been selected based on their law enforcement experience, in particular state troopers who had patrolled the US border with Mexico. The 2-23 IN commander, then Lieutenant Colonel Tom Feltey, recalled collective support to Janan's Border Police in this case as 'Afghan IO' (information operations), a kind of public relations campaign.

The destruction of reeds and bushes along an arid riverbed was not likely to prevent insurgents from using the desert terrain of Shorabak as an infiltration route. They were more apt to hide in the compounds of sympathetic villagers than among the river reeds. Likewise, Afghan intelligence was based more on human sources than on satellite or drone imagery.

But Hajji Janan, true to his nature as a 'diva' partner, wanted to put on an ostentatious display. He intended the American-supplied bulldozers and air support as evidence to area residents that he had taken steps to safeguard them. Feltey recalled, 'He's going to take action, and tear that thing down, and help the locals.' The US partner used the 'Afghan Robin Hood' moniker for Janan that his predecessors in Spin Boldak had applied to Raziq. Both of these leaders used foreign resources for the benefit – either imagined or in real security terms – of ordinary Afghans. In addition to the destruction of vegetation, the week-long operation installed a new checkpoint to be manned by the Border Police.[12]

As the Americans ended their combat mission in 2014, Kandahar seemed as secure a republican stronghold as it had ever been. The Taliban movement struggled to maintain any momentum. Mullah Omar had died of illness in the spring of 2013, though spokesmen continued to make statements on his behalf for the next two years. Omar's secret successor, Mullah Mansour, fell to a drone attack in Pakistan in 2016.[13] But the movement, despite issues at the top level of governance, proved resilient.

The Taliban was able to re-emerge after years of dormancy due to the decentralization of its organization and the diversity of its participants. One intelligence analyst broke down the resistance into three distinct entities: top-level administrators based in Quetta and Miran Shah, a large pool of manpower opposed to the Kabul government known as 'local Taliban,' and agents of the 'narco Taliban,' which opposed government forces and competed among their rackets to facilitate drug shipments. The drug lords only affiliated with the Taliban when it suited their business interests.[14] The high council members who held titles and offices in Pakistan had little sway over local and narco insurgent leaders, since the Taliban operated with a local, cellular franchise model rather than a traditional governing hierarchy. Moreover, no matter how many heads the US was able to chop off, new ones sprouted up, since Taliban grievances against the republican government remained.[15] This was a lesson that some American officials had already learned, or should have should have learned before. According to a document published by the U.S. Marine Corps, over two years of the 'decapitation' strategy of killing 'high value' leaders beginning in 2006 had regulated in September 2008 as the month with the 'highest number of security incidents and casualties in Southern Afghanistan'. The Kabul government had allied with Western infidels, allowed them to occupy the country, and permitted unspeakable acts against Muslims. Now that the foreigners were preparing to leave, Taliban officials and sympathetic mullahs across the region urged that it was time to exact revenge.

Some of the Afghan security forces were frank with their American allies about the developing situation. Though foreign support had given the republic some control over the cities and the major highways, the Taliban maintained a quiet presence in the rural areas. One commander in Kandahar told his American partner that the insurgents were 'one terrain feature away,' from their point of view on a combat outpost (COP). The Afghan warned, 'If you guys end up closing this COP down, and I have to stay here . . . I don't want to tell you. I respect you guys, but I'm going to have to grow a beard [i.e. become a Taliban commander].'[16] For those toward the bottom of the new republican security apparatus, survival meant flexibility in one's allegiance.

Political and Operational Trends

From 2014 on, Raziq balanced his adoption of increasing patronage responsibilities with the demands of Taliban offensives. Throughout these years, his forces managed to preserve Kandahar as one of the few provinces where the insurgency could not re-establish itself. At the level of national politics, 2014 was a troubled year. Abdul Ghani won a contested presidential election in June but was not sworn in until September, due to allegations of rampant fraud. Even then, Ghani took power as the leader of a Unity front, in which his rival at the ballot box, Abdullah Abdullah, served alongside him in a top ministerial role as 'chief executive.'

The new President had campaigned on firing 'warlords' such as Raziq, but Ghani's narrow victory forced him to keep the police chief at his post. After all, Kandahar Province was one of the few where the Taliban had failed to make inroads in recent years. One of Raziq's mentors from the 7th Special Forces group, who had deployed to Kandahar in 2002 and 2009, assessed that by 2015, the province was 'the safest I'd ever seen it.' A leading Taliban researcher agreed that by this point, insurgent activity was 'entirely underground' in Kandahar, whereas recruitment occurred in the open throughout the neighboring provinces.[17] Part of the difference, Raziq's partner argued, was that he had his base of power 'wired tight,' due to his tactical prowess and political savvy, both enabled by a superior network of intelligence.

Though the Afghan National Army's 205th Corps had more combat power in Kandahar, Raziq's informants kept him on a faster operational pace. He was able to mobilize forces to encircle and trap enemy fighters as they began to occupy outposts to the north and west of Kandahar City. His partner summed up the reputation that gained him such a willing following: 'He was not selfish and not scared.'[18] Raziq often led from the front on these operations, and his subordinates knew of his generosity in sharing the spoils of American patronage and captured insurgent caches. A lawyer in Kandahar City framed Raziq's accomplishments in a different way: 'If the Taliban or anyone having links with them is being found, he would be immediately executed and buried in the desert, in the outskirts of Kandahar. That is why people praise Raziq.'[19] But his forces did more than defend the province against suspected anti-government agents.

Throughout 2014, as the American forces dwindled, Raziq and a host of hand-picked units stepped up operations outside of Kandahar Province. Pakistani officials blamed him for secret operations across the border in Baluchistan that killed several prominent pro-Taliban mullahs. Whether or not Raziq accompanied the militants across the border in person, he had taken the lead in supporting the Baluch insurgency from safe havens in his home district.[20] Within Afghanistan, he could be more hands-on. In the summer of 2015, Raziq led Afghan forces that lifted a Taliban siege in Helmand. The next year, he performed a similar feat to the north of Kandahar, where local police and army units had abandoned district centers to the insurgents. Tiny and remote Uruzgan had been the domain of another Popalzai strongman, Matiullah Khan, who had been the province's chief of police from 2010 until his 2015 assassination in Kabul. Some claimed he had been killed by a suicide bomber disguised in a *burqa*. Other witnesses insisted it had been an inside job, in which Khan's vehicle had been abducted and his corpse discovered with execution-style wounds.[21]

As another province lost its stabilizing iron fist, Raziq's forces leveraged material assistance from their Special Forces friends. Border Police from Kandahar began to take over the security problems that Matiullah Khan had handled in the past. Sometimes Raziq's personal appearance at compounds amid intense fire emboldened government forces to maintain their positions and drive Taliban units from their own defenses. But just as often, by this late point in his career, Raziq contributed through his coordination with partners at Kandahar Airfield for the apt operational deployment of the region's diminishing military resources, to respond to local crises across the South.[22]

Adviser Rotations

Raziq's final US advisers, from 2016 until his assassination two years later, bore witness to the increasing obstacles to effective partnership. One Texas National Guard officer, who served in Kandahar both in 2013 and 2017, commented on the difference in access to his Afghan partner during Operation Enduring Freedom compared to the rebranded Operation New Dawn that began in 2014. Prior to the change in mission, the US adviser lived at FOB Walton, adjacent to Raziq's police headquarters on the eastern side of Kandahar City. The adviser had access to his own MP platoon to serve as a security detail, with vehicles to shuttle him to Raziq's personal suite at Mandigak Palace on demand. By 2017, FOB Walton itself was 'gone,' transferred to the Afghan forces. US advisers lived on a section of Kandahar Airfield, and they had to schedule a personal security detachment that they shared with other units. Advisers could expect to meet with their allies only twice per week.[23] Raziq's primary role in these meetings was no longer to learn from the Americans, but to provide them with intelligence.

The Texas Guard officer alongside Raziq in 2017 had been a Full Bird Colonel (O6). His replacement was a Lieutenant Colonel from California's 40th Infantry Division, David Craig. This was Craig's third overseas deployment, a sign of the times that featured frequent downrange rotations for the Guard. He had volunteered in 2005 for an artillery slot that went unfilled from a Georgia unit on its way to Iraq. That year, California had more than half of its 20,000 personnel overseas: most in Iraq, but others in the Sinai Peninsula and Guantanamo.[24] Craig deployed again in 2009 to Kosovo. Now, with his combined experience overseas and as an LAPD detective, he had been entrusted to make the vital strategic link with Raziq.

Craig described his role as less of an adviser than a 'collector.' Raziq was now coordinating the efforts of the National Police, Highway Police, and National Civil Order Police, in addition to his primary Border Police force. The Afghan leader called Craig every day with intelligence that the Californian could take to senior officials at KAF. Almost every night, Craig was woken to respond to a Taliban attack on one of Raziq's outposts. Those near the Pakistan border were especially vulnerable.

As violence accelerated against Raziq's forces, the Americans continued to withdraw. After a grievous vehicle-borne IED incident struck the 82nd Airborne Division in Kandahar, the US advisers stayed off the roads for the rest of their nine-month rotation. They took only helicopter rides between their quarters on the airfield and Raziq's Mandigak Palace. In doing so, they abided by policies that sacrificed access to the host-nation partner in favor of the security of armed air patrols. The lack of available air support reduced opportunities for exchange between the Americans and their Afghan partners.[25] Lieutenant Colonel Kincy Clark, a Civil Affairs officer from the California Army National Guard who replaced Craig as Raziq's adviser, recalled the strict limitations on meeting with Afghan partners upon his arrival in 2018. The Afghan leader was limited in his time, as every agency in the South sought him out. The Americans were limited in their tolerance of the IED threat on the roads.

The advisers had to find a new way to meet with Raziq, who suggested they try the Kandahar Airport (KDH), a civilian agency which was part of the larger Kandahar Airfield complex. Technically, the airport came under the purview of the Ministry of Interior, but Raziq's forces controlled its security. Kandahar's airspace constituted another mode of border crossing over which Raziq claimed authority. Since KDH was a 'little island' within the American security bubble at KAF, the Americans did not need to coordinate for their own combat patrols through the city. Partnership found a workaround at the airport.

Kincy Clark's relationship with Raziq in Kandahar grew over the course of their weekly meetings. At one point, Raziq said he wanted to take a vacation in Europe, and he asked Clark where to go. His American adviser suggested Switzerland, a land of peace with mountain vistas. He hoped that Raziq would benefit from the calm Swiss neutrality and the familiarity of hills in the background. But Raziq returned to his adviser with a dismissive report of Switzerland. He also shared that he had diverted his trip to South-Eastern Europe.

Raziq expounded on his newfound love of Croatia. 'The food is cheap, the people are nice,' his adviser recalled. Raziq was trying to downplay the true motivation for the trip. It was in the Balkans that Raziq had found arms dealers who would sell him affordable night vision goggles. 'For a poor boy like me,' Raziq implored, 'Croatia is the best place in Europe. Did I mention the food?' Clark had to pry out of Raziq, through extended discussions about this 'vacation,' the real purpose of his European trip. True to Raziq's reputation, what he explained first as a personal indulgence actually resulted from his desire to improve the fighting capacity of his forces. The Taliban lacked night vision capability as a rule, though Raziq alleged that some insurgents had acquired it of late. He was determined at least to match his opponents, if not gain an advantage over them during the hours of darkness.[26]

Raziq's travel abroad put him in a tiny minority of Afghan politicians who gained foreign contacts after demonstrating their leadership within the country. But Raziq's trip had little in common with those of his predecessors. For example, Ahmad Shah Massoud had spoken French with European statesmen when he warned them about the Taliban and Al Qaeda before the 9/11 attacks. Raziq did not have the elder warlord's background as the son of a royal army officer, socialized at French boarding schools. He had catapulted from regional to international power thanks to the effectiveness of his intelligence network. Though Raziq's wealth and experience could get him an audience with European arms dealers, they could not gain him the entrance to the halls of power in Brussels or Paris that Massoud had achieved.[27]

Nevertheless, the scale of Raziq's international connections set him apart from other contemporary strongmen. He had long cultivated connections within Pakistan, through his Achakzai kinsman's political party and through support for Baluch insurgents. Of late, he had developed contacts in Indian intelligence who were likewise interested in weakening their Pakistani neighbors. Along the way, Raziq had cooperated with his brother Tadin Khan to establish a business network in Dubai. Now he forged new paths for arms supply partnerships in Europe.[28] Kandahar's other security forces leader, 205th Army Corps commander General Nazar, had by comparison a more circumscribed foreign network. The army leader had built his reputation in the Northern Alliance, prior to the US invasion in 2001. Like his patron Abdul Rashid Dostum, Nazar was an ethnic Uzbek with ties to Afghanistan's northern neighbors and to Turkey, unlike Raziq's wide connections, west to the Balkans and east to India.

Raziq understood the cultural differences within the Afghan borderlands, the different motivations of the northerners in the army and the local southerners in the police. He said at one meeting in 2018, 'The Taliban fights for Allah; the army fights for each other; the police fight for money. No one is fighting for Afghanistan.'[29] These hints at political fragmentation provoked American fears about the imminent break-up of the fragile republican government. Raziq's comments also demonstrated his awareness of the difficulties that creating national sentiment posed in Central Asia, which had long been a meeting place of diverse cultures.

Afghan Aides

After 2016, Raziq's closest aides were no longer his Achakzai kinsmen and family members. He had promoted, in place of the assassinated Ramazan Agha, three young Border Policemen who were skilled in foreign languages. Of his three aides, only one was an Achakzai. Another was a fellow southerner from the Barakzai tribe, and a third aide was an Afridi, from the east. These men became Raziq's right hands, secretaries constantly at his side, who helped him to prioritize and react to the constant crises that came to his attention. The aides noticed their leader's suffering from the stress of his job and from memories of fallen subordinates. Raziq's rapid rise to prominence affected his health, which became a growing concern to his inner circle of supporters. During one mission in 2017, Raziq and his comrades did not sleep for several days while under siege from Taliban fighters. Afterward, Raziq experienced episodes in which he became paralyzed and could not speak. He visited India for psychological treatment and returned with medicine to assuage his nerves.[30]

Raziq set an intention to back off from leading operations in person during his last years. He relied on many subordinate commanders to take the lead in police matters. This delegation of authority allowed Raziq to hold court. He established himself as a source of conflict resolution and resource distribution at Mandigak Palace.[31] Raziq's offer to administer justice was an attempt to narrow the cultural gap between the Afghan government and the Taliban. In the eyes of many Kandaharis, it was preferable to live under the harsh but immediate justice of the Taliban rather than under the corruptible justice of distant Kabul. Raziq's settling of disputes corresponded to his spirit of reform, albeit in his own Afghan context.

The republic and its officers would continue to face tension so long as the Taliban remained outside of a political settlement in Kandahar, where they had regained territory as the Americans and their NATO partners backed out. Raziq, in the midst of his diminished support from abroad, began to propose a new effort at reconciliation with Taliban elders. He called it his 'Taliban retirement program,' based in Aino Mena. As the neighborhood known as 'Little America' was drained of its foreign clientele, the Taliban who had been hiding in Pakistan could take their place. Here Raziq was perhaps too optimistic; Taliban leadership sensed that the NATO members had decided to leave. It was only a matter of waiting until they could seize the whole country, rather than settle for a mere district of Kandahar City.[32]

Chapter 16

GHOST TOWN (2015–21)

Kandahar Airfield had long served as the southern headquarters of the foreign coalition. After 2014, in compliance with Wild West chronology, the base began to resemble a ghost town. The sprawling complex housed upward of 30,000 soldiers and contractors during the surge. Since then, it had become a shell of its former self with fewer than 10,000 residents. Of the half dozen coffee shops that once dotted the boardwalk, only one survived. TGI Friday's had closed.[1] The Airfield, though home to fewer businesses catering to creature comforts, remained a desirable place for Americans to be stationed. The sturdy housing built by Navy Seabees for NATO's senior personnel stayed in place; its plumbing system still worked. In the last years of the war, smaller and smaller American contingents made use of the lavish living spaces. Captain Marshall Rogers recalled, 'I finally had [indoor] plumbing. On my fourth deployment.' In 2015, Rogers was an intelligence officer attached to Task Force South. It would turn out to be a wild rotation in country for several reasons, but the junior officer recalled the plush living conditions as 'the wildest thing that I'd ever experienced.' Outside the barracks, the atmosphere was eerily quiet. All that was missing to complete the desolate aesthetic was a rolling tumbleweed.

Physical comforts could not dispel the sinking feeling that Rogers experienced in the aftermath of the American troop surge. Reports from Afghan partners filtered into the intelligence cell and revealed the extent to which Kandahar City had become an isolated bubble of security within a chaotic region. There had been one spectacular Taliban attack on the Airfield, in December 2015, in which over one hundred civilians lost their lives. But for the most part, KAF was the safest place to be in Afghanistan. It was the center of NATO brass and contractor dollars, and therefore the last well in the region to dry up.

For those Afghan military forces who manned the outposts of the periphery, the American withdrawal resulted in an abrupt increase in mortality. The ANSF in 2015 lost over 7,000 soldiers killed in action, or more than the US total over twenty years. The next year, the death toll hovered around the same level, but in 2017 it jumped to over 9,000. Rogers suspected that Raziq himself had arranged some of those casualties. Evidence suggested that he used American resources in late 2015 to take out commanders within the ANSF who were rival smugglers. Even as the Taliban closed in, republican leaders continued to feud over the shrinking pot of resources.

In the process of harping on these dubious developments, Rogers lost the ear of his command. They labeled him a 'sky-is-falling S2 [intelligence officer],' even when events seemed to bear out his analysis. Afghan Special Forces had to be substituted for regular troops in defense of district centers, as entire 'ghost' units existed only on paper and had ceased to function in neighboring provinces. In October 2015, disgruntled Afghan soldiers hijacked military aircraft sent to evacuate their wounded comrades from northern Helmand. When the helicopters landed at KAF, the defectors scattered and disappeared. Another incident of the same kind happened early the next year. Rogers often attended meetings interrupted by rocket attacks on the base during the last months of the deployment. The insurgents had breached the former oasis of security at the heart of Kandahar.[2]

As the Americans withdrew, how long could Raziq hold onto their professed ideals? In particular, how long could he continue to push for gender equality? Women serving in government gave mixed messages about political trends. On one hand, Raziq had defended individual women on Kandahar's Provincial Council. He had encouraged one of them to run for the position and supported her campaign. He rebuked an Achakzai elder who had threatened one of the female representatives on the Council and forced him to apologize to the offended member. Raziq, moreover, made effusive public statements that differentiated his policies on gender from the Taliban's. On the other hand, some believed in the cynical explanation for Raziq's strong words on the matter. These critics claimed that he was only appeasing the Western press. He made a few public displays of support toward women in the service of preserving an otherwise misogynistic status quo, since the provincial government continued to reward a narrow clique of men who controlled military resources.[3]

As the American departure became more apparent every day, Raziq looked to forge his own, independent foreign contacts. In addition to his new arms dealer accomplices in Europe, Raziq flaunted connections with the Indian intelligence service. He developed friendships during the course of extended medical visits, for himself and members of his family. Furthermore, he sent wounded subordinates to India to ensure their safety as they recovered. He established a school in that country, where the orphans of his fallen Border Policemen received scholarships. Raziq was brash in making these new liaisons apparent to the Pakistani intelligence service, as his visits to India became more frequent and more public in the last year of his life.[4] These developing relationships served as a threat of encirclement to Pakistani agents, who sought to maintain Afghanistan as a pliant Islamic ally against the Hindu powerhouse to the east.

But Raziq faced hostility even amid his conciliatory efforts at international politics. In January 2017, the Police Chief attended a meeting at the governor's compound in Kandahar City with a peace delegation from the United Arab Emirates. During a session in the Governor's guesthouse, Raziq stepped out to take a phone call. Moments later, a bomb planted under a couch in the room exploded. Eleven people died in the blast, including American MPs, Afghan republic officials, and five diplomats from the Emirates. Some observers suspected that the attack had been planned against Raziq and had missed its target. If so, it was among the last of some two dozen attempts on Raziq's life, each of which augmented his reputation.

The Taliban and Haqqani networks denied responsibility for the attack. To harm members of an Islamic government who sought to mediate in the Afghan conflict could draw negative reactions from potential supporters of the insurgency. Still, one republican official described the incident as a bungled Taliban attack. He claimed that the Governor's personal chef had taken bribes from three unidentified men in Chaman, Pakistan, who gave him explosives to hide in his employer's guesthouse. Taliban spokesmen dismissed the bombing as the result of personal grudges. Others blamed the attack on foreign intelligence agents, who may have resented the growing power of the Emiratis in Afghanistan. Raziq claimed that the scheme was the work of a Haqqani network cell linked to the Pakistani intelligence service (ISI), whereas others believed a Taliban cell connected to Iran was responsible.[5] The event raised suspicion on all sides of the diplomatic efforts underway.

Throughout 2018, Raziq returned from trips abroad to a homeland where political trends were turning against him. For four years, his patron Hamid Karzai had been absent from the Kabul government. While the new president Abdul Ghani was a fellow Pashtun, he drew authority from technocratic skills rather than aristocratic lineage. Ghani's main political talking points were to criticize Karzai's corruption and reliance on 'warlords' to rule the provinces. This stance set him at odds with Raziq, who began to support the northern strongmen of the Ankara group. These politicians held that Kabul had become an interfering agent between the people and their rightful regional leaders.[6] Afghans had begun to wonder how long these local enclaves could hold out without the support of American fuel, mechanics, and bombers.[7]

Raziq's final American advisers arrived in Kandahar during a summer of diplomatic transition. The Taliban and the Afghan government had agreed to a ceasefire for the Ramadan holiday. The Americans sought to extend the agreement, but the Taliban refused to continue negotiations with the republic. It was the beginning of an eighteen-month process, nine rounds long, from which came the Doha Agreement that concluded the war. In the end, the Taliban got its way and negotiated a two-party deal with the United States. During negotiations, at the end of the 2018 Ramadan ceasefire, the Afghan government began a new offensive based from Kandahar, north into Uruzgan and west into Helmand. The republican officials used the leverage of American airpower, while they still had it, to hold the insurgency at bay.

Pomegranates, 18 October 2018

At the Governor's palace in Kandahar City, General Raziq met with the top US commander in Afghanistan, General Scott Miller. The American leader wanted to show international solidarity in the days preceding nation-wide Afghan elections. Raziq walked shoulder-to-shoulder (*shona-ba-shona*) with his American counterpart. The two men sauntered slowly to allow for some last-minute conversation after the meeting. Both were short in stature, but both possessed the aura of command. As the Pashto proverb goes, Miller and Raziq were 'as much below the ground as they were above it.'[8] They strolled through garden courtyards, among a crowd of Afghan and American officers, who began to separate by nationality. The American group had a helicopter to catch, while Raziq and the Afghans prepared to depart in armored cars.

General Miller was among his nation's most decorated and experienced combat leaders. He had commanded in Delta Force, the most selective special missions unit in the military. After thirty-five years in the army, just over half of that during the Global War on Terrorism, Miller had reached his top operational command: of the few thousand United States, NATO, and other Coalition forces who remained in Afghanistan. Miller's command philosophy was aggressive pursuit of the Taliban, to ensure their cooperation in diplomatic agreements that would end the war with the United States. The Afghan government was no longer privy to these negotiations.

A bodyguard of the provincial Governor followed Miller and Raziq as they walked to the helicopter pad. Along with a ceremonial, chrome-plated AK-47 rifle slung across his chest, the guard carried two boxes of pomegranates. The fruit was a gift, to be handed over to a member of the staffs that flocked around their commanders like circling birds. The bodyguard, a dark-haired youth with rounded jowls, had been working at the Governor's palace for two months.

On this day, having accepted his fateful assignment, he dropped the boxes of pomegranates and opened fire on Raziq's back from two meters. Four bullets from the AK-47 struck the Police Chief in his legs and lower torso. Blood spread over the landing zone's cracked concrete, pooling and mixing with the lighter red juice of the broken pomegranates.[9]

Lieutenant Colonel Kincy Clark, Raziq's adviser, was checking radio equipment at the palace when he heard the rattle of an AK-47. He bolted toward the nearby landing zone. Everyone was shouting. People dashed from all directions seeking cover. Confusion reigned as startled soldiers tried to piece together whether the brief attack was over, in one spurt of fire, or whether it was merely the opening salvo in a complex ambush.

Before the Americans could organize a helicopter to airlift the wounded, Raziq's aides hustled his stiff, bloodied body into a white Toyota Landcruiser. The driver sped off through the crowded courtyard of the Governor's Palace to a local hospital. 'They drove it like they stole it,' Clark recalled. Despite the haste, he knew the attempt to save their boss was a lost cause. This time, Raziq's American adviser had arrived too late to help him.

After the Afghan convoy sped off, US forces took about an hour to re-secure the compound. An Afghan intelligence officer died from injuries suffered in that day's spray of gunfire, too. The Governor, an American general, an Afghan general, and a British-Afghan interpreter all survived gunshot wounds to their arms and legs. The killer, disguised in the uniform of the Governor's guards, fell alongside his victims, as the US security detail riddled his body with M-4 rounds from close range.

He was known to fellow guards as Gulbuddin, and to the Taliban as Abu Dujana, but later investigations found other names: Raz Mohammad or Mujahid Hafiz Zabihullah. The Taliban maintained a strict policy against publicizing their operatives, even after successful operations removed the need for secrecy. Part of the movement's strength, and an indication of its anti-modern political project, was a rejection of worldly fame in favor of what one insightful UN observer called the 'hegemony of their anonymous cadres.'[10] The assassin's obscurity after death reflected the manner of his short life, as his most important quality was to be unremarkable. He had been hired as a guard by the Governor's cousin and lately promoted, from watching the towers to a post within the Governor's office.

The Quetta Shura Taliban claimed to have trained and deployed the young assassin. During the Governor's meeting, the guard received a phone call from Pakistan that relayed his orders. Raziq had expressed some concerns about the trip, but he assumed that insurgents would attack his convoy outside the Governor's palace, on the road, with a suicide bomber on a motorbike or a car loaded with explosives.[11] General Miller escaped the attack unharmed. Despite the American's prominence, he had not been the primary target of the attack. Instead, it had been the final, successful attempt of twenty-eight on the life of the Achakzai Police Chief. By 2018, the Taliban assessed that Raziq was the more significant element of an Afghan–American partnership that had already sounded its own death knell.

Rumor

Rumors began to form mere seconds after the fatal burst of gunfire on 18 October. The shooting had come from inside the Governor's compound, where only

Americans were supposed to be armed. The Afghan soldiers guarding the outer cordon, who had their backs to the meetings that had taken place, turned around and began to shoot at the Americans who had killed the insider threat. Had the Americans set Raziq up? Who had sent this insider? Was he really an agent of the Taliban, as claimed? Had the Pakistani government been involved?

Long after October 2018, some Afghans continued to believe that the Americans had sacrificed Raziq, either by arranging the murder or by stepping back and allowing him to be killed. His troubled past had become too much of a liability for the foreigners, and Raziq had stoked fresh problems with recent skirmishes at the border against Pakistani scouts.[12] The Americans were giving billions of dollars in aid to Pakistan, and yet everyone knew that Pakistan also supported the Taliban. So perhaps the US cut Raziq down to clear the way for their Pakistani friends, official and clandestine. There was a certain logic, perverse yet satisfying, to the rumors. Even the most outlandish claims about Raziq's Kandahar contained a kernel of truth that allowed conspiratorial theories to gain credence and spread.[13]

Others who speculated about Raziq's death pointed fingers at Zalmay Wesa, the Governor of Kandahar, who had himself been injured in the attack. Still, a member of the Governor's guard had killed Raziq. On some level, it had been Wesa's responsibility to vet his own security staff. Then, too, the Governor had been suspected of foul play while he was commander of the 209th Corps in Mazar-i Sharif. In 2011, an assassin succeeded in killing a rival general after what was supposed to be a routine meeting, while Wesa had been spotted nearby on the phone. Despite the wounding of the Governor in this more recent killing, some believed the gunshot to his foot had been a purposeful ploy to throw people off the scent.[14]

According to these rumors, Zalmay Wesa might have coordinated the assassination to please President Ghani. The President had lately taken a hardline stance against regional 'warlords.' About a year before the assassination, Raziq hosted an anti-Ghani rally at which he announced his support for one of the Governors the president had removed on charges of corruption. Raziq believed his power, like the former Governor's, derived from the loyalty of the people. 'I was not appointed by this government, and it cannot fire me.' Raziq proclaimed, 'I am serving because the people of Kandahar want me to serve, and I will only leave this post if they tell me to do so.'[15] In any standoff between him and Ghani, the Americanized academic tucked away in Kabul, Raziq was confident about who would emerge victorious.

Raziq's statements might have been the first step toward his joining the camp of the Ankara group, which formed in the summer of 2017 to oppose Ghani's Pashtun coalition. The Ankara politicians sought to split the ethnic coalition by recruiting Raziq to their ranks.[16] Had the President ordered Kandahar's Governor to cut down a popular rival? Rumors spread that other former patrons in Kabul were happy to see Raziq go at last. Did Karzai and Ghani shake hands and forget past differences in celebration of their surviving the young upstart? The last few years had spread fear and jealousy among entrenched authorities in the capital. The Achakzai commander had become too powerful for the comfort of elites at the national level.

These rumors, which lacked concrete evidence, spread like wildfire across the Afghan-Pakistan borderlands. Even if false, the tales illustrated the depths of mistrust that had developed between the United States and some of its former Afghan supporters in the closing years of their partnership.

Things Fall Apart

One of Donald Trump's campaign promises had been to dial back American military obligations abroad. After he took office, he began to drop the 'America first' angle of getting out of Afghanistan at all costs, in favor of a dealmaker approach to negotiations. Trump tapped an experienced Afghan diplomat, Zalmay Khalilzad, to lead the peace talks. Khalilzad had been a heavyweight player in Afghan politics since 2003, when he helped to demobilize rebellious warlords on Hamid Karzai's behalf.[17] Trump had little patience, and perhaps even less respect, for the negotiations. He said of his chief diplomat, 'I hear he's a con man, although you need a con man for this.'[18] While Trump likely meant that one needed to be wily in order to trick the Taliban, the Republic of Afghanistan became the conned party. Khalilzad had been absent from his homeland for so long that many Afghans believed he had lost touch with reality.[19]

After the signing of the Doha Agreement in February 2020, there was nothing to hold Taliban fighters back. By July, nearly all the 17,000 civilian contract workers who kept the aircraft and heavy weapons working had left the country. It was now only a matter of time before the Taliban recognized their soldiers could roam the countryside with impunity, now that the Afghan government could not bring a technological advantage to bear on the battlefield.

Trump was out of office the next year when the situation reached its crisis point, but his diplomatic choices ensured a fatal loss of capability for the Afghan Republic. As Marine General Frank McKenzie, who oversaw the evacuation, recalled, 'The signing of the Doha agreement had a really pernicious effect on the government of Afghanistan and on its military, psychological more than anything else,' by setting a concrete date for the ultimate American withdrawal.[20]

Throughout 2021, the clock continued to tick. Afghan commanders, who saw the writing on the wall, began to hoard paychecks and supplies. Afghan soldiers began to face the choice of eating grass or going hungry. President Biden delayed pulling out the final 2,500 US troops from May until September, but the new Commander-in-Chief agreed with Trump that the longest American war should come to an end. Biden, who had been a critic of Obama's surge from the beginning, allowed his hands to remain tied by Trump's deal.

In the meantime, the Afghan government prioritized its five largest military bases in the country from which to continue to coordinate the trickle of American resources that still functioned. US airstrikes increased through the end of the Trump presidency, as the administration sought sensational bombing – i.e. MOAB, the 'Mother of All Bombs' – to deny terrain to enemy fighters.[21] But even as the number of airstrikes increased, the nature of US support in Afghanistan became more circumscribed. Foreign support could only come as a defensive measure, within 800m of a government outpost. Taliban fighters in some instances stepped over predictable lines drawn in the sand, as they bided their time on neutral territory until the political deal ran its course.[22]

No amount of bombing could reverse the irredeemable blow that the Doha deal struck against the legitimacy of the Afghan government. In the words of one veteran-author, it was a 'betrayal' akin to President Nixon's abandonment of South Vietnam in the 1970s. H.R. McMaster called Doha a 'surrender agreement.' The United States negotiated in terms of 'Orwellian doublespeak,' as if anyone believed the Taliban would share power with Ghani's regime that had been bombing its camps and fighters into submission just months before.[23] In addition to the material and political obstacles that the Doha Agreement created, the Afghan government had lost one of its primary human assets in Abdul Raziq Achakzai, who had been killed at the beginning of this lengthy period of US-Taliban negotiations.

Taliban Return

After a few tense days, during which Americans wondered what authorities in Kabul would decide, President Ghani agreed to support Raziq's younger brother as heir to the top security post in southern Afghanistan. Tadin Khan, though his experience comprised smuggling rather than official government work, became the Chief of Police for Kandahar. He inherited the somewhat grudging support of the Americans, Raziq's former advisers.[24]

Many saw this transition as the last in a long line of missed opportunities. These critics reasoned that somewhere along the way, in an ideal world, the United States should have backed away from reinforcing Raziq's power. His rise had resulted in the concentration of power in a family rather than a bureaucratic office. Perhaps that family had been ill-equipped to handle power in a responsible manner.

Tadin Khan tried to lead as his elder brother had, but he had neither a history of combat operations nor personal charm to support him. The demands that Raziq had made with harsh rhetoric began to fall on deaf ears. Many elders and military commanders in Kandahar decided to go their own way, without consulting the new Police Chief. In this gradual way, official power became hollowed out throughout the government of Afghanistan.[25]

The Taliban swept rapidly through Kandahar in August 2021. In some cases, they settled old scores. Each Afghan side accused the other of playing puppet for a foreign master: either the Punjabis of Pakistan or the American infidels. On 12 August, a journalist based in Pakistan posted a sarcastic tweet that suggested public opinion had turned toward the Taliban as they retook the South. 'Dozens of undercover [Pakistani] ISI agents have been spotted throwing stones at Afghan warlord Raziq's posters in Kandahar city.' The agents in question were a group of local children. One of them sported the same Sindhi cap visible on the tattered billboard in the background. Only the top of Raziq's head, from the bridge of his nose up, is visible. The rest of the image had been torn down. So the very recognition of the billboard as a depiction of Raziq spoke to his enduring yet polarizing legacy in Kandahar.[26]

Those who supported the Afghan government over the years chafed under accusations that they had abandoned the fight. The Biden administration had only modest hopes for their ally Ghani, but even the dourest predictions held that his regime would hang on for at least a few months, through the end of the year. Though the collapse of the Afghan government was precipitous by the Western media's timetable, those who lived in the region remembered time in a different way, mediated through their memory of Raziq. At the end of 2021, Twitter user Pashtana Zalmai Khan Dorani posted: 'All those "why southerners didn't fight." I think I need to refresh your memory with General Raziq and how he fought to protect everything. While y'all didn't even know Afghanistan existed. South gave sons like him to protect Afghanistan.' Since 2014, when the American drawdown accelerated during Operation New Dawn, an estimated 45,000 Afghan security forces had been killed in action.[27]

Dorani's tweet received a ferocious reply from another account. @Yas_Al_Zmn responded, 'CIA propped warlords who ran torture dungeons and raked in 1,000,000+ a month from drug revenue overlooking Spin Boldak are your heroes. Morally bankrupt *qaum* (tribe).'[28] The moral indignation apparent, whether fabricated by the ISI or the result of authentic local anger at Raziq's former regime, became manifest in more than the adolescent casting of stones.

Most of those who had worked with Raziq went into hiding. They sought friends or relatives in Kabul, or they fled to another province, somewhere in the Afghan countryside. Speculative reports claimed that the Taliban had killed anywhere from four hundred to several thousand people, mostly security forces and their family members, in reprisals against the old regime. A former republican official from Kandahar noted, 'People are being killed merely for carrying a picture of General Raziq.' There were an estimated 18,000 policemen in Kandahar at the time of the province's occupation, and about 1,000 became prisoners of the new Taliban regime.[29] Some of Raziq's supporters who had the means went abroad. Those who remained in Kandahar risked retaliation.

Spin Boldak stood out among Afghan districts for its high number of revenge killings in Afghanistan as the republic fell. Across most of the country, the Taliban took control with little need for violence.

As power changed hands in 2021, Afghans once more unearthed mass graves. Allegations emerged to explain who these people had been, and how they ended up dead in the desert. Authorities produced twelve bodies, now just piles of broken bones, in Spin Boldak district. The Taliban claimed that with these remains they had discovered more victims of Raziq's Border Police.[30] But they may have belonged to Achakzai opponents of the Taliban, or to ancestors buried long before the modern era of civil war. In this case, as in many, it was impossible to be certain about the details of the deceased.

AFTERLIVES

I visited Afghanistan from April 2011 until the following spring, a year that overlapped with Raziq's promotion to provincial Chief of Police. My unit deployed to Nangarhar Province, whose Governor was Raziq's early patron Gul Agha Sherzai. Still, I was unaware of the dynamic Police Chief from Kandahar. Though Raziq's story had been integral to mine, I had not recognized it at the time.

I did not find out about General Raziq from my own experiences, but from an internet meme. It was the second week of January 2021. The US was in political crisis, in part due to the spread of rumors on social media. Misinformation about the COVID health crisis combined with doubts about the legitimacy of the presidential election that favored Joe Biden over Donald Trump. An unruly mob forced its way into the Capitol and threatened Congress while its members were certifying the peaceful transfer of power. The State Department noted that the incident might hurt American abilities to promote democracy, both 'at home and abroad.'[1]

Many insurrectionists were military veterans.[2] Some wore helmets mounted with optics. They carried ka-bar knives and other military paraphernalia. A few brought plastic zip-ties, a standard element of kit downrange, in the hopes of bagging a captive Congressman or -woman. At the time, the US still had troops stationed in Afghanistan. They were in the last stages of a partnership, some twenty years old, that would end with the Taliban takeover in September.

The meme spread through veteran-run accounts in the days after the riot. In the guise of 'Breaking News,' the caption announced: 'Afghanistan sends 1300 troops to US: Our allies need help restoring democracy.' The image portrays General Raziq at a lectern, in front of a gold-painted microphone. In a twist of irony, the image depicts Raziq's speech at a June 2012 graduation ceremony for Afghan police who had undergone a fourteen-week course on literacy and

This meme first appeared on the social media sites of "Pop Smoke," curated by Marine infantry veterans, on 10 January 2021.

tactical training.[3] It was the kind of institutionalization that Raziq's advisers hoped might outlive him in Afghanistan.

At this early stage in his rise to power, Raziq still looked rough around the edges. He had not yet acquired his ease with Western dress. His Border Police uniform featured a retro-looking chocolate-chip-cookie pattern. His patrol cap sat askew atop his head, and his facial hair was patchy. The plastic water bottle and paper signs taped to the wall in the background betrayed the slapdash, improvised aesthetic of his era in Kandahar.

This is the visual punchline of the meme: Raziq appears to be the last person that Americans would want to help restore democracy. From behind the microphone, Raziq seems ready to declare, as a European strongman once did, '*Après moi, le déluge.*' His image exposes the thinness of civilization's veneer. What was lost on website administrators who shared the meme was that Raziq had been among the most effective of the men that the United States had entrusted of late to help spread representative government abroad.

Though the American meme mocked Raziq, he remained a martyr figure to his many Afghan supporters. His time as Kandahar Police Chief was cut short, but something about Raziq continued to inspire people in the years after his assassination. He had emerged as a national hero. The dramatic way in which he lived and died made him a symbol for the youngest generation of Afghans. He represented a kind of Kandahari utopia, as he led a province that seemed at once open to the ways of outsiders, yet authentic to local traditions. Neither attribution was entirely accurate, but each was true at certain times, to certain people.

Legacy

At its best, Raziq's time as Police Chief was more peaceful and more profitable than what had passed over the previous generation. But for those neglected by the spoils system, young men from marginalized tribes in particular, Kandahar under Raziq could be hellish. The inconsistency of his power had less to do with the man himself than with the difficulty of his task of translation. Raziq sought to make unpopular American concepts palatable to Kandaharis while they were courted by an opposing Taliban worldview. To his credit, Raziq was able to convince many throughout the South to accept aspects of the foreign program. He enabled governance by district councils (*shura*), and he encouraged the admittance of girls and women into schools and positions of public authority.

The Americans in Afghanistan organized their worldview according to linear time, which advanced toward progress. The Taliban, on the other hand, believed time was cyclical. Paradise, rather than progress, was an exclusive reward for believers. Raziq accepted the US mindset for its attendant benefits in creating wealth and fostering public health. But his actions suggest that he did not share the American concept of inclusive development, the ideal of progress to benefit society as a whole. Raziq's idea of progress depended instead upon the relative elevation of some groups above others, in concentric circles of loyalty from his immediate family, outward to his tribe, and the Afghan nation, defined in a negative sense as those opposed to the Punjabi-dominated government of Pakistan.

Raziq was amenable to some aspects of American law-based rule. After all, he used his position in the Border Police to gain power outside of the tribal hierarchy that kept his Achakzai network below Popalzai and Barakzai elites. But Raziq transcended the credentials that institutions could provide. He also knew how to demonstrate his antecedents as a Pashtun village boy, and his simple religiosity, to locals in Kandahar. Western agents tended to see religion as a personal matter, rather than the basis for public authority. Raziq believed that religion should be a guide for action and integrated into the function of the state.

Yet Raziq distinguished himself from the Taliban in terms of religion, because he saw Islam as just one potential source of wisdom, and furthermore a source that required expert interpretation. The Achakzai had a reputation in the region as a less religious, more commercial tribe. They were people who benefited from variable readings of scripture and a laissez-faire approach to morality. The Taliban, taking a lead from the Salafist tradition of Islam, believed in strict Quranic literalism, which was so simple that it could be understood by low-level students on motorcycles, armed with AK-47s.

Raziq was constrained as well by conflicting viewpoints on security. The US proposed a centralized state, backed by a monopoly of violence, to enable governance reform. The Taliban countered with promises of decentralized local governance and claims that Afghans could not experience true peace until all foreigners had been expelled. The anti-imperial message resonated with the memories of Soviet and British domination. Raziq, for his part, saw the foreigners as a means of gaining resources and dispensing patronage to bolster his power. Ordinary Kandaharis, struggling with few options for security, could turn either toward purity in a religious sense with the Taliban, or toward material wealth with Raziq and his partners.

Song

Raziq's critics claimed that he gained support only through bribery and fear. They bristled at heroic depictions of Raziq. In their eyes, he was a false idol, who could only have been mistaken for a hero after four decades of disastrous warfare.[4] But this critical sentiment belied the outpouring of emotion upon his death in the form of songs, composed by slick professionals as well as crude amateurs on social media. An internet fan page, *Raziq Showqi*, posted an auto-tuned, trance-like chant to YouTube entitled 'Martyr (*Shaheed*) General Raziq':

> The borders are crying. People cry after him.
> Every Afghan cries. Afghanistan is trembling.
> He was the voice of the poor nation, sacrificed to the motherland.
> We weep for our hopes. Malala's flag is lowered. Maiwand cries.
> The country's belt is cut. All the military cries.[5]

A song in Dari, rather than Pashto, demonstrated the Kandahari leader's national reach by the time of his assassination. Despite its macabre lyrics, the song became popular at weddings across Afghanistan:

> Why did heaven allow this to happen?
> Suddenly Raziq was separated from us.
> As soon as they took your coffin,
> The earth and the sky were crying for you...
>
> The whole nation of Afghans is set on fire.
> Their roofs and doors are set ablaze.
> They martyred the lion of the nation,
> And grieved the mother of the nation.[6]

Abdul Raziq's mother had attended her son's funeral alongside a host of officials from the republican government. On the way home, she said that, *Insh'allah*, she would give all her children for a free Afghanistan. One of her sons, Tadin Khan, had already taken Raziq's place in the line of fire as Kandahar Chief of

Police. Her other surviving son had never entered politics. He had sworn off public life, and he had tried to convince Raziq to retire. Government offices lead only to scandal and ruin. Come back to us, Raziq's younger brother had implored, and enjoy life among your family.[7]

A popular folk musician dedicated one of his most-watched videos to the late police chief. The young man sang in praise:

> He was raised by the milk of the Pashtun mother.
> He was raised in the family of lions.
> He is a victor, a hero, a protector.[8]

Before Raziq's followers lowered him into the grave, they wrapped him in the flag of the Afghan Republic. It was a fitting tribute to one of its last nationalist leaders.

BIBLIOGRAPHY

Interviews conducted by author
(Rank indicates interviewee's position at the time of their interaction with General Raziq.)

Aadland, Erik. CPT U.S. Army, 8-1 CAV. 4 May 2021.
Achakzai, Tadin Khan. Kandahar Chief of Police. 14 August 2024.
Achakzai, Tadin Khan #2. 27 August 2024.
Achakzai, Tadin Khan #3. 29 October 2024.
Afridi, Ghorzang. Raziq aide. 28 May 2022.
Afridi, Ghorzang #2. 31 May 2022.
Aggus, Matthew. CPT Canadian Army, Kandahar OMLT. 12 April 2022.
Arian, Basir. Linguist. 9 April 2021.
Arian, Basir #2. 10 May 2021.
Arian, Basir #3. 12 August 2021.
Bass, Jordan. 1LT U.S. Army, 4-2 CAV. 16 April 2021.
Beckman, Steven, Jr. CPT U.S. Army, 8-1 CAV. 23 April 2021.
Beckman, Steven, Sr. COL U.S. Army, RC South J2. 12 May 2021.
Browne, W. Scott. 1LT U.S. Army, 4-2 CAV. 11 May 2021.
Carroll, Dustin. SFC U.S. Army, 4-2 CAV. 13 October 2021.
Clark, Kincy. LTC California NG. 15 December 2021.
Clark, William. LTC U.S. Army, 8-1 CAV. 26 March 2021.
Clark, William #2. 17 May 2021.
Chayes, Sarah. ISAF staff. 23 June 2021.
Craig, David. LTC California NG. 14 January 2022.
Counts, Billy. CSM U.S. Army, 503 MP. 7 September 2022.
Crow, David. CPT U.S. Army, 8-1 CAV. 29 April 2021.
Davis, Brad. CPT U.S. Army, 201 BfSB. 16 September 2022.
Davis, Brad #2. 20 October 2022.

Den Harder, Edwin. 1LT U.S. Army, 4-2 CAV. 29 April 2021.

Duwors, Joseph. Chaplain U.S. Army, 4-2 CAV. 5 August 2022.

Edwards, James. COL U.S. Army, 525 BfSB. 25 March 2021.

Fazel, Najib. Linguist. 26 March 2021.

Feltey, Thomas. LTC U.S. Army, 2-23 IN. 26 October 2021.

Flannery, James. 1LT U.S. Army, 1-187 IN. 18 March 2022.

Fletcher, William. MAJ Canadian Army, TF Orion. 20 August 2021.

Formica, Anthony. 1LT U.S. Army, 1-5 IN. 25 May 2021.

Fortune, James. 1LT U.S. Army, 4-2 CAV. 7 April 2021.

Fox, Thaddeus. 1LT U.S. Army, 4-2 CAV. 28 February 2021.

Fox, Thaddeus #2. 14 August 2021.

Freakley, Sam. CPT U.S. Army, 1-32 IN. 3 November 2022.

Freakley, Sam #2. 15 November 2022.

Fritz, Jeffery. CPT U.S. Army, 4-2 CAV. 27 June 2021.

Ges, Bertrand. LTC U.S. Army, 3-319 FA. 2 March 2022.

Green, Andrew. LTC U.S. Army, 4-2 CAV. 22 March 2021.

Gregory, Andrew. 1LT U.S. Army, 4-2 CAV. 13 May 2021.

Grenier, Stephen. LTC U.S. Army, Special Forces. 11 October 2022.

Griffiths, Stephen. CPT U.S. Army, 1-26 IN. 13 October 2021.

Haimidi, Rangina. Afghan Education Minister. 30 June 2022.

Hope, Ian. LTC Canadian Army, TF Orion. 26 July 2021.

Johnson, David. MAJ U.S. Army, 8-1 CAV. 9 April 2021.

Johnston, Gary. COL U.S. Army, 504 BfSB. 16 November 2021.

Kelley, Matthew. CPT U.S. Army, 4-2 CAV. 19 March 2021.

Kirby, Owen. U.S. State Department. 19 March 2021.

Kohler, Patrick. 1LT U.S. Army, 8-1 CAV. 19 May 2021.

Kough, Kris. LTC California NG. 29 January 2022.

LaPlante, Joseph. 1LT U.S. Army, 8-1 CAV. 5 May 2021.

Lerch, Slade. MAJ Canadian Army, 3-319 FA Liaison. 14 March 2022.

Lerch, Slade #2. 20 March 2022.

Leydet, David. 1LT U.S. Army, 8-1 CAV. 28 May 2021.

Lowe, James. LTC U.S. Army, 3-7 FA. 19 April 2021.

Malgarai, Ahmad Shah. Linguist. 11 June 2022.

Markert, Daniel. MAJ California NG. 27 January 2022.

Markus, Danny. U.S. Department of Agriculture, Nuristan PRT. 30 September 2021.

Miakhel, Shahmahmood. Governor of Nangarhar Province. 28 June 2021.

Michaelis, Patrick. LTC U.S. Army, 8-1 CAV. 13 August 2021.

Mirzada, Naqib. MAJ ANSF Special Operations. 6 October 2022.

Mirzada, Naqib #2. 14 October 2022.

Nihart, Terry. LTC U.S. Army, 503 MP. 5 November 2021.

Nihart, Terry #2. 24 November 2021.

Payne, Leslie. Human Terrain System. 16 August 2021.

(Redacted). Achakzai tribe member. 24 July 2025.

(Redacted). Afghan Blackwater employee. 18 September 2021.
(Redacted). COL U.S. Army. 9 July 2021.
(Redacted). CPT U.S. Army 1. 21 April 2021.
(Redacted). CPT U.S. Army 2. 6 July 2022.
(Redacted). CPT U.S. Army 3. 7 July 2022.
(Redacted). Law Enforcement Professional. 1 February 2022.
(Redacted). Linguist 1. 2 November 2021.
(Redacted). Linguist 2. 21 March 2022.
(Redacted). Linguist 2 #2. 28 March 2022.
(Redacted). Linguist 2 #3. 12 April 2022.
(Redacted). Linguist 3. 16 April 2022.
(Redacted). Linguist 4. 26 April 2022.
(Redacted). Linguist 5. 20 September 2022.
(Redacted). Senior NATO government official. 14 April 2021.
(Redacted). Senior U.S. government official 1. 22 June 2021.
(Redacted). Senior U.S. government official 2. 20 December 2021.
(Redacted). Senior U.S. government official 3. 23 December 2021.
(Redacted). U.S. Special Forces Officer. 15 February 2022.
Reed, Kenneth. MAJ U.S. Army, 4-2 CAV. 15 June 2022.
Ringgenberg, Dirk. CPT U.S. Army, 2-503 IN. 16 March 2022.
Ringgenberg, Dirk #2. 12 April 2022.
Ritchie, Robert. MAJ Canadian Army, Kandahar PRT, OMLT. 2 September 2021.
Rogers, Marshall. CPT U.S. Army, TF South deputy J2. 28 July 2022.
Rogers, Marshall #2. 1 September 2022.
Safi, Abraham. Linguist. 10 February 2022.
Saqib, Najibullah. Raziq aide. 8 August 2022.
Savage, Ronald. USAID Spin Boldak. 15 July 2022.
Scheidt, Kenneth. LTC U.S. Army, AfPak Hands. 29 June 2021.
Smiley, Jeffrey. BG California NG. 12 January 2022.
Tomola, Mark. MAJ U.S. Army, 7 SF. 23 February 2022.
Wali, Akbar. Linguist and contractor. 3 July 2021.
Wali, Akbar #2. 26 July 2021.
Wesa, Tooryalai. Governor of Kandahar Province. 29 July 2021.
Wesa, Tooryalai #2. 5 August 2021.
Wolusmal, Roshaan. Mayor of Kandahar City. 10 July 2021.
Xiong, Tou. SPC U.S. Army, 525 BfSB. 26 May 2022.

Primary Sources and Other Unpublished Materials

2-23 IN. 'WARNO 4 to OPORD 13-01: Tomahawk Freedom.' 31 October 2012
5/2 SBCT Intelligence. 'Special Assessment: COL Abdul Razziq.' 13 March 2010.
525 BfSB. Operations Summary (OPSUM). 9 September 2011.

Afghanistan Ministry of Urban Development Affairs. 'State of Afghan Cities 2015.' Kabul: United Nations Report, 2015.

'Canadian Forces in Afghanistan: Report of the Standing Committee on National Defence,' 39th Canadian Parliament, 1st session. June 2007.

Cardinalli, Anna Maria. 'Pashtun Sexuality.' Human Terrain Team AF-6. Research Update and Findings. 2009.

'Commander Massoud to visit European Parliament in Strasbourg on 5 April 2001.' Press Release. President of the European Union.

Congressional Research Service Division.
- 'Department of Defense Contractor and Troop Levels in Afghanistan and Iraq: 2007-2020.' Updated 22 February 2021.
- Thomas, Clayton. 'Afghanistan: Background and U.S. Policy: In Brief.' 1 November 2018.

Crisostomo, Renee. 'Abdul Raziq in 2012.' 18th Wing Public Affairs. U.S. Air Force photo. 9 June 2012.

CTF Lightning Intelligence. 'Spin Boldak Corruption.' 12 September 2010.

CTF Lightning Intelligence. 'Spin Boldak HUMINT.' 5 October 2010.

Duffy, Sean. 'Shell Game: The U.S.-Afghan Opium Relationship.' PhD dissertation. University of Arizona, 2011.

Edwards, James. 'Brigade Commander's After Action Notes.' 525 BfSB. 9 September 2011.

Edwards, James. Contemporary Operations Study Team Interview. 13 February 2013.

Field Manual (FM) 3-24: *Counterinsurgency.* 13 May 2014.

Human Rights Watch. 'World Report: Afghanistan.' 2010-2015.

Kandahar Intelligence Fusion Cell (KIFC). 'Taking Stock of COL Abdul Razziq, ABP.' 19 November 2009.

M/4-2 CAV Intelligence. 'Notes from Recent Interactions with ANSF.' 22 September 2010.

M/4-2 CAV Intelligence. 'Spin Boldak Inbrief.' 25 September 2010.

M/4-2 CAV Intelligence. 'Notes from Recent Interactions with GIRoA.' 27 September 2010.

M/4-2 CAV Intelligence. 'Bismillah Arghestani Interview.' 13 November 2010.

M/4-2 CAV Intelligence. 'How Spin Boldak Works.' 19 November 2010.

M/4-2 CAV Intelligence. 'M Troop 4/2 Personalities.' Undated c. 2010.

Obama, Barack. 'The New Way Forward - The President's Address.' 1 December 2009.

'Special Committee on the Canadian Mission in Afghanistan.' 40th Canadian Parliament, 2nd session. 18 November 2009.

Special Inspector General for Afghanistan Reconstruction (SIGAR). 'Quarterly Reports to Congress.' 2008-2018.
- 'Counternarcotics: Lessons from the U.S. Experience in Afghanistan.' June 2018.

– 'Lessons Learned: Police in Conflict.' June 2022.

– 'Why the Afghan Security Forces Collapsed.' February 2023.

United Nations. 'Provincial Overview: Kandahar Province,' UN International Organization of Migration. 2021.

United Nations. 'UNODC Opium Survey 2010.'

United Nations Assistance Mission Afghanistan (UNAMA). 'Treatment of Conflict-Related Detainees in Afghan Custody.' October 2011.

– 'Treatment of Conflict-Related Detainees in Afghan Custody: One Year On.' January 2013.

– Reports on the Protection of Civilians in Armed Conflict. 2010-2014.

U.S. Army Training and Doctrine Command. Ft. Leavenworth: *Warrior Ethos Staff Primer*. 2003.

U.S. Department of State. Country Report on Human Rights Practices, Afghanistan. 2010-2015.

– 'International Narcotics Control Strategy Report.' 1984.

– 'Dissent Channel Cable.' 7 January 2021.

U.S. Military Academy. *Register of Graduates*.

Books

Acemoglu, Daron and James A. Robinson, *Why Nations Fail: The Origins of Power, Prosperity, and Poverty*. New York: Crown, 2012.

Ackerman, Elliot. *The Fifth Act: America's End in Afghanistan*. New York: Penguin, 2022.

Adamec, Ludwig, ed. *Historical and Political Gazetteer of Afghanistan*. Volume 5: Kandahar and South-Central Afghanistan. Graz: Akademische Druck, 1980.

Ahmed, Akbar S. *Pukhtun Economy and Society: Traditional Structure and Economic Development in a Tribal Society*. New York: Routledge, 1980.

Alexievich, Svetlana. *Zinky Boys: Soviet Voices from the Afghanistan War*. New York: W.W. Norton, 1992.

Barfield, Thomas. *Afghanistan: A Cultural and Political History*. Princeton: Princeton University Press, 2010.

Bercuson, David. *Significant Incident: Canada's Army, the Airborne and the Murder in Somalia*. Toronto: McClelland and Stewart, 1996.

Blum, David and J. Edward Conway, (eds). *Counterterrorism and Threat Finance Analysis During Wartime*. Lanham: Lexington Books, 2015.

Bradford, James T. *Poppies, Politics, and Power: Afghanistan and the Global History of Drugs and Diplomacy*. Ithaca: Cornell University Press, 2019.

Braithwaite, Rodric. *Afghantsy: the Russians in Afghanistan, 1979-89*. Oxford: Oxford University Press, 2011.

Brooks, Michael, (ed) *Eyewitness to War, Vol. III: US Army Advisors in Afghanistan*. Ft. Leavenworth: Combat Studies Institute Press, 2010.

Caroe, Olaf. *The Pathans 550 BC - AD 1957*. Oxford: Oxford University Press, 1958.

Cassidy, Robert. *War, Will, and Warlords: Counterinsurgency in Afghanistan and Pakistan, 2001-2011*. Quantico: Marine Corps University Press, 2012.

Chandrasekaran, Rajiv. *Little America: The War within the War for Afghanistan.* New York: Vintage, 2012.

Chayes, Sarah. *The Punishment of Virtue: Inside Afghanistan after the Taliban.* New York: Penguin, 2006.

Churchill, Winston. *The Story of the Malakand Field Force*. London: Thomas Nelson, 1916.

Clarke, R.C. *Hashish!* New York: Red Eye Press, 1998.

Coll, Steve. *Directorate S: The CIA and America's Secret Wars in Afghanistan and Pakistan*. New York: Penguin, 2018.

Daddis, Gregory. *Withdrawal: Reassessing America's Final Years in Vietnam.* Oxford: Oxford University Press, 2017.

— *Pulp Vietnam: War and Gender in Cold War Men's Adventure Magazines.* Cambridge: Cambridge University Press, 2020.

Daudzai, Haqmal. *The State-Building Dilemma in Afghanistan: The State Governmental Design at the National Level and the Role of Democratic Provincial Councils in Decentralization at the Sub-National Level.* Berlin: Budrich Academic Press, 2021.

Dawson, Grant. *'Here is Hell': Canada's Engagement in Somalia.* Vancouver: University of British Columbia Press, 2007.

Deloria, Philip. *Indians in Unexpected Places*. New Haven: Yale University Press, 2004.

Dorronsoro, Gilles. *Revolution Unending: Afghanistan, 1979 to the Present.* London: Hurst, 2005.

Drinnon, Richard. *Facing West: the Metaphysics of Indian-Hating and Empire Building*. Minneapolis: University of Minnesota Press, 1980.

Dupree, Louis. *Afghanistan*. Princeton: Princeton University Press, 1973.

DuPrez, Scott. *One Night's Shelter (From Home to Homelessness): The Autobiography of an American Buddhist Monk*. Sri Lanka, 1985.

Edwards, David. *Heroes of the Age: Moral Fault Lines on the Afghan Frontier.* Berkeley: University of California Press, 1996.

— *Caravan of Martyrs: Sacrifice and Suicide Bombing in Afghanistan.* Berkeley: University of California Press, 2017.

Elphinstone, Mountstuart. *An Account of the Kingdom of Caubul*. London: Longman, Hurst, Orme, and Brown, 1815.

— *An Account of the Kingdom of Caubul*. London: Richard Bentley, 3rd ed. 1842

Emerson, Ralph Waldo. *English Traits*. Boston: Phillips, Sampson, and Company, 1858.

Felbab-Brown, Vanda. *Shooting Up: Counterinsurgency and the War on Drugs.* Washington: Brookings, 2010.

Fergusson, James. *Taliban: the Unknown Enemy*. New York: Hachette, 2011.

Gall, Sandy. *Afghan Napoleon: The Life of Ahmad Shah Massoud*. London: Haus Publishing, 2021.

Gannon, Kathy. *I is for Infidel: From Holy War to Holy Terror in Afghanistan*. New York: Hachette, 2006.

Gant, James. *One Tribe at a Time: The Paper that Changed the War in Afghanistan*. New York: Black Irish Entertainment, 2014.

Gemie, Sharif and Brian Ireland. *The Hippie Trail: A History, 1957-1978*. Manchester: Manchester University Press, 2017.

Giustozzi, Antonio. *Empires of Mud: War and Warlords in Afghanistan*. New York: Columbia University Press, 2009.

— *Decoding the New Taliban: Insights from the Afghan Field*. London: Hurst, 2009.

— *The Taliban at War: 2001-2018*. Oxford: Oxford University Press, 2019.

Goodson, Larry. *Afghanistan's Endless War: State Failure, Regional Politics, and the Rise of the Taliban*. Seattle: University of Washington Press, 2001.

Grad, Marcela. *Massoud: An Intimate Portrait of the Legendary Leader*. St. Louis: Webster University Press, 2009.

Granatstein, J.L. *Who Killed the Canadian Military?* Toronto: Harper Collins, 2004.

Grau, Lester, (ed). *The Bear Went Over the Mountain: Soviet Combat Tactics in Afghanistan*. Washington: National Defense University Press, 1996.

— (with Dodge Billingsley). *Operation Anaconda: America's First Major Battle in Afghanistan*. Lawrence: University of Kansas Press, 2011.

Gregorian, Vartan. *The Emergence of Modern Afghanistan: Politics of Reform and Modernization, 1880- 1946*. Stanford: Stanford University Press, 1969.

Hastings, Michael. *The Operators: The Wild and Terrifying Inside Story of America's War in Afghanistan*. New York: Blue Rider Press, 2012.

Hazelton, Jacqueline. *Bullets Not Ballots: Success in Counterinsurgency Warfare*. Ithaca: Cornell University Press, 2021.

Hopkins, B.D. *The Making of Modern Afghanistan*. New York: Palgrave MacMillan, 2008.

Horn, Bernd. *No Lack of Courage: Operation Medusa, Afghanistan*. Toronto: Dundurn Press, 2010.

Hymel, Kevin. *Strykers in Afghanistan: 1st Battalion, 17th Infantry Regiment in Kandahar Province, 2009*. Ft. Leavenworth: Combat Studies Institute, 2014.

Jacobsen, Annie. *First Platoon: a Story of Modern War in the Age of Identity Dominance*. New York: Penguin, 2021.

Jalali, Ali Ahmad. *A Military History of Afghanistan: From the Great Game to the Global War on Terror*. Lawrence: University of Kansas Press, 2017.

— and Lester Grau, (eds). *The Other Side of the Mountain: Mujahidin Tactics in the Soviet-Afghan War*. Quantico: USMC Press, 1998.

Johnson, Robert. *The Afghan Way of War: How and Why They Fight.* Oxford: Oxford University Press, 2012.

Junger, Sebastian. *Tribe: On Homecoming and Belonging.* New York: Hachette, 2016.

Kakar, Hasan. *Government and Society in Afghanistan: The Reign of Amir 'Abd Al-Rahman Khan.* Austin: University of Texas Press, 1979.

Kalyvas, Stathis. *The Logic of Violence in Civil War.* Cambridge: Cambridge University Press, 2006.

Kaldor, Mary. *New and Old Wars: Organized Violence in a Global Era.* Stanford: Stanford University Press, 1999.

Khan, Muhammad Hayat. *Afghanistan and its Inhabitants.* Delhi: Indian Public Press, 1874.

Khan, Sultan Mahomed, (ed). *Life of Abdur Rahman.* London: John Murray, 1900.

Kilcullen, David and Greg Mills. *The Ledger: Accounting for Failure in Afghanistan.* London: Hurst, 2021.

Koontz, Christopher N., (ed). *Enduring Voices, Oral Histories of the US Army in Afghanistan 2003-2005.* Washington: Center for Military History, 2008.

Krakauer, Jon. *Three Cups of Deceit.* New York: Anchor, 2011.

Lee, Jonathan. *Afghanistan: a History from 1260 to the Present.* London: Reaktion Books, 2019.

Levi, Peter. *The Light Garden of the Angel King: Journeys in Afghanistan.* London: Eland, 2013.

Maguire, Peter and Mike Ritter. *Thai Stick: Surfers, Scammers, and the Untold Story of the Marijuana Trade.* New York: Columbia University Press, 2014.

Malkasian, Carter. *The American War in Afghanistan: A History.* Oxford: Oxford University Press, 2021.

Malejacq, Romain. *Warlord Survival: The Delusion of State Building in Afghanistan.* Ithaca: Cornell University Press, 2019.

Maloney, Sean M. *Enduring the Freedom: A Rogue Historian in Afghanistan.* Sterling: Potomac, 2005.

– *Confronting the Chaos: a Rogue Military Historian Returns to Afghanistan.* Washington DC: Naval Institute Press, 2009.

Mansfield, David. *A State Built on Sand: How Opium Undermined Afghanistan.* Oxford: Oxford University Press, 2016.

Martin, Mike. *An Intimate War: An Oral History of the Helmand Conflict, 1978-2012.* Oxford: Oxford University Press, 2014.

Marten, Kimberley. *Warlords: Strong-arm Brokers in Weak States.* Ithaca: Cornell University Press, 2012.

Mattox, Gale and Stephen Grenier. *Coalition Challenges in Afghanistan: The Politics of Alliance.* Stanford: Stanford University Press, 2015.

Mestrovic, Stjepan. *Strike and Destroy: When Counter-Insurgency (COIN) Doctrine Met Hellraiser's Brigade or, The Fate of Corporal Morlock.* New York: Algora Publishing, 2012.

Mortenson, Greg and David Oliver Relin. *Three Cups of Tea: One Man's Mission to Fight Terrorism and Build Nations . . . One School at a Time.* New York: Penguin, 2006.

Mukhopadhyay, Dipali. *Warlords, Strongman Governors, and the State in Afghanistan.* Cambridge: Cambridge University Press, 2014.

Napoleoni, Loretta. *Terror Incorporated.* New York: Penguin, 2003.

Naylor, Sean. *Not a Good Day to Die: the Untold Story of Operation Anaconda.* New York: Berkeley, 2005.

Noelle, Christine. *State and Tribe in Nineteenth-Century Afghanistan: The Reign of Amir Dost Muhammad Khan (1826-1863).* New York: Routledge, 1997.

Partlow, Joshua. *A Kingdom of Their Own: The Family Karzai and the Afghan Disaster.* New York: Knopf, 2016.

Porter, Patrick. *Military Orientalism: Eastern War through Western Eyes.* New York: Columbia University Press, 2009.

Rashid, Ahmed. *Taliban: Militant Islam, Oil, and Fundamentalism in Central Asia.* New Haven: Yale University Press, 2000.

– *Descent into Chaos: The United States and the Failure of Nation Building in Pakistan, Afghanistan, and Central Asia.* New York: Viking, 2008.

Reardon, Mark and Jeffrey A. Charleston. *From Transformation to Combat: The First Stryker Brigade at War.* Washington DC: Center for Military History, 2007.

Rico, Johnny. *Blood Makes Grass Grow Green: a Year in the Desert with Team America.* New York: Random House, 2007.

Robinson, Linda. *One Hundred Victories: Special Ops and the Future of American Warfare.* New York: Public Affairs, 2013.

Roy, Olivier. *Islam and Resistance in Afghanistan.* Cambridge: Cambridge University Press, 1985.

Rubin, Barnett. *The Fragmentation of Afghanistan.* New Haven: Yale University Press, 1995.

– *Afghanistan from the Cold War to the Global War on Terror.* Oxford: Oxford University Press, 2013.

Rumsfeld, Donald. *Known and Unknown: A Memoir.* New York: Penguin, 2011.

Sands, Chris and Fazelminallah Qazizai. *Night Letters: The Secret History of Gulbuddin Hekmatyar and the Afghan Islamists Who Changed the World.* London: Hurst, 2019.

Schou, Nicholas. *Orange Sunshine: The Brotherhood of Eternal Love and its Quest to Spread Peace, Love, and Acid to the World.* New York: St. Martin's, 2010.

Slotkin, Richard. *Gunfighter Nation: The Myth of the Frontier in Twentieth-Century America.* Norman: University of Oklahoma Press, 1998.

Smucker, Philip. *Al Qaeda's Great Escape: the Military and the Media on Terror's Trail.* Washington: Potomac Books, 2004.

Sorley, Lewis. *A Better War: The Unexamined Victories and Final Tragedy of America's Last Years in Vietnam*. London: Harcourt and Brace, 1999.

Steele, Jonathan. *Ghosts of Afghanistan: the Haunted Battlefield*. Berkeley: Counterpoint Press, 2011.

Stone, Damien. *Pomegranate: a Global History*. London: Reaktion Books, 2017.

Suhrke, Astri. *When More is Less: The International Project in Afghanistan*. New York: Columbia University Press, 2011.

Tanguy, Jean-Marc. *Les Scorpions de Spin Boldak*. Paris: Nimrod, 2013.

Terkel, Studs. *'The Good War': an Oral History of World War Two*. New York: Penguin, 1986.

Thier, J. Alexander, (ed). *The Future of Afghanistan*. Washington: US Institute of Peace, 2009.

Tunnell IV, Harry D. *Red Devils: Tactical Perspectives from Iraq*. Ft. Leavenworth: Combat Studies Institute Press, 2006.

Tyson, Ann Scott. *American Spartan: The Promise, the Mission, and the Betrayal of Special Forces Major Jim Gant*. New York: Harper Collins, 2014.

Urban, Mark. *War in Afghanistan*. London: MacMillan Press, 1990.

Vick, Alan, et al. *The Stryker Brigade Combat Team: Rethinking Strategic Responsiveness and Assessing Deployment Options*. Santa Monica: RAND, 2002.

Wattie, Chris. *Contact Charlie: The Canadian Army, the Taliban, and the Battle for Afghanistan*. Toronto: Key Porter Books, 2010.

Whitlock, Craig. *The Afghanistan Papers: The Secret History of the War*. New York: Simon and Schuster, 2021.

Williams, Brian. *The Last Warlord: The Life and Legend of Dostum, the Afghan Warrior Who Led U.S. Special Forces to Topple the Taliban Regime*. Chicago: Chicago Review Press, 2013.

Zaeef, Mullah Abdul Salam. *My Life with the Taliban*. London: Hurst, 2011.

Articles and Book Chapters

'15 Taliban dead in clash with Afghan troops.' *CBC News*. 22 March 2006.

'A timeline of the U.S. military presence in Afghanistan.' *AP News*. 8 September 2019.

Abdi, Ali. 'The Afghan *Bachah* and its Discontents: An Introductory History.' *Iranian Studies*. Vol. 56, no. 1 (January 2023): 161-80.

Ables, Micah. 'Ally, Bad Guy, or Both? Thoughts on Reconciling American Values and Questionable Partners, Two Years after the Death of Abdul Raziq.' West Point Modern War Institute. 19 November 2020.

'Afghan bombers attack police force.' *Al Jazeera*. 7 September 2008.

'Afghan governor's rights abuses known in '07.' *CBC News*. 12 April 2010.

'Afghan troops kill suspected Taliban rebels at Pakistan border.' *New York Times*. 22 March 2006.

Ahmad, Jibran. 'Taliban's Mullah Omar Died of Natural Causes in Afghanistan, Son Says.' *Reuters*. 14 September 2015.

– 'Taliban seeks to reassure UAE over Afghanistan attack.' *Reuters*. 19 January 2017.

Ahmed, Azam and Matthieu Aikins, 'America's Monster: How the U.S. Backed Kidnapping, Torture and Murder in Afghanistan.' *New York Times*. 22 May 2024.

Ahram, Ariel and Charles King. 'The Warlord as Arbitrageur.' *Theory and Society*. Vol. 41, no. 2 (March 2012): 169-86.

Aikins, Matthieu. 'America's Monster: Who was Abdul Raziq?' *New York Times Magazine*. 22 May 2024.

– 'Contracting the Commanders: Transition and the Political Economy of Afghanistan's Private Security Industry.' NYU Center on International Cooperation. October 2012.

– 'Our Man in Kandahar.' *The Atlantic*. November 2011.

– 'The Master of Spin Boldak.' *Harper's Magazine*. December 2009.

Armitage, David. 'Every Great Revolution is a Civil War.' In *Scripting Revolution: A Historical Approach to the Comparative Study of Revolutions*, ed. Keith Baker and Dan Edelstein. Stanford: Stanford University Press, 2015: 57-68.

Assmann, Karin, John Goetz, and Marc Hujer. '"Let's Kill": Report Reveals Discipline Breakdown in Kill Team Brigade.' *Der Spiegel International*. 4 April 2011.

Barfield, Thomas. 'Afghanistan is Not the Balkans: Ethnicity and its Political Consequences from a Central Asian Perspective.' *Central Eurasian Studies Review*. Vol. 4, no. 1 (Winter 2005): 2-8.

– 'Problems in Establishing Legitimacy in Afghanistan.' *Iranian Studies*. Vol. 37, no. 2 (June 2004): 263-93.

Barrett, Devlin et al. 'A Sprawling Investigation: What we know so far about the Capitol mob arrests.' *Washington Post*. 13 May 2021.

Bartholet, Jeffrey and Steve LeVine. 'The Holy Men of Heroin.' *Newsweek*. 5 December 1999.

Becatoros, Elena and Tarek El-Tablawy. '17 killed in suicide blast in southern Afghanistan.' *Denver Post*. 7 January 2011.

'Bernier clarifies comments over Kandahar's governor.' *CBC News*. 14 April 2008.

Bezhan, Frud. 'Afghans Laud, Rights Groups Concerned by "Take No Prisoners" Orders.' *Radio Free Europe*. 24 August 2014.

Boal, Mark. 'The Kill Team: How US Soldiers in Afghanistan Murdered Innocent Civilians.' *Rolling Stone*. 28 March 2011.

Booth, Nathan. 'Brigade Holds Memorial for 32 lost in 2009.' *DVIDS*. 1 January 2010.

Bowman, Tom. 'He Calmed Kandahar, But at What Cost?' *National Public Radio*. 21 May 2015.

Bradford, James and David Mansfield. 'Known Unknowns and Unknown Knowns: What we know about the cannabis and the hashish trade in Afghanistan.' *EchoGeo*. Vol. 48. April-June 2019.

Brewster, Murray. 'Canadian diplomat Glyn Berry's Afghanistan murder unsolved after 10 years.' *Toronto Star*. 15 January 2016.

Campbell, William. 'Shorawak Valley and the Toba Plateau.' *Proceedings of the Royal Geographical Society and Monthly Record of Geography*. Vol. 2, no. 10 (Oct. 1880): 620-6.

'Canadian diplomat killed in Afghan blast.' *NBC News*. 15 January 2006.

Cervera, Guillermo. '10 Years of Afghan War: How the Taliban Go On.' *Newsweek*. 2 October 2011.

Cesaretti, Laura and Fazelminallah Qazizai. 'Democracy at any cost: How the West supported an Afghan general who ruled through fear.' *The New Arab*. 22 November 2018.

Chandrasekaran, Rajiv 'The Afghan Robin Hood.' *Washington Post*. 4 October 2010.

– (with John Pomfret). 'Aided by US, Pashtun Militias Move Closer to Kandahar.' *Washington Post*. 27 November 2001.

Chappell, Bill. 'US Soldier Sentenced to Life in Afghan Village Attacks.' *National Public Radio*. 23 August 2013.

Chayes, Sarah. 'Afghanistan's Future, Lost in the Shuffle.' *New York Times*. 1 July 2003.

Cloud, David. 'Letting Go in Afghanistan as Mission Winds Down.' *Los Angeles Times*. 9 December 2012.

Coburn, Noah. 'Merchant-Warlords: Changing Forms of Leadership in Afghanistan's Unstable Political Economy.' In *Modern Afghanistan: The Impact of Forty Years of War*. Nazif Shahrani, (ed). Bloomington: Indiana University Press, 2018.

Coll, Steve and Adam Entous. 'The Secret History of the U.S. Diplomatic Failure in Afghanistan.' *The New Yorker*. 10 December 2021.

Collins, Joseph. 'The Rise and Fall of Major Jim Gant.' *War on the Rocks*. 14 April 2014.

Collins, Shannon. 'What to Know About the GBU-43/B, "Mother of All Bombs."' *DVIDS*. 14 April 2017.

Cooper, Kenneth. 'Afghans Cultivate Islamic State, but Ignore Illicit Harvest.' *Washington Post*. 11 May 1997.

Cordesman, Anthony R. 'The Afghan Narcotics Industry: A Summary.' *Center for Strategic and International Studies*. 12 November 2009.

Crews, Robert. 'Moderate Taliban?' In *The Taliban and the Crisis of Afghanistan*. Crews and Amin Tarzi, (eds). Cambridge: Harvard University Press, 2008.

Crowley, Michael. 'Trump's Deal with the Taliban Draws Fire from his Former Allies.' *New York Times*. 19 August 2021.

Cullather, Nick. 'Damming Afghanistan: Modernization in a Buffer State.' *Journal of American History.* Vol. 89, no. 2 (September 2002): 512-37.

'DEA Releases Photos of Record-Breaking Seizure in Afghanistan.' DEA.gov website. 13 June 2008.

'Deadly suicide bombing wrecks Afghan bathhouse.' *France24.* 7 January 2011.

Deveau, Scott. 'Saskatchewan soldier killed in IED Blast.' *Windsor Star.* 6 September 2008.

Di Manno, Rosie. 'Taking the Fight Back to Kandahar City,' *Toronto Star.* 14 August 2009.

Dickerson, Matthew. 'Treebeard.' In Michael Drout, (ed). *J.R.R. Tolkien Encyclopedia: Scholarship and Critical Assessment.* New York: Taylor and Francis, 2007.

Dominique, Bryan. 'Unit gives women voice in Southern Afghanistan.' *Fayetteville Observer.* 23 August 2012.

Dreisbach, Tom and Meg Anderson. 'Nearly 1 in 5 Defendants in Capitol Riot Cases Served in the Military'. *National Public Radio.* 21 January 2021.

Dupee, Matt. 'Kandahar Drug Bust: Narco-Penetration of the State.' *Long War Journal.* 5 September 2009.

Dupree, Louis. 'Afghanistan in 1983: And Still No Solution.' *Asian Survey.* Vol. 24, no 2 (February 1984): 229-39.

Edwards, David. '"The Perfect Counterinsurgent." Reconsidering the Case of Major Jim Gant.' *Small Wars and Insurgencies.* Vol. 31, no. 2 (February 2020): 420-44.

Entous, Adam and Jessica Donati. 'How the U.S. Tracked and Killed the Leader of the Taliban.' *Wall Street Journal.* 25 May 2016.

Faramarz, Samim. 'Noor Receives Huge Support from Kabul Gathering,' *Tolo News,* 29 December 2017.

Fisher, Luke. 'Airborne's Hazing Exposed.' *Maclean's.* 30 January 1995.

Flynn, Michael T., Matt Pottinger, and Paul Batchelor. 'Fixing Intel: A Blueprint for Making Intelligence Relevant in Afghanistan.' *Center for a New American Security.* January 2010.

Forsberg, Carl. 'Afghanistan report 3, The Taliban's Campaign for Kandahar.' *Institute for the Study of War.* 2009.

– 'Counterinsurgency in Kandahar: Evaluating the 2010 Hamkari Campaign,' *Institute for the Study of War.* 2010.

Fowler, David C. 'Rymes of Robin Hood.' In *Literary History of the Popular Ballad.* Fowler, (ed). Durham: Duke University Press, 1968.

Giustozzi, Antonio and Noor Ullah. 'Tribes and Warlords in Southern Afghanistan, 1980-2005.' *Crisis States Working Papers.* Series 2, no. 7 (September 2006).

Goetz, John and Marc Hujer. 'The Good Boy and the "Kill Team."' *Der Spiegel International.* 31 March 2011.

Goldstein, Joseph. 'U.S. soldiers told to ignore sexual abuse of boys by Afghan allies.' *New York Times.* 21 September 2015.

Goodhand, Jonathan. 'Frontiers and Wars: the Opium Economy in Afghanistan.' *Journal of Agrarian Change.* Vol. 5, no. 2 (April 2005): 191-216.

— 'From Holy War to Opium War? A Case Study of the Opium Economy in North-eastern Afghanistan.' *Central Asian Survey.* Vol. 19, no. 2 (February 2000): 265-80.

Gopal, Anand. 'Kandahar's Mystery Executions.' *Harper's Magazine.* September 2014.

Gossman, Patricia. 'Will Afghanistan Prosecute Kandahar's Torturer in Chief?' Human Rights Watch. 17 May 2017.

Graff, Peter. 'US troops leave border to Afghan boss accused of graft.' *Reuters.* 17 March 2010.

Grau, Lester and Ali Ahmad Jalali, 'Underground Combat: Stereophonic Blasting, Tunnel Rats and the Soviet-Afghan War.' *Engineer.* Vol. 28 (1998): 20-3.

Graham-Harrison, Emma. 'Afghanistan officials sanctioned murder, torture and rape, says report.' *The Guardian.* 3 March 2015.

Green, Nile. 'Tribe, Diaspora, and Sainthood in Afghan History.' *Journal of Asian Studies.* Vol. 67, no. 1 (2008): 171-211.

Hamid, Tamim. 'Paris Unveils Plaque in Honor of Ahmad Shah Massoud.' *Tolo News.* 27 March 2021.

Haq, Ikramul. 'Pak-Afghan Drug Trade in Historical Perspective.' *Asian Survey.* Vol. 36, no. 10 (October 1996): 945-63.

Harmon, Jeff. 'Toe to toe with Russians in Kandahar's holy war.' *Sunday Times.* 11 August 1985.

Hastings, Michael. 'King David's War.' *Rolling Stone.* 2 February 2011.

Hawkins, John M. 'The Costs of Artillery: Eliminating Harassment and Interdiction Fire during the Vietnam War.' *Journal of Military History.* Vol. 70 (January 2006): 91-122.

Houston, Whitney. 'FOB Walton closes: A step in the right direction.' *DVIDS.* 20 July 2014.

Hughes, Paul. 'Engineers generate power at FOB Walton.' *DVIDS.* 11 August 2011.

Islami, Modaser. 'Afghans demand justice for war victims after mass grave discovery.' *Arab News.* 27 September 2022.

Jackson, Ashley. 'Politics and Governance in Afghanistan: The Case of Kandahar.' *AREU* working paper 34. June 2015.

Jeong, May. 'The U.S. Lost a Key Ally in Southern Afghanistan, but Abdul Raziq Was No Hero.' *The Intercept.* 30 October 2018.

Johnson, Kirk. 'Guilty Plea by Sergeant in Killing of Civilians.' *New York Times.* 5 June 2013.

Johnson, Robert. 'Upstream Engagements and Downstream Entanglements: The Assumptions, Opportunities, and Threats of Partnering.' *Small Wars and Insurgencies.* Vol. 25, no. 3 (2014): 647-68.

Johnson, Thomas H. and Matthew C. DuPee. 'Analysing the new Taliban Code of Conduct (*Layeha*): an assessment of changing perspectives and strategies of the Afghan Taliban.' *Central Asian Survey.* Vol. 31, no. 1 (March 2012): 77-91.

Kalyvas, Stathis. '"New" and "Old" Civil Wars: a Valid Distinction?' *World Politics.* Vol. 54 (October 2001): 99-118.

Kaplan, Robert. 'Indian Country.' *Wall Street Journal.* 21 September 2004.

'Killings of 15 Afghans to Be Probed.' *Los Angeles Times.* 23 March 2006.

Lamb, Christina. 'Afghan police: all's fair in love and war.' *The Times.* 25 July 2010.

Latifi, Ali. 'Mother of All Bombs.' *New York Times.* 20 April 2017.

– (with Abdullah Shahood). 'Afghan rage over Kandahar massacre sentence.' *Al Jazeera.* 1 September 2013.

Lieven, Anatol. 'Mujahidin fail to subdue the pirate turncoat.' *The Times.* 26 January 1988.

Londono, Ernesto. 'Afghanistan sees rise in "dancing boys" exploitation.' *Washington Post.* 4 April 2012.

– 'US soldier charged in Kandahar massacre showed no remorse, comrade says.' *Washington Post.* 5 November 2012.

Lowe, Miranda Summers. 'The Gradual Shift to an Operational Reserve: Reserve Component Mobilizations in the 1990s.' *Military Review* (May-June 2019): 120-6.

– 'The National Guard and Reserves.' In *Understanding the U.S. Military.* Katherine Carroll and William Hickman, (eds). New York: Routledge, 2023.

Lubold, Gordon. 'In Afghanistan's Troubled South.' *Christian Science Monitor.* 30 April 2008.

Malkasian, Carter, Jerry Meyerle, and Megan Katt. 'The War in Southern Afghanistan, 2001-2008.' *CNA Strategic Studies.* July 2009.

Manchanda, Nivi. 'The Imperial Sociology of the "Tribe" in Afghanistan.' *Millennium: Journal of International Studies.* Vol. 46, no. 2 (2018): 165-89.

Mansfield, David. 'Coping Strategies, Accumulated Wealth, and Shifting Markets: The Story of Opium Poppy Cultivation in Badakhshan 2000-2003.' *Agha Khan Development Network.* January 2004.

Mashal, Mujib. 'Afghan Police Chief, Long a Taliban Target, Faces a New Emotion: Fear.' *New York Times.* 31 May 2015.

– (with Thomas Gibbons-Neff), 'How a Taliban Assassin Got Close Enough to Kill a General.' *New York Times.* 2 November 2018.

McCarten, James. 'Bernier's Afghan Bombshell.' *Toronto Star.* 14 April 2008.

McGeough, Paul. 'Who Killed Australia's Warlord in Afghanistan?' *Sydney Morning Herald.* 26 June 2015.

McMaster, H.R. 'The Battle of 73 Easting.' In *Leaders in War.* Frederick Kagan and Chris Kubik, (eds). New York: Frank Cass, 2005.

Minoia, Giulia and Adam Pain. '90% Real – The Rise and Fall of a Rentier Economy: Stories from Kandahar, Afghanistan.' *AREU* working paper 38. November 2015.

Myerson, Roger. 'Stabilization Lessons from the British Empire.' *Texas National Security Review.* Vol. 6, no. 1 (Winter 2022/23): 35-50.

'No US Charges over Afghan Bodies.' *BBC South Asia.* 26 November 2005.

Nordland, Rod. 'Afghans Plan to Stop Recruiting Children as Police.' *New York Times.* 30 January 2011.

O'Hara, Jane. 'Rape in the military.' *MacLean's.* 25 May 1998.

Packer, George. 'The Lesson of Tal Afar.' *The New Yorker.* 3 April 2006.

Partlow, Joshua. 'Kandahar governor faced allegation in job with contractor'. *Washington Post.* 26 May 2010.

Peter, Tom. 'Assassinated Kandahar Police chief was optimistic about security.' *Christian Science Monitor.* 15 April 2011

Peters, Gretchen. 'Traffickers and Truckers: Illicit Afghan and Pakistani Power Structures with a Shadowy but Influential Role.' In *Impunity: Countering Illicit Power in War and Transition.* Michelle Hughes and Michael Miklaucic, (eds). Washington: National Defense University Press, 2017.

Peuch, Jean-Christophe. 'Afghanistan: Warlord's Role as Political Leader Remains Questionable.' *Radio Free Europe.* 12 April 2001.

Pugliese, David. '"Man Love Thursday" Returns.' *Ottawa Citizen.* 6 October 2008.

Rennie, Steve. 'Over veggies and cherry juice, life changed for new Kandahar governor.' *Canadian Press.* 19 December 2008.

Reynolds, Maura. 'Kandahar's Lightly Veiled Homosexual Habits.' *Los Angeles Times.* 3 April 2002.

Roggio, Bill. 'General Raziq's assassin trained at a Taliban camp.' *Long War Journal.* 21 October 2018.

Rosenberg, Matthew and Maria Abi-Habib. 'Afghanistan Blunts Anticorruption Efforts.' *Wall Street Journal.* 12 September 2010.

Saboory, Ghafoor. 'Raziq Says Government Cannot Remove Him from His Post.' *Tolo News.* 2 January 2018.

Sadat, Sami. 'I commanded Afghan troops this year. We were betrayed.' *New York Times.* 25 August 2021.

Saifullah, Masood. 'Who Carried Out the Kandahar Bombing?' *Deutsche Welle.* 11 January 2017.

Sanger, David. 'A Test for the Meaning of Victory in Afghanistan.' *New York Times.* 13 February 2010.

Sara, Sally. 'Taliban claims Afghan bomb attack.' *Australian Broadcasting Corporation.* 15 April 2011.

Schmitt, Eric. 'Army Examining an Account of Abuse of 2 Dead Taliban.' *New York Times.* 20 October 2005.

Schonfeld, Reese. 'Afghanistan: Robin Hood and the Sheriff of Nottingham.' *Huffington Post.* 29 November 2009.

Shachtman, Noah. 'Marjah's "Government in a Box" Flops as McChrystal Fumes.' *Wired.* 25 May 2010.

Shah, Taimoor and Carlotta Gall. 'Key Taliban Leader is Killed in Joint Operation.' *New York Times.* 14 May 2007.

Shinseki, Eric. 'The Army Transformation: A Historic Opportunity.' *Army Magazine.* October 2000.

Siddique, Abubakar. '"Afghanistan Is Hell": Supporters of Late Afghan General Claim Taliban Killings, Persecution.' *Radio Free Europe.* 2 November 2022.

Silliman, Stepen. 'The "Old West" in the Middle East: U.S. Military Metaphors in Real and Imagined Indian Country.' *American Anthropologist.* Vol. 110, no. 2 (June 2008): 237-47.

Simonsen, Richard. 'Kandahar PRT, State Dept. Visit Spin Boldak,' *DVIDS.* 26 June 2011.

Smith, Craig. 'Kandahar Journal: Shh, it's an Open Secret: Warlords and Pedophilia.' *New York Times.* 21 February 2002.

Smith, Graeme. 'Inspiring Tale of Triumph over Taliban not all it Seems.' *Globe and Mail.* 23 September 2006.

– 'A Country Where Blood is Everything.' *Globe and Mail.* 11 December 2006.

– 'The Afghan Mission, Knowing the Enemy: The Taliban.' *Globe and Mail.* 13 January 2007.

– (with Omar el Akkad). 'Mullah's death leaves Kandahar exposed.' *Globe and Mail.* 13 October 2007.

Smith, Thomas W. 'Protecting Civilians . . . or Soldiers? Humanitarian Law and the Economy of Risk in Iraq,' *International Studies Perspectives.* Vol. 9 (2008): 144-64.

Soloman, Andy. 'Looters Raid Relief Stores in Afghan Border Town.' *Reuters.* 27 November 2001.

Stanski, Keith. '"So These Folks are Aggressive": An Orientalist Reading of "Afghan Warlords."' *Security Dialogue.* Vol. 40, no. 1 (February 2009): 74-94.

Starkey, Jerome. 'Afghan commandos discover 230 tonnes of cannabis in the desert.' *Belfast Telegraph.* 10 July 2008.

Sturcke, James. 'US soldiers "desecrated Taliban bodies."' *The Guardian.* 20 October 2005.

'Suicide bombers kill 6 police officers in Kandahar.' *New York Times.* 7 September 2008.

Synovitz, Ron. 'Afghanistan: Reports Claim "War on Terror" Used to Hide Blood-Feud Killings.' *Radio Free Europe.* 31 March 2006.

'Taliban attacks kill at least 24 in Afghanistan.' *CBC News.* 16 January 2006.

Tan, Michelle. 'Boredom in rogue platoon leads to murder.' *Army Times.* 28 November 2011.

Tanzeem, Ayesha. 'Afghan Intel Chief: Suspects that Killed UAE Ambassador Living in Pakistan.' *Voice of America*. 15 June 2017.

Tarzi, Amin. 'Tarikh-i Ahmad Shah: The First History of Afghanistan.' In *Afghan History Through Afghan Eyes*. Niles Green, (ed). Oxford: Oxford University Press, 2015.

Thomas, Paul. 'Ambush in Gumbad Valley.' *Infantry Magazine* (January-February 2008): 27-31.

Thompson, Mark. 'The Fall of the Green Berets' Lawrence of Afghanistan.' *Time Magazine*. 25 June 2014.

Tilly, Charles. 'Warmaking and State making as Organized Crime.' In *Bringing the State Back in*. Theda Skocpol et al., (eds). Cambridge: Cambridge University Press, 1985. 169-91.

'"Today We Shall All Die." Afghanistan's Strongmen and the Legacy of Impunity.' *Human Rights Watch*. 3 March 2015.

Trofimov, Yaroslav and Matthew Rosenberg. 'In Afghanistan, US Turns "Malignant Actor" Into Ally. *Wall Street Journal*. 18 November 2010.

Tunnell IV, Harry D. 'Developing a Unit Language Capability for War.' *Joint Forces Quarterly*. No. 51 (2008): 114-16.

Tyson, Ann Scott and Jim Gant. 'Afghanistan, in person: From tribal ties to pleas for help.' *Christian Science Monitor*. 23 August 2021.

Walsh, Declan. 'Powerful Afghan Police Chief Puts Fear in Taliban and Their Enemies.' *New York Times*. 8 November 2014.

Watson, Paul. 'Credibility eludes Kandahar police force.' *Toronto Star*. 20 June 2011.

Weber, Max. 'Politics as a Vocation.' In *Weber: Selections in Translation*. Cambridge: Cambridge University Press, 1978. 212-25.

Wellman, Philip Walter. 'Conspiracy theories abound over US role in Kandahar police chief's killing.' *Stars and Stripes*. 26 October 2018.

Wright, Robin. 'Trump Drops the Mother of All Bombs on Afghanistan.' *The New Yorker*. 14 April 2017.

Yousafzai, Sami. 'The Taliban's Oral History of the Afghanistan War.' *Newsweek*. 25 September 2009.

Ziezulewicz, Geoff and Jon Simkins. 'Here be giants – outlandish tales of the military and the Afghan colossi.' *Military Times*. 31 October 2002.

Zimmerman, Rebecca. 'The Afghan Warlord with a Cheshire Cat Grin.' *Newsweek*. 29 April 2015.

Films

Amiri, Sharif. 'Documentary on Gen. Raziq's Assassination.' *Tolo News*. 9 November 2018.

Kiazand, Gelareh. 'Inside the Afghan National Army, Part 4/5, Killing Time in Kandahar.' *Vice News.* 27 February 2014.

Krauss, Dan. *The Kill Team.* Documentary film (2013).

– *The Kill Team.* A24 studio feature film (2019).

Quraishi, Najibullah. *The Dancing Boys of Afghanistan.* Documentary film (2010).

Online Resources

Afghan Analysts Network

– Adili, Ali Yawar and Thomas Ruttig. '"The Ankara Coalition:" Opposition from within the government.' 25 July 2017.

– Sabawoon, Ali Mohammad. 'The Gates of Friendship: How Afghans cross the Afghan-Pakistani border.' 28 January 2020.

– Ruttig, Thomas. 'The Killing of Razeq: Removing the Taleban's strongest foe in Kandahar, an indirect hit at elections.' 19 October 2018.

– Semple, Michael. 'Not Everybody's Hero.' 31 October 2018.

Lieber Institute at West Point

– Fetchik, Janine and Matt Montazolli. 'Unobserved Fires and the Law of Armed Conflict.' 3 March 2023.

September 11th Sourcebooks, vol. VII: The Taliban File. Sajit Gandhi, (ed). National Security Archive. George Washington University.

– US Consulate (Peshawar) cable. 'New Fighting and New Forces in Kandahar.' 3 November 1994.

– US Embassy (Islamabad) cable. 'The Taliban – Who Knows What the Movement Means?' 28 November 1994.

– US Embassy (Islamabad) cable, 'Believe Pakistan is Backing Taliban,' 6 December 1994.

– US Embassy (Islamabad) cable. 'Finally a Talkative Talib.' 20 February 1995.

Washington Post Afghanistan Papers

– SIGAR Lessons Learned Interviews.

Wikileaks

(in chronological order of report)

– Norland. US Embassy (Kabul) cable. 'Kandahar: A Governor's Intentions.' 24 January 2006.

– Neumann. US Embassy (Kabul) cable. 'PRT/Kandahar – Dealing with the Taliban "Spring Offensive."' 24 April 2006.

- RC South. 'Direct Fire Spin Buldak.' 15 June 2006.
- Norland. US Embassy (Kabul) cable. 'PRT Kandahar/Helmand: Security Concerns Take Center Stage.' 16 October 2006.
- US Embassy (Kabul) cable. 'PRT Kandahar: Six Month Assessment.' 25 July 2007.
- US Embassy (Kabul) cable. 'Pakistanis at Kandahar Border Flag Meeting – The Quetta Shura is a Fabrication.' 7 October 2009.
- 5/2 SBCT, RC South. 'Friendly Action. Cache Found/Cleared.' 10 November 2009.
- US Embassy (Kabul) cable. 'Kandahar Politics Complicate U.S. Objectives in Afghanistan.' 6 December 2009.
- TF Saint. 'Non-Combat Event.' 16 December 2009.
- US Embassy (Kabul) cable. 'Spin Boldak: a Stability and Security Balancing Act.' 17 December 2009.
- US Embassy (Kabul) cable. 'Spin Boldak Powerbroker Encourages Modernization of Customs Operations.' 3 February 2010.
- US Embassy (Kabul) cable, 'Bedlam and Corruption Permeate Customs Process at Spin Boldak.' 7 February 2010.
- US Embassy (Kabul) cable. 'Powerbroker and Governance Issues in Spin Boldak.' 7 February 2010.
- US Embassy (Kabul) cable. 'Kandahar: Corruption Reforms by the Master of Spin?' 17 February 2010.
- Diplomatic (Washington) cable. 'Relationship Dynamics, Afghan Border Police Colonel Abdul Razaq.' 16 November 2010.
- Diplomatic (Washington) cable. 'Afghan Border Police in the Spin Boldak District, Kandahar Province.' 26 November 2010.

ENDNOTES

Prologue: Pomegranates (2010)

1. For the ancient world, see Damien Stone, *Pomegranate: a Global History* (London: Reaktion Books, 2017), 14-52; *Quran*, Sura LV, verse 68; for modern Kandahar, see Tooryalai Wesa Interview, Governor of Kandahar Province, 29 July 2021; Ahmed Rashid, *Taliban* (New Haven: Yale University Press, 2000), 20.
2. M/4-2 CAV Intelligence, 'Recent Interactions with ANSF,' 22 September 2010; Basir Arian Interview, Linguist, 9 April 2021; W. Scott Browne Interview, 1LT U.S. Army, 4-2 CAV, 11 May 2021; Najibullah Saqib Interview, Raziq aide, 8 August 2022.
3. Owen Kirby Interview, U.S. State Department, 19 March 2021; David Johnson Interview, MAJ U.S. Army, 8-1 CAV, 9 April 2021.
4. Abdul Raziq's birth date, like that of most Afghans of his generation, is unknown. His name appears variably in English as: Razaq, Razeq, Razik, and Razziq. Those closest to him seem to pronounce his name RAH-zik, though many put heavy emphasis on the last syllable: rah-ZEEK. The disagreement on accent is again typical of Afghanistan, whose capital is pronounced by most insiders as KAH-bul and by most outsiders as kah-BOOL.
5. For pomegranates, see Matthew Kelley Interview, CPT U.S. Army, 4-2 CAV, 19 March 2021; Edwin Den Harder Interview, 1LT U.S. Army, 4-2 CAV, 29 April 2021; Steven Beckman, Sr. Interview, COL U.S. Army, RC South J2, 12 May 2021; for Raziq's mulling of retirement, see Andrew Green Interview, LTC U.S. Army, 4-2 CAV, 22 March 2021; James Edwards Interview, COL U.S. Army, 525 BfSB, 25 March 2021; William Clark Interview, LTC U.S. Army, 8-1 CAV, 26 March 2021; (Redacted) Interview, U.S. Army Special Forces Officer, 15 February 2022.

Introduction: Biography of a Police Chief

1. Najib Fazel Interview, Linguist, 26 March 2021; Marshall Rogers Interview #2, CPT U.S. Army, TF South deputy J2, 1 September 2022; (Redacted) Interview, U.S. Special Forces Officer, 15 February 2022.

2. The list includes: Ahmad Shah Massoud and Mohammed Fahim (Panjshir), Abdul Rasul Sayyaf (Kabul), Abdul Rashid Dostum (Jozjan), Atta Mohammad Nur (Balkh), Ismail Khan (Herat), and Sher Mohammad Akhundzada (Helmand). For an early criticism of warlord governance, see Sarah Chayes, 'Afghanistan's Future, Lost in the Shuffle,' *New York Times*, 1 July 2003; for biographical monographs that feature warlords, see Brian G. Williams, *The Last Warlord: The Life and Legend of Dostum, the Afghan Warrior Who Led U.S. Special Forces to Topple the Taliban Regime* (Chicago: Chicago Review Press, 2013); Sandy Gall, *Afghan Napoleon: The Life of Ahmad Shah Massoud* (London: Haus Publishing, 2021); Marcela Grad, *Massoud: An Intimate Portrait of the Legendary Leader* (St. Louis: Webster University Press, 2009); the lone example of a Pashtun commander appears to be on the insurgent side: see Chris Sands and Fazelminallah Qazizai, *Night Letters: The Secret History of Gulbuddin Hekmatyar and the Afghan Islamists Who Changed the World* (London: Hurst, 2019).

3. Linda Robinson, *One Hundred Victories: Special Ops and the Future of American Warfare* (New York: Public Affairs, 2013), 39-44, 59-64.

4. Kandahar Intelligence Fusion Cell (KIFC), 'Taking Stock of COL Abdul Razziq, ABP,' 19 November 2009; 5/2 SBCT, 'Special Assessment: COL Abdul Razziq,' 13 March 2010; Thaddeus Fox Interview, 1LT U.S. Army, 4-2 CAV, 2 February 2021; Green Interview, 22 March 2021; Ghorzang Afridi Interview, Raziq aide, 28 May 2022.

5. Steven Beckman, Jr. Interview, CPT U.S. Army, 8-1 CAV, 23 April 2021; Edwin Den Harder Interview, 1LT U.S. Army, 4-2 CAV, 29 April 2021; Andrew Gregory Interview, 1LT U.S. Army, 4-2 CAV, 13 May 2021; (Redacted), Senior U.S. Government Official 1, 22 June 2021; Jeffery Fritz Interview, CPT U.S. Army, 4-2 CAV, 27 June 2021.

6. Philip Smucker, *Al Qaeda's Great Escape: the Military and the Media on Terror's Trail* (Sterling: Potomac, 2004); Lester Grau and Dodge Billingsley, *Operation Anaconda: America's First Major Battle in Afghanistan* (Lawrence: University of Kansas, 2011); for a popular account, see Sean Naylor, *Not a Good Day to Die: the Untold Story of Operation Anaconda* (New York: Berkley, 2005).

7. No official census has been completed in Afghanistan since an attempt in 1979. The movement of war refugees since then has made reliable figures unobtainable. One UN report counted 60,000 dwellings in Kandahar City and estimated 7.5 people per dwelling for a population of 460,000

(Afghanistan Ministry of Urban Development Affairs, 'State of Afghan Cities 2015,' 11). But in 2009, Canadian BG Jonathan Vance estimated that up to 85% of the province's one million people had relocated to greater Kandahar City for safety (Rosie Di Manno, 'Taking the Fight Back to Kandahar City,' *Toronto Star*, 14 August 2009). The population of Spin Boldak was still more in flux. The Kandahar PRT in 2011 estimated the population of Spin Boldak district at 250,000, including 100,000 internally displaced persons; Richard Simonsen, 'Kandahar PRT, State Dept. Visit Spin Boldak,' *DVIDS*, 26 June 2011; 525 BfSB Operations Summary (OPSUM), 9 September 2011, 10; the most recent estimate of population for Kandahar Province is 1.9 million, with 550,000 in Kandahar City and about 200,000 in Spin Boldak district (UN International Organization of Migration, 'Provincial Overview: Kandahar Province' (2021), 4).

8. Azam Ahmed and Matthieu Aikins, 'America's Monster: How the U.S. Backed Kidnapping, Torture and Murder in Afghanistan,' *New York Times*, 22 May 2024; Matthieu Aikins, 'America's Monster: Who was Abdul Raziq?' *New York Times Magazine*, 22 May 2024.

9. The 'better war' myth that claimed humanitarianism as the goal of a new strategy developed during the Vietnam War; Gregory Daddis, *Withdrawal: Reassessing America's Final Years in Vietnam* (Oxford: Oxford University Press, 2017), xi-xii; Lewis Sorley, *A Better War: The Unexamined Victories and Final Tragedy of America's Last Years in Vietnam* (London: Harcourt and Brace, 1999).

10. FM 3-24: *Counterinsurgency*, 13 May 2014, 1-11.

11. Jacqueline Hazelton, *Bullets Not Ballots: Success in Counterinsurgency Warfare* (Ithaca: Cornell University Press, 2021), 5-6.

12. Brad Davis Interview, CPT U.S. Army, 201 BfSB, 16 September 2022; Anthony Formica Interview, 1LT U.S. Army, 1-5 IN, 25 May 2021; Stephen Grenier Interview, LTC U.S. Army, Special Forces, 11 October 2022; Leslie Payne Interview, Human Terrain System, 16 August 2021; (Redacted), Senior U.S. government official 1, 22 June 2021; (Redacted), Senior U.S. government official 2, 20 December 2021.

13. Stathis Kalyvas, *The Logic of Violence in Civil War* (Cambridge: Cambridge University Press, 2006), 12-13.

14. Barnett Rubin, *The Fragmentation of Afghanistan* (New Haven: Yale University Press, 1995), x, 13-15.

15. May Jeong, 'The U.S. Lost a Key Ally in Southern Afghanistan, But Abdul Raziq Was No Hero,' *The Intercept*, 30 October 2018.

16. Roger Myerson, 'Stabilization Lessons from the British Empire,' *Texas National Security Review* 6, no. 1 (Winter 2022/2023), 35-50; Daron Acemoglu and James A. Robinson, *Why Nations Fail: The Origins of Power, Prosperity, and Poverty* (Crown, 2012).

17. Ralph Waldo Emerson, *English Traits* (Boston: Phillips, Sampson, and Company, 1858), 176.

18. Charles Tilly, 'Warmaking and State making as Organized Crime,' in *Bringing the State Back In* (Cambridge: Cambridge University Press, 1985), 169-191; Max Weber, 'Politics as a Vocation,' in *Weber: Selections in Translation*, (Cambridge: Cambridge University Press, 1978), 212-25.

19. Kimberly Marten, *Warlords: Strong-arm Brokers in Weak States* (Ithaca: Cornell University Press, 2012).

20. Ariel Ahram and Charles King, 'The Warlord as Arbitrageur,' *Theory and Society* 41, no. 2 (March 2012), 169-86, here 172-4.

21. Antonio Giustozzi and Noor Ullah, "'Tribes' and Warlords in Southern Afghanistan, 1980-2005,' Crisis States Working Papers, Series 2, no. 7 (September 2006), 5.

22. Keith Stanski, "So These Folks are Aggressive': An Orientalist Reading of 'Afghan Warlords," *Security Dialogue* 40, no. 1 (February 2009), 74-94, here 75-6, 89; Patrick Porter, *Military Orientalism: Eastern War through Western Eyes* (New York: Columbia University Press, 2009), 29-37.

23. Antonio Giustozzi, *Empires of Mud: War and Warlords in Afghanistan* (New York: Columbia University Press, 2009); Dipali Mukhopadhyay, *Warlords, Strongman Governors, and the State in Afghanistan* (Cambridge: Cambridge University Press, 2014); Romain Malejacq, *Warlord Survival: The Delusion of State Building in Afghanistan* (Ithaca: Cornell University Press, 2019).

24. Raziq's brother and Kandahar Police Chief Tadin Khan Achakzai, Afghan Education Minister Rangina Haimidi, Ambassador and Nangarhar Governor Shahmahmood Miakhel, Kandahar Governor Tooryalai Wesa, and Kandahar City Mayor Roshaan Wolusmal.

25. Studs Terkel, *'The Good War': an Oral History of World War Two* (New York: Penguin, 1986), 42.

26. For outstanding examples of oral histories on Afghanistan, which served as inspirations for research, see Svetlana Alexievich, *Zinky Boys: Soviet Voices from the Afghanistan War* (New York: W.W. Norton, 1992); Lester Grau, ed., *The Bear Went Over the Mountain: Soviet Combat Tactics in Afghanistan* (Washington DC: National Defense University, 1996); Ali Ahmad Jalali and Lester Grau, eds., *The Other Side of the Mountain: Mujahidin Tactics in the Soviet-Afghan War* (Quantico: USMC Press, 1998); David Edwards, *Heroes of the Age: Moral Fault Lines on the Afghan Frontier* (University of California, 1996); Edwards, *Caravan of Martyrs: Sacrifice and Suicide Bombing in Afghanistan* (Berkeley: University of California Press, 2017); Mike Martin, *An Intimate War: An Oral History of the Helmand Conflict, 1978-2012* (Oxford: Oxford University Press, 2014).

27. Matthieu Aikins, 'The Master of Spin Boldak,' *Harper's Magazine*, December 2009; Peter Graff, 'US troops leave border to Afghan boss accused of graft,' *Reuters*, 17 March 2010; Paul Watson, 'Credibility

eludes Kandahar police force,' *Toronto Star*, 20 June 2011; Aikins, 'Our Man in Kandahar,' *The Atlantic*, November 2011; Human Rights Watch, "Today We Shall All Die': Afghanistan's Strongmen and the Legacy of Impunity,' Human Rights Watch, 3 March 2015; Emma Graham-Harrison, 'Afghanistan officials sanctioned murder, torture and rape, says report,' *The Guardian*, 3 March 2015; Tom Bowman, 'He Calmed Kandahar, But at What Cost?' *National Public Radio*, 21 May 2015; Patricia Gossman, 'Will Afghanistan Prosecute Kandahar's Torturer in Chief?' Human Rights Watch, 17 May 2017; Laura Cesaretti and Fazelminallah Qazizai, 'Democracy at any cost: How the West supported an Afghan general who ruled through fear,' *The New Arab*, 22 November 2018; Micah Ables, 'Ally, Bad Guy, or Both? Thoughts on Reconciling American Values and Questionable Partners, Two Years After the Death of Abdul Raziq,' 19 November 2020, West Point Modern War Institute.

28. Richard Drinnon, *Facing West: the Metaphysics of Indian-Hating and Empire Building* (Minneapolis: University of Minnesota Press, 1980), 449-65; Philip Deloria, *Indians in Unexpected Places* (New Haven: Yale University Press, 2004), Chapter 2; Richard Slotkin, *Gunfighter Nation: The Myth of the Frontier in Twentieth-Century America* (Norman: University of Oklahoma Press, 1998); for more on popular evocations of Indian Country in Vietnam, see Gregory Daddis, *Pulp Vietnam: War and Gender in Cold War Men's Adventure Magazines* (Cambridge: Cambridge University Press, 2020), 144, 187.

29. The dilemma Raziq posed is evident in the accounts of participant-observers; Micah Ables, 'Ally, Bad Guy, or Both?'; Carter Malkasian, *The American War in Afghanistan: A History* (Oxford: Oxford University Press, 2021), 292; for civil war typology, see David Armitage, 'Every Great Revolution is a Civil War,' in *Scripting Revolution: A Historical Approach to the Comparative Study of Revolutions*, ed. Keith Baker and Dan Edelstein (Stanford: Stanford University Press, 2015), 57-68; for a debate about morality of civil wars, see Mary Kaldor, *New and Old Wars: Organized Violence in a Global Era* (Stanford: Stanford University Press, 1999); and the rebuttal by Stathis Kalyvas, '"New" and "Old" Civil Wars: a Valid Distinction?' *World Politics*, vol. 54 (Oct. 2001), 99-118.

Chapter 1: Tribe (1747–2010)

1. Robert Johnson, 'Upstream Engagements and Downstream Entanglements: The Assumptions, Opportunities, and Threats of Partnering,' *Small Wars and Insurgencies* 25, no. 3 (2014), 647-68; Johnson, *The Afghan Way of War: How and Why They Fight* (Oxford: Oxford University Press, 2012), 23; Porter, *Military Orientalism*, 6-7.

2. Nivi Manchanda, 'The Imperial Sociology of the 'Tribe' in Afghanistan,' *Millennium: Journal of International Studies* 46, no. 2 (2018), 165-89.

3. Mountstuart Elphinstone, *An Account of the Kingdom of Caubul* (London: Longman, Hurst, Orme, and Brown, 1815), 173-4.

4. B.D. Hopkins, *The Making of Modern Afghanistan* (New York: Palgrave MacMillan, 2008), 17-20; Nivi Manchanda, 'Imperial Sociology,' 173-7; Stanski, "So These Folks are Aggressive," 85-9.

5. Hopkins, *Modern Afghanistan*, 17.

6. Winston Churchill, *The Story of the Malakand Field Force* (London: Thomas Nelson, 1916), 3.

7. James Gant, *One Tribe at a Time* (New York: Black Irish Entertainment, 2014), 22.

8. U.S. Army, *Warrior Ethos Staff Primer* (Ft. Leavenworth: Training and Doctrine Command, 2003).

9. Ann Scott Tyson, *American Spartan: The Promise, the Mission, and the Betrayal of Special Forces Major Jim Gant* (Harper Collins, 2014); a man incapable of defending the honor of his women (*namus*) is known as a cuckold (*daus*), see Edwards, *Heroes of the Age*, 58.

10. Gant, *One Tribe*, pp. 19, 52, 61; David Edwards, "The Perfect Counterinsurgent': Reconsidering the Case of Major Jim Gant,' *Small Wars and Insurgencies* 31, no. 2 (February 2020), 420-44. Gant's misunderstanding only came to light by coincidence. Anthropologist David Edwards happened to have an informant whose family lived in the same Mangwal village where Gant had been.

11. Joseph Collins, 'The Rise and Fall of Major Jim Gant,' *War on the Rocks*, 14 April 2014; 'Top Green Beret Officer Forced to Resign Over Affair with WaPo Reporter,' *ABC News*, 24 June 2014; Mark Thompson, 'The Fall of the Green Berets' Lawrence of Afghanistan,' *Time Magazine*, 25 June 2014; Ann Scott Tyson and Jim Gant, 'Afghanistan, in person: From tribal ties to pleas for help,' *Christian Science Monitor*, 23 August 2021.

12. Dirk Ringgenberg Interview, CPT U.S. Army, 2-503 IN, 16 March 2022.

13. Sebastian Junger, *Tribe: On Homecoming and Belonging* (New York: Hachette, 2016).

14. *Life of Abdur Rahman*, ed. Sultan Mahomed Khan (London: John Murray, 1900) 2: 215-217; Olaf Caroe, *The Pathans 550 BC - AD 1957* (Oxford: Oxford University Press, 1958), 255; Vartan Gregorian, *The Emergence of Modern Afghanistan: Politics of Reform and Modernization, 1880- 1946* (Stanford: Stanford University Press, 1969), 46; Louis Dupree, *Afghanistan* (Princeton: Princeton University Press, 1973), 332-334; Amin Tarzi, 'Tarikh-i Ahmad Shah: The First History of 'Afghanistan," in *Afghan History Through Afghan Eyes* (Oxford: Oxford University Press, 2015).

15. Thomas Barfield, *Afghanistan: A Cultural and Political History* (Princeton: Princeton University Press, 2010), 53-6; Christine Noelle, *State and Tribe*

in *Nineteenth-Century Afghanistan: The Reign of Amir Dost Muhammad Khan (1826-1863)* (New York: Routledge, 1997), 136; Akbar S. Ahmed, *Pukhtun Economy and Society: Traditional Structure and Economic Development in a Tribal Society* (New York: Routledge, 1980), 117-18; Rubin, *Fragmentation*, 28.

16. Noelle, *State and Tribe*, xvii; Jonathan Lee, *Afghanistan: a History from 1260 to the Present* (London: Reaktion Books, 2019), 113-14.

17. Ludwig Adamec, ed., *Historical and Political Gazetteer of Afghanistan* 5: Kandahar and South-Central Afghanistan (Graz: Akademische Druck, 1980), 18.

18. (Redacted) Interview, Linguist 2, 21 March 2022.

19. Durrani tribes split into two branches: the more privileged Zirak and the more marginalized Panjpai. Within the Zirak group, the Popalzai and Barakzai tribes treat the Achakzai as poor relatives, but connections to these dominant clans conferred a historic benefit to the Achakzai compared to the Noorzai.

20. Hopkins, *Modern Afghanistan*, 92-93; Noelle, *State and Tribe*, 129, 230-2; Olivier Roy, *Islam and Resistance in Afghanistan* (Cambridge University Press, 1985), 12-15; Thomas Barfield, 'Afghanistan is Not the Balkans: Ethnicity and its Political Consequences from a Central Asian Perspective,' *Central Eurasian Studies Review* 4, no. 1 (Winter 2005), 2-8, here 5.

21. Rashid, *Descent into Chaos: The United States and the Failure of Nation Building in Pakistan, Afghanistan, and Central Asia* (New York: Viking, 2008), 7-8; for 'military labor market,' see Hopkins, *Modern Afghanistan*, 70-75. For more on Durrani, see Elphinstone, *Caubul* (1815), 553-5, 557; Lee, *Afghanistan*, 118-28; Roy, *Islam and Resistance*, 12- 13; Muhammad Hayat Khan, *Afghanistan and its Inhabitants* (Delhi: Indian Public Press, 1874), 57-64; Hopkins, *Modern Afghanistan*, 94-5; Caroe, *Pathans*, 259; Gregorian, *Modern Afghanistan*, 49.

22. Abraham Safi Interview, Linguist, 10 February 2022.

23. Akbar Wali Interview, Linguist and contractor, 3 July 2021; Roshaan Wolusmal Interview, Mayor of Kandahar City, 10 July 2021; Safi Interview, 10 February 2022; Ahmad Shah Malgarai Interview, Linguist, 11 June 2022; (Redacted) Interview, Linguist 5, 20 September 2022

24. Malkasian, *American War*, 9; Edwards, *Caravan of Martyrs*, 142; Ahmed, *Pukhtun Economy*, 181.

25. Fazel Interview, 26 March 2021; Roy, *Islam and Resistance*, 23; Elphinstone, *Caubul*, 295.

26. Beckman, Jr. Interview, 23 April 2021; Greg Mortenson and David Oliver Relin, *Three Cups of Tea: One Man's Mission to Fight Terrorism and Build Nations...One School at a Time* (New York: Penguin, 2006); Jon Krakauer, *Three Cups of Deceit* (New York: Anchor, 2011).

27. Gregorian, *Modern Afghanistan*, 41; Dupree, *Afghanistan*, 126; Ahmed, *Pukhtun Economy*, 3; Rubin, *Fragmentation*, 23; Safi Interview, 10 February 2022; (Redacted) Interview, Linguist 5, 20 September 2022.

28. Edwards, *Heroes*, 48; Ahmed, *Pukhtun Economy*, 182.

29. Shahmahmood Miakhel Interview, Governor of Nangarhar Province, 28 June 2021; Roy, *Islam and Resistance*, 13; Ahmed, *Pukhtun Economy*, 194-5; Edwards, *Heroes*, 241, fn. 9.

30. Elphinstone, *Caubul*, 299.

31. Elphinstone, *Caubul*, 422.

32. Sarah Chayes, *The Punishment of Virtue: Inside Afghanistan After the Taliban* (New York: Penguin, 2006), 33.

33. James Edwards Interview, COL U.S. Army, 525 BfSB, 25 March 2021; Den Harder Interview, 29 April 2021; (Redacted) Interview, COL U.S. Army, 9 July 2021.

34. Adamec, *Gazetteer*, pp. 21, 366-7; William Campbell, 'Shorawak Valley and the Toba Plateau,' *Proceedings of the Royal Geographical Society and Monthly Record of Geography* 2, no. 10 (Oct. 1880), 620-6, here 624-5.

35. Another major group was led by Hajji Karim Khan. (M/4-2 CAV Intelligence, 'M Troop 4/2 Personalities,' 6; M/4-2 CAV Intelligence, 'Recent Interactions with GIRoA,' 27 September 2010.) The founder of the lineage, Achak Khan, had two sons: Gujan and Badin, whose descendants now number in the hundreds of thousands. Raziq's Adozai clan descended from the Gujanzai (Adamec, *Gazetteer*, 18.)

36. The Noorzai AHP leader was Lal Jan; the Achakzai Taliban leader was Abdur Razzaq Akhundzada; Kirby Interview, 19 March 2021; Fox Interview #2, 14 August 2021; US Embassy (Kabul) cable, 'Spin Boldak Powerbroker Encourages Modernization of Customs Operations,' Wikileaks, 3 February 2010.

Chapter 2: Soviet War (1976–1994)

1. 5/2 SBCT, 'Special Assessment,' 2; Afridi Interview, 28 May 2022; Tadin Khan Achakzai Interview, Kandahar Chief of Police, 14 August 2024.

2. Gretchen Peters, 'Traffickers and Truckers: Illicit Afghan and Pakistani Power Structures with a Shadowy but Influential Role,' in *Impunity: Countering Illicit Power in War and Transition*, eds. Michelle Hughes and Michael Miklaucic (Washington: National Defense University Press, 2017), 127; Loretta Napoleoni, *Terror Incorporated* (New York: Penguin, 2003), 119-20.

3. (Redacted) Interview, Linguist 2, 21 March 2022.

4. Larry Goodson, *Afghanistan's Endless War: State Failure, Regional Politics, and the Rise of the Taliban* (Seattle: University of Washington, 2001), 92-5; Rodric Braithwaite, *Afghantsy: the Russians in Afghanistan,*

1979-89 (Oxford, 2011), 331; for initial purge, see Mullah Abdul Salam Zaeef, *My Life with the Taliban* (London: Hurst, 2011), 175; Louis Dupree, 'Afghanistan in 1983: And Still No Solution,' *Asian Survey* 24, no 2 (February 1984), 229-39, for 'rubbleization,' 234.

5. Aikins, 'America's Monster.' (Redacted) Achakzai tribe member. 25 July 2025.

6. Tadin Khan Interview, 14 August 2024. (Redacted) Achakzai tribe member. 25 July 2025.

7. Giustozzi and Ullah, 'Tribes' and Warlords,' pp. 7-9; M/4-2 CAV Intelligence, 'Notes from Recent Interactions with GIRoA,' 27 September 2010.

8. Ronald Savage Interview, USAID Spin Boldak, 15 July 2022; Vanda Felbab-Brown, *Shooting Up: Counterinsurgency and the War on Drugs* (Washington DC: Brookings, 2010), 116-17, 145; for the Soviet war in Afghanistan as a 'kiriz war,' see: Alexievich, *Zinky Boys*, 111; Lester Grau and Ali Ahmad Jalali, 'Underground Combat: Stereophonic Blasting, Tunnel Rats and the Soviet-Afghan War,' *Engineer* 28 (1998), 20-3.

9. Ikramul Haq, 'Pak-Afghan Drug Trade in Historical Perspective,' *Asian Survey* 36, no. 10 (October 1996), 945-63; U.S. Department of State, 'International Narcotics Control Strategy Report,' (Washington DC, 1984), 4.

10. Kirby Interview, 19 March 2021; Miakhel Interview, 28 June 2021; Jeff Harmon, 'Toe to toe with Russians in Kandahar's holy war,' *Sunday Times*, 11 August 1985; Mark Urban, *War in Afghanistan* (London: MacMillan Press, 1990), 140, 241; Gilles Dorronsoro, *Revolution Unending: Afghanistan, 1979 to the Present* (London: Hurst, 2005), 187; Anatol Lieven, 'Mujahidin fail to subdue the pirate turncoat,' *The Times*, 26 January 1988; Giustozzi, *Empires of Mud*, 62-4.

11. Rubin, *Fragmentation*, 159.

12. Kirby Interview, 19 March 2021.

Chapter 3: Civil War (1994–2001)

1. Tadin Khan Interview, 14 August 2024; Afridi Interview, 28 May 2022; Fazel Interview, 26 March 2021.

2. Malkasian, *American War*, 37-38; Rashid, *Taliban*, 25; U.S. Embassy (Islamabad) Cable, 'Finally a Talkative Talib,' 20 February 1995, 6, in *September 11th Sourcebooks* VII: The Taliban File, ed. Sajit Gandhi, National Security Archive, George Washington University.

3. For more on the origins of the Taliban movement, see Zaeef, *Life with the Taliban*, 58-69; U.S. Consulate (Peshawar) Cable, 'New Fighting and New Forces in Kandahar,' 3 November 1994; U.S. Embassy (Islamabad) Cable, 'The Taliban – Who Knows What the Movement Means?' 28 November 1994, in *September 11th Sourcebooks*; Sam Freakley Interview, CPT U.S. Army, 1-32 IN, 3 November 2022; Freakley Interview #2, 15 November 2022.

4. U.S. Consulate (Peshawar) Cable, 'New Fighting'; U.S. Embassy (Islamabad) Cable, 'The Taliban – Who Knows'; U.S. Embassy (Islamabad) Cable, 'Believe Pakistan is Backing Taliban,' 6 December 1994.

5. Barnett Rubin, *Afghanistan from the Cold War to the Global War on Terror* (Oxford: Oxford University Press, 2013), 58-9.

6. Zaeef, *Life with the Taliban*, 154-5.

7. Mullah Naqib of the Alokozai tribe; see U.S. Consulate, 'New Fighting'; U.S. Embassy, 'Who Knows'; U.S. Embassy, 'Talkative Talib.'

8. The two commanders were Amir Lalai and Ustad Halim.

9. Rashid, *Taliban*, 27-29; 5/2 SBCT, 'Special Assessment,' 2.

10. U.S. Embassy, 'Taliban – Who Knows,' 10.

11. Afridi Interview, 31 May 2022.

12. Tadin Khan Interview, 14 August 2024; 5/2 SBCT, 'Special Assessment,' 2; Michael Hastings, *The Operators: The Wild and Terrifying Inside Story of America's War in Afghanistan* (New York: Blue Rider Press, 2012), 362.

Chapter 4: Militias (2001–5)

1. Matthieu Aikins, 'Contracting the Commanders: Transition and the Political Economy of Afghanistan's Private Security Industry,' NYU Center on International Cooperation, October 2012, 8.

2. Zaeef, *Life with the Taliban*, 161-2.

3. Rajiv Chandrasekaran and John Pomfret, 'Aided by US, Pashtun Militias Move Closer to Kandahar,' *Washington Post*, 27 November 2001; Andy Soloman, 'Looters Raid Relief Stores in Afghan Border Town,' *Reuters*, 27 November 2001; Sean M. Maloney, *Enduring the Freedom: A Rogue Historian in Afghanistan* (Sterling: Potomac, 2005), pp. 202-4, 290; Ali Ahmad Jalali, *A Military History of Afghanistan: From the Great Game to the Global War on Terror* (Lawrence: University of Kansas Press, 2017), 478-9.

4. 5/2 SBCT, 'Special Assessment.'

5. (Redacted), Linguist 2, 21 March 2022; Sean Maloney, *Confronting the Chaos: a Rogue Military Historian Returns to Afghanistan* (Washington DC: Naval Institute Press, 2009), 149; US Embassy (Kabul) cable, 'Spin Boldak Powerbroker Encourages Modernization of Customs Operations,' Wikileaks, 3 February 2010.

6. Sarah Chayes Interview, ISAF staff, 23 June 2021.

7. 5/2 SBCT, 'Special Assessment.'

8. Aikins, 'Master of Spin Boldak.'

9. Saqib Interview, 8 August 2022; (Redacted) Interview, Linguist 2, 21 March 2022; Malgarai Interview, 11 June 2022; Ian Hope Interview, LTC Canadian Army, TF Orion, 26 July 2021.

10. Wali Interview, 3 July 2021.
11. Fazel Interview, 26 March 2021.
12. Green Interview, 22 March 2021.
13. Kirby Interview, 19 March 2021; Chayes Interview, 23 June 2021.
14. Ahram and King, 'Warlord as Arbitrageur.'
15. Edwards Interview, 25 March 2021.
16. U.S. Embassy (Kabul) cable, 'Powerbroker and Governance Issues in Spin Boldak,' Wikileaks, 7 February 2010; U.S. Embassy (Kabul) cable, 'Kandahar: Corruption Reforms by the Master of Spin?,' Wikileaks, 17 February 2010.

Chapter 5: Wild West (2005–6)

1. Between 1967 and 1970, the Army reduced 'H&I' missions from about half of all artillery ammunition expended to a negligible percentage. The driving reason for commanders, rather than humanitarian concerns, was to save money on ammunition. See John M. Hawkins, 'The Costs of Artillery: Eliminating Harassment and Interdiction Fire During the Vietnam War,' *Journal of Military History* 70 (January 2006), 91-122. The doctrine and training of U.S. artillery between the Vietnam War and the GWoT stipulated observed fires only. During the invasion of Iraq in 2003, unobserved fires were prohibited unless for 'immediate defense of friendly forces.' Approval authority for fires in Afghanistan rested with ground force commanders. In August 2010, GEN David Petraeus issued a directive that stated 'Prior to the use of fires, the commander approving the strike must determine that no civilians are present. If unable to assess the risk of civilian presence, fires are prohibited,' though the following passage qualified that the directive did not prevent commanders from protecting their own or Afghan government forces, see 'Gen. Petraeus updates guidance on use of force,' 4 August 2010, CENTCOM; for Iraq, see Thomas W. Smith, 'Protecting Civilians…or Soldiers? Humanitarian Law and the Economy of Risk in Iraq,' *International Studies Perspectives* 9 (2008), 144-64; for an international comparison of doctrine, see Janine Fetchik and Matt Montazolli, 'Unobserved Fires and the Law of Armed Conflict,' Lieber Institute, West Point.
2. Bertrand Ges Interview, LTC U.S. Army, 3-319 FA, 2 March 2022.
3. Slade Lerch Interview, MAJ Canadian Army, 3-319 FA Liaison, 14 March 2022.
4. Ges Interview, 2 March 2022.
5. JP 3-24: *Counterinsurgency*, V-8 - V-9. Many distinct institutions arose to support partnership: Task Force Phoenix, a training brigade from the 10th Mountain Division, was developed in 2002 when army leaders realized there were not enough US Special Forces to train army and police forces

across Afghanistan. By July 2003, the official mandate for training had shifted from JSOC to TF Phoenix, which created and oversaw embedded training teams (ETT), which after the Iraq invasion were often staffed by the National Guard rather than active-duty units. Non-U.S. NATO trainers organized as Operational Mentoring and Liaison Teams (OMLT). More interest in partnership during the 2009-2012 surge led to more intensive but smaller scale projects, such as Human Terrain Teams and AfPak Hands. The sustained use of SFAT in Afghanistan gave rise to the first Security Forces Assistance Brigades (SFAB) by 2018; see *Eyewitness to War, Vol. III: US Army Advisors in Afghanistan*, ed. Michael Brooks Ft. Leavenworth: Combat Studies Institute Press, 2010, 50-1; *Coalition Challenges*, eds. Mattox and Grenier, 52-3; Grenier Interview, 11 October 2022.

6. *Eyewitness to War*, 324.

7. Dirk Ringgenberg Interview #2, 12 April 2022; (Redacted) Interview, U.S. Special Forces Officer, 15 February 2022.

8. Ges Interview, 2 March 2022.

9. Paul Thomas, 'Ambush in Gumbad Valley,' *Infantry Magazine*, January-February 2008, 27-31.

10. Eric Schmitt, 'Army Examining an Account of Abuse of 2 Dead Taliban,' *New York Times*, 20 October 2005; James Sturke, 'US soldiers 'desecrated Taliban bodies,'' *The Guardian*, 20 October 2005.

11. *Enduring Voices, Oral Histories of the U.S. Army in Afghanistan 2003-2005*, ed. Christopher N. Koontz (Washington DC: Center for Military History, 2008), 76-7.

12. Ges Interview, 2 March 2022; 'No US Charges over Afghan Bodies,' *BBC*, 26 November 2005.

13. *Eyewitness to War*, 313-14.

14. Ges Interview, 2 March 2022; Jean-Marc Tanguy, *Les Scorpions de Spin Boldak* (Paris: Nimrod, 2013), 34-6; 'Direct Fire Spin Buldak,' RC South, Wikileaks, 15 June 2006.

15. Norland, 'Kandahar: A Governor's Intentions,' U.S. Embassy (Kabul), Wikileaks, 24 January 2006.

Chapter 6: Massacre (2006)

1. Jonathan Steele, *Ghosts of Afghanistan: the Haunted Battlefield* (Berkeley: Counterpoint Press, 2011), 14.

2. Geoff Ziezulewicz and Jon Simkins, 'Here be giants – outlandish tales of the military and the Afghan colossi,' *Military Times*, 31 October 2002.

3. Mountstuart Elphinstone, *An Account of the Kingdom of Caubul* (London: Richard Bentley, 3d ed. 1842), 292. On the prevalence of ghost stories in

Afghanistan: 'Sunnis and Shi'as alike believed in ghosts, demons, fairies, *dajjal* (Anti-Christ), fortunetellers, and particularly shrines, numerous all over Afghanistan.' Hasan Kakar, *Government and Society in Afghanistan: The Reign of Amir 'Abd Al-Rahman Khan* (Austin: University of Texas Press, 1979), 148; 'Khan Jahan Lodi is said to have patronized this first work [of Afghan history] on the genesis and past glory of the Afghans after an Irani at the Mughal court made derogatory statements about the origins of the Afghans, claiming they were descended not from Adam but from fire-spirits (*jinn*).' Nile Green, 'Tribe, Diaspora, and Sainthood in Afghan History,' *Journal of Asian Studies* 67, no. 1 (2008), 171-211, here 185).

4. Edwards, *Caravan of Martyrs*, 3.

5. 'Afghan troops kill suspected Taliban rebels at Pakistan border,' *New York Times*, 22 March 2006; '15 Taliban dead in clash with Afghan troops,' *CBC News*, 22 March 2006; Ron Synovitz, 'Afghanistan: Reports Claim 'War on Terror' Used to Hide Blood-Feud Killings,' *Radio Free Europe*, 31 March 2006.

6. Lalai came from the Hamidzai clan of the Achakzai tribe, whereas Raziq came from the Adozai; these factions often feuded over resources and positions of power.

7. Matthieu Aikins, 'Our Man in Kandahar,' *The Atlantic*, November 2011.

8. Malgarai Interview, 11 June 2022; (Redacted) Interview, Linguist 3, 16 April 2022; Green Interview, 22 March 2021.

9. (Redacted), Linguist 3, correspondence with author, 25 March 2023; 'Killings of 15 Afghans to Be Probed,' *Los Angeles Times*, 23 March 2006.

10. Carl Forsberg, 'Counterinsurgency in Kandahar: Evaluating the 2010 Hamkari Campaign,' Institute for the Study of War, 2010, 48-9.

11. Aikins, 'Our Man in Kandahar.'

12. Aikins, 'Master of Spin Boldak.'

Chapter 7: Canadians in Kandahar (2006–9)

1. Ges Interview, 2 March 2022.

2. Luke Fisher, 'Airborne's Hazing Exposed,' *MacLean's*, 30 January 1995; David Bercuson, *Significant Incident: Canada's Army, the Airborne and the Murder in Somalia* (Toronto: McClelland and Stewart, 1996); Jane O'Hara, 'Rape in the military,' *Maclean's*, 25 May 1998; Grant Dawson, *'Here is Hell': Canada's Engagement in Somalia* (Vancouver: University of British Columbia, 2007); see also Howard Coombs, 'The Evolution of a New Canadian Way of War,' in Mattox and Grenier, *Coalition Challenges*, 65-6; J.L. Granatstein, *Who Killed the Canadian Military?* (Toronto: Harper Collins, 2004).

3. Robert Ritchie Interview, MAJ Canadian Army, Kandahar PRT, OMLT, 2 September 2021.

4. Hope Interview, 26 July 2021.

5. Giustozzi, *Taliban at War*, 44, 53.

6. William Fletcher Interview, MAJ Canadian Army, TF Orion, 20 August 2021; Carl Forsberg, 'Afghanistan report 3, The Taliban's Campaign for Kandahar,' *Institute for the Study of War* (2009), 22-6.

7. Hope Interview, 26 July 2021.

8. Chris Wattie, *Contact Charlie: The Canadian Army, the Taliban, and the Battle for Afghanistan* (Toronto: Key Porter Books, 2010), 52.

9. (Redacted) Interview, Senior NATO government official, 14 April 2021; 'Canadian diplomat killed in Afghan blast,' *NBC News*, 15 January 2006; Graeme Smith, 'A Country Where Blood is Everything,' *Globe and Mail*, 11 December 2006; Murray Brewster, 'Canadian diplomat Glyn Berry's Afghanistan murder unsolved after 10 years,' *Toronto Star*, 15 January 2016; 'Taliban attacks kill at least 24 in Afghanistan,' *CBC News*, 16 January 2006.

10. Wattie, *Contact Charlie*, pp. 40, 85.

11. Antonio Giustozzi, *Decoding the New Taliban: Insights from the Afghan Field* (London: Hurst, 2009), 138-139; Malkasian, *War in Afghanistan*, 142-4; Wattie, *Contact Charlie*, 46; Forsberg, 'Campaign for Kandahar,' 24.

12. Fletcher Interview, 20 August 2021.

13. Neumann, 'PRT/Kandahar – Dealing with the Taliban 'Spring Offensive,'' U.S. Embassy (Kabul), Wikileaks, 24 April 2006.

14. Hope Interview, 26 July 2021; Wattie, *Contact Charlie*, 265-6.

15. Graeme Smith, 'Inspiring Tale of Triumph over Taliban not all it Seems,' *Globe and Mail*, 23 September 2006; Malkasian, *American War*, 147.

16. Bernd Horn, *No Lack of Courage: Operation Medusa, Afghanistan* (Toronto: Dundurn Press, 2010); 46, 114-15; Malkasian, *American War*, 151-2.

17. The villages in question were Siah Choy, Pashmul, and Zangabad; Norland, 'PRT Kandahar/Helmand: Security Concerns Take Center Stage,' US Embassy (Kabul), Wikileaks, 16 October 2006.

18. Graeme Smith, 'The Afghan Mission, Knowing the Enemy: The Taliban,' *Globe and Mail*, 13 January 2007.

19. Taimoor Shah and Carlotta Gall, 'Key Taliban Leader is Killed in Joint Operation,' *New York Times*, 14 May 2007.

20. 'Special Committee on the Canadian Mission in Afghanistan,' 40th Canadian Parliament, 2nd session, no. 15, 18 November 2009.

21. 'Afghan governor's rights abuses known in '07,' *CBC News*, 12 April 2010.

22. James McCarten, 'Bernier's Afghan Bombshell,' *Toronto Star*, 14 April 2008; 'Bernier clarifies comments over Kandahar's governor,' *CBC News*, 14 April 2008.

23. Forsberg, 'Counterinsurgency in Kandahar,' 44; Joshua Partlow, 'Kandahar governor faced allegation in job with contractor, *Washington Post*, 26 May 2010.

24. Forsberg, 'Counterinsurgency in Kandahar,' 43-4; Steve Rennie, 'Over veggies and cherry juice, life changed for new Kandahar governor,' *Canadian Press*, 19 December 2008.

25. Polio has since returned to the Afghan-Pakistan borderlands. The first confirmed cases in Kandahar appeared in 2018 after Taliban-controlled districts refused the vaccine.

26. Wesa Interview, 29 July 2021; Wesa Interview #2, 5 August 2021.

27. Ritchie Interview, 2 September 2021.

28. Ritchie Interview, 2 September 2021; Matthew Aggus Interview, CPT Canadian Army, Kandahar OMLT, 12 April 2022.

29. Green Interview, 22 March 2021; Wesa Interview, 29 July 2021; (Redacted) Interview, Linguist 2, 21 and 28 March 2022.

30. Wesa Interview #2, 5 August 2021.

31. Omar el Akkad and Graeme Smith, 'Mullah's death leaves Kandahar exposed,' *Globe and Mail*, 13 October 2007; for the Karzai family's role in the tribal politics of Kandahar, see US Embassy (Kabul) cable, 'Kandahar Politics Complicate U.S. Objectives in Afghanistan,' 6 December 2009.

32. Carl Forsberg, 'Campaign for Kandahar,' 37-45; 'Suicide bombers kill 6 police officers in Kandahar,' *New York Times*, 7 September 2008; 'Afghan bombers attack police force,' *Al Jazeera*, 7 September 2008; Scott Deveau, 'Saskatchewan soldier killed in IED Blast,' *Windsor Star*, 6 September 2008; for a similar attack the next year, see 'Twin Blasts Hit Police HQ in Kandahar,' *Voice of America*, 1 November 2009.

33. James Flannery Interview, 1LT U.S. Army, 1-187 IN, 18 March 2022; Adamec, *Gazetteer*, 504.

34. 'Canadian Forces in Afghanistan: Report of the Standing Committee on National Defence,' 39th Canadian Parliament, 1st session (June 2007), 57; Aggus Interview, 12 April 2022.

Chapter 8: Arrival of the Surge (2009)

1. Renanah Miles, 'Russia: Friend or Foe on Afghanistan?' in Mattox and Grenier, *Coalition Challenges*, 278-280.

2. James Lowe Interview, LTC U.S. Army, 3-7 FA, 19 April 2021; Ali Mohammad Sabawoon, 'The Gates of Friendship: How Afghans cross the Afghan-Pakistani border,' *Afghan Analysts Network*, 28 January 2020.

3. US Embassy (Kabul) cable, 'Bedlam and Corruption Permeate Customs Process at Spin Boldak,' Wikileaks, 7 February 2010.

4. W. Clark Interview, 26 March 2021; Fritz Interview, 27 June 2021; US Embassy (Kabul) cable, 'Spin Boldak Powerbroker Encourages Modernization of Customs Operations,' Wikileaks, 3 February 2010.

5. Jordan Bass Interview, 1LT U.S. Army, 4-2 CAV, 16 April 2021; Fritz Interview, 27 June 2021; at the end of the following year, in December 2010, the local U.S. unit spent $8.1 of CERP funds for another highway improvement project. 525 BfSB, OPSUM, 9 September 2011, 12.

6. J. Alexander Thier, ed. *The Future of Afghanistan* (US Institute of Peace, 2009), 11; Guillermo Cervera, '10 Years of Afghan War: How the Taliban Go On,' *Newsweek*, 2 October 2011; (Redacted) Interview, Linguist 5, 20 September 2022.

7. Lowe Interview, 19 April 2021; Fox Interview #2, 14 August 2021.

8. Matthew Dickerson, 'Treebeard,' in Michael Drout, ed., *J.R.R. Tolkien Encyclopedia: Scholarship and Critical Assessment* (New York: Taylor and Francis, 2007), 678.

9. Eric Shinseki, 'The Army Transformation: A Historic Opportunity,' *Army Magazine*, October 2000, 23; Alan Vick et. al., *The Stryker Brigade Combat Team: Rethinking Strategic Responsiveness and Assessing Deployment Options* (RAND, 2002), 4-8.

10. Billy Counts Interview, CSM U.S. Army, 503 MP, 7 September 2022; Hymel, *Strykers in Afghanistan*, 1; see also Mark Reardon and Jeffrey A. Charleston, *From Transformation to Combat: The First Stryker Brigade at War* (Washington DC: Center for Military History, 2007), 19.

11. Patrick Kohler Interview, 1LT U.S. Army, 8-1 CAV, 19 May 2021; Fox Interview #2, 14 August 2021.

12. W. Clark Interview, 26 March 2021; Donald Rumsfeld, *Known and Unknown: A Memoir* (New York: Penguin, 2011).

13. The incremental surges of U.S. troops in Afghanistan: December 2007, 25,000 troops; May 2009, 50,000 troops; December 2009, 67,000 troops; August 2010; 100,000 troops, see 'A timeline of the US military presence in Afghanistan,' *AP News*, 8 September 2019.

14. David M. Blum and J. Edward Conway, eds., *Counterterrorism and Threat Finance Analysis During Wartime* (Lanham: Lexington Books, 2015), 130.

15. Aikins, 'Master of Spin Boldak.'

16. Blum and Conway, *Finance Analysis*, 131; in Helmand, the Governor had been Sher Mohammad Akhundzada; in Uruzgan, Jan Mohammad Khan was removed from his post.

17. Harry D. Tunnell IV, 'Developing a Unit Language Capability for War,' *Joint Forces Quarterly*, no. 51 (2008), 114-16.

18. W. Clark Interview, 26 March 2021; Erik Aadland Interview, CPT U.S. Army, 8-1 CAV, 4 May 2021; (Redacted) Interview, CPT U.S. Army 3, 7 July 2022.

19. Kirby Interview, 19 March 2021; W. Clark Interview, 26 March 2021.

20. Kirby Interview, 19 March 2021; Kohler Interview, 19 May 2021; US Embassy (Kabul) cable, 'Spin Boldak: a Stability and Security Balancing Act,' Wikileaks, 17 December 2009.

21. Kohler Interview, 19 May 2021; U.S. Embassy, 'Spin Boldak: Stability and Security.'

22. Johnson, *Afghan Way of War*, 269; for shift in tactics in 2004, and Arab advisers, see Sami Yousafzai, 'The Taliban's Oral History of the Afghanistan War,' *Newsweek*, 25 September 2009; for suicide attackers as mentally challenged or psychologically traumatized, see James Fergusson, *Taliban: the Unknown Enemy* (New York: Hachette, 2011), 140; for evidence that Mullah Omar only allowed Pakistanis rather than Afghans for use as suicide bombers, see Forsberg, 'Campaign for Kandahar,' 24.

23. (Redacted) Interview, Senior NATO government official, 14 April 2021; Malgarai Interview, 11 June 2022.

24. Anna Maria Cardinalli, 'Pashtun Sexuality,' HTT AF-6 Research Update and Findings, 2009; Craig Smith, 'Kandahar Journal: Shh, It's an Open Secret: Warlords and Pedophilia,' *New York Times*, 21 February 2002; Ernesto Londono, 'Afghanistan sees rise in 'dancing boys' exploitation,' *Washington Post*, 4 April 2012.

25. (Redacted) Interview, CPT U.S. Army 3, 7 July 2022; Joseph Goldstein, 'U.S. soldiers told to ignore sexual abuse of boys by Afghan allies,' *New York Times*, 21 September 2015.

26. U.S. State Department, Country Report on Human Rights Practices, Afghanistan, 2010, 47.

27. Najibullah Quraishi, *The Dancing Boys of Afghanistan*, documentary film (2010).

28. Maura Reynolds, 'Kandahar's Lightly Veiled Homosexual Habits,' *Los Angeles Times*, 3 April 2002; Ali Abdi, 'The Afghan *Bachah* and its Discontents: An Introductory History,' *Iranian Studies* 56, no. 1 (January 2023), 161-80.

29. Thomas H. Johnson and Matthew C. DuPee, 'Analysing the new Taliban Code of Conduct (*Layeha*): an assessment of changing perspectives and strategies of the Afghan Taliban,' *Central Asian Survey* 31, no. 1 (March 2012), 77-91, here 82.

30. Rod Nordland, 'Afghans Plan to Stop Recruiting Children as Police,' *New York Times*, 30 January 2011.

31. Beckman, Sr. Interview, 12 May 2021; David Leydet Interview, 1LT U.S. Army, 8-1 CAV, 28 May 2021; (Redacted) Interview, CPT U.S. Army 3, 7 July 2022; David Pugliese, "Man Love Thursday' Returns,' *Ottawa Citizen*, 6 October 2008; Christina Lamb, 'Afghan police: all's fair in love and war,' *The Times*, 25 July 2010.

32. Hope Interview, 26 July 2021; (Redacted) Interview, Senior NATO government official, 14 April 2021; Kandahar would have been more like The Sopranos if Tony (Ahmed Wali Karzai) had been killed off in an early season and Christopher (Raziq), had to take on mafia operations beyond his capacity.

Chapter 9: Airstrike (2009)

1. 5/2 SBCT, 'Friendly Action, Cache Found/Cleared,' RC South, Wikileaks, 10 November 2009.

2. NATO officials in the summer of 2007 posited that Raziq 'controls large-scale narcotics trafficking' on behalf of regional power brokers such as Ahmed Wali Karzai (Raziq's patron), against Arif Khan Noorzai (Raziq's rival). U.S. Embassy (Kabul) cable, 'PRT Kandahar: Six Month Assessment,' Wikileaks, 25 July 2007.

3. Aadland Interview, 4 May 2021.

4. 5/2 SBCT, 'Friendly Action.'

5. Aadland Interview, 4 May 2021; Kohler Interview, 19 May 2021.

6. 5/2 SBCT, 'Friendly Action.'

7. Fazel Interview, 26 March 2021; W. Clark Interview, 26 March 2021; W. Clark Interview #2, 17 May 2021.

8. Kirby Interview, 19 March 2021; W. Clark Interview, 26 March 2021.

9. COL Sharif, in Raziq's chain of command as deputy commander of the 3rd ABP Zone, 'credited Blackwater training for the detailed list of seizures' obtained from Pakistani infiltrators in Spin Boldak, see U.S. Embassy (Kabul) cable, 'Pakistanis at Kandahar Border Flag Meeting - The Quetta Shura is a Fabrication,' Wikileaks, 7 October 2009.

10. Sean Duffy, 'Shell Game: The U.S.-Afghan Opium Relationship,' PhD diss., University of Arizona, 2011, 80-2; James T. Bradford, *Poppies, Politics, and Power: Afghanistan and the Global History of Drugs and Diplomacy* (Ithaca: Cornell University Press, 2019), 68-9, 74; Nick Cullather, 'Damming Afghanistan: Modernization in a Buffer State,' *Journal of American History* 89, no. 2 (Sep. 2002), 512-537, here 523-4.

11. Sharif Gemie and Brian Ireland, *The Hippie Trail: A History, 1957-1978* (Manchester: Manchester University Press, 2017).

12. Scott DuPrez, *One Night's Shelter: The Autobiography of an American Buddhist Monk* (Sri Lanka, 1985), 77-83; Peter Levi, *The Light Garden of the Angel King: Journeys in Afghanistan* (London: Eland, 2013), 15, 107.

13. Nicholas Schou, *Orange Sunshine: The Brotherhood of Eternal Love* (New York: St. Martin's, 2010), 88-89; R.C. Clarke, *Hashish!* (New York: Red Eye Press, 1998), 137.

14. Peter Maguire and Mike Ritter, *Thai Stick: Surfers, Scammers, and the Untold Story of the Marijuana Trade* (New York: Columbia University Press, 2014), 18-19, 26, 29; Bradford, *Poppies, Politics*, 118-9, 155-60, 197-8; Cullather, 'Damming Afghanistan,' 535-6.

15. David Mansfield, *A State Built on Sand: How Opium Undermined Afghanistan* (Oxford: Oxford University Press, 2016), 107-8.

16. Felbab-Brown, *Shooting Up*, 126; Jonathan Goodhand, 'Frontiers and Wars: the Opium Economy in Afghanistan,' *Journal of Agrarian Change* 5, no. 2 (April 2005), 191-216, here 199, 203; Rashid, *Taliban*, 118.

17. Felbab-Brown, *Shooting Up*, 129, Kenneth Cooper, 'Afghans Cultivate Islamic State, but Ignore Illicit Harvest,' *Washington Post*, 11 May 1997.

18. Green Interview, 22 March 2021; Jeffrey Batholet and Steve LeVine, 'The Holy Men of Heroin,' *Newsweek*, 5 December 1999, 40-43; Jonathan Goodhand, 'From Holy War to Opium War? A Case Study of the Opium Economy in North-eastern Afghanistan,' *Central Asian Survey* 19, no. 2 (February 2000), 265-80.

19. Mansfield, *State Built on Sand*, 122-3, 131- 8; Robert Crews, 'Moderate Taliban?' in Crews and Amin Tarzi, The Taliban and the Crisis of Afghanistan (Cambridge: Harvard University Press, 2008), 238-73; Kathy Gannon, *I is for Infidel: From Holy War to Holy Terror in Afghanistan* (New York: Hachette, 2006), 55-60; Rashid, *Taliban*, 103-4.

20. David Mansfield, 'Coping Strategies, Accumulated Wealth, and Shifting Markets: The Story of Opium Poppy Cultivation in Badakhshan 2000-2003,' Agha Khan Development Network Report, January 2004.

21. James Bradford and David Mansfield, 'Known Unknowns and Unknown Knowns: What we know about the cannabis and the hashish trade in Afghanistan,' *EchoGeo,* vol. 48, (Apr-Jun 2019), 3; Savage Interview, 15 July 2022.

22. Bass Interview, 16 April 2021; Arian Interview, 9 April 2021; Arian Interview #3, 12 August 2021.

23. Gregory Interview, 13 May 2021; see also Freakley Interview, 3 November 2022.

24. Formica Interview 25 May 2021.

25. Steve Coll, *Directorate S: The CIA and America's Secret Wars in Afghanistan and Pakistan* (New York: Penguin, 2018), 272-7.

26. Felbab-Brown, *Shooting Up*, 141-4; Mansfield, *State Built on Sand*, 114; (Redacted) Interview, Afghan Blackwater employee, 18 September 2021.

27. Coll, *Directorate S*, 268-72.

28. In May 2009, there were more than 50,000 U.S. troops in Afghanistan, and when President Obama announced his surge in December, there were 67,000. Obama's increase that arrived in 2010 brought the total number of U.S. troops to about 100,000. See 'A timeline of U.S. troop levels in Afghanistan since 2001,' *AP News*, 6 July 2016.

29. UNODC Opium Survey 2010; Anthony H. Cordesman, 'The Afghan Narcotics Industry: A Summary,' Center for Strategic and International Studies, 12 November 2009.

30. Lerch Interview #2, 20 March 2022.

31. Mansfield, *State Built on Sand*, 114-115; SIGAR, 'Quarterly Report to Congress,' 30 October 2014, 11; Freakley Interview, 3 November 2022.

32. SIGAR, 'Counternarcotics: Lessons from the U.S. Experience in Afghanistan,' June 2018, 53; Partlow, *Kingdom of Their Own*, 104-107; Matthew Rosenberg and Maria Abi-Habib, 'Afghanistan Blunts Anticorruption Efforts,' *Wall Street Journal*, 12 September 2010.

33. 'DEA Releases Photos of Record-Breaking Seizure in Afghanistan,' *DEA. gov*, 13 June 2008; Jerome Starkey, 'Afghan commandos discover 230 tonnes of cannabis in the desert,' *Belfast Telegraph*, 10 July 2008; Matt Dupee, 'Kandahar Drug Bust: Narco-Penetration of the State,' *Long War Journal*, 5 September 2009.

Chapter 10: Trials (2009–10)

1. H.R. McMaster, 'The Battle of 73 Easting,' in *Leaders in War*, Frederick Kagan and Chris Kubik, eds. (New York: Frank Cass, 2005), 105-117; Harry D. Tunnell IV, USMA Register of Graduates, Class: 1984, Cullum number 41704.

2. George Packer, 'The Lesson of Tal Afar,' *The New Yorker*, 3 April 2006.

3. Harry D. Tunnell IV, *Red Devils: Tactical Perspectives from Iraq* (Ft. Leavenworth: Combat Studies Institute Press, 2006), 52-3; see also Hazelton, *Bullets not Ballots*, 2-6. The difference between Hazelton's conclusions and Tunnell's is the emphasis on the host-nation government. Tunnell's Afghan partners were means to his end of killing insurgents. Hazelton concludes that capacity of the indigenous government is more important than the military strength of the great power supporting it.

4. Hymel, *Strykers*, 43; Aikins, 'Master of Spin Boldak.'

5. Nathan Booth, 'Brigade Holds Memorial for 32 lost in 2009,' *DVIDS*, 1 January 2010; Hymel, *Strykers*, 47-9.

6. Stjepan Mestrovic, *Strike and Destroy: When Counter-Insurgency (COIN) Doctrine Met Hellraiser's Brigade or, The Fate of Corporal Morlock* (New York: Algora Publishing, 2012), 67.

7. (Redacted) Interview, CPT U.S. Army 3, 7 July 2022; Mestrovic, *Strike and Destroy*, 155.

8. Karin Assmann, John Goetz, Marc Hujer, "Let's Kill': Report Reveals Discipline Breakdown in Kill Team Brigade,' *Der Spiegel International*, 4 April 2011; Aadland Interview, 4 May 2021; (Redacted) Interview, CPT U.S. Army 3, 7 July 2022.

9. Mark Boal, 'The Kill Team: How US Soldiers in Afghanistan Murdered Innocent Civilians,' *Rolling Stone*, 28 March 2011.

10. Boal, 'Kill Team'; John Goetz and Marc Hujer, 'The Good Boy and the 'Kill Team,'' *Der Spiegel International*, 31 March 2011; Michelle Tan, 'Boredom in rogue platoon leads to murder,' *Army Times*, 28 November 2011; for interviews with participants see Dan Krauss, *The Kill Team*,

documentary film (2013); for the dramatized version, see Dan Krauss, *The Kill Team*, A24 studio feature (2019).

11. 'Let's Kill,' *Der Spiegel*, 4 April 2011.

12. Johnson Interview, 9 April 2021.

13. Boal, 'Kill Team;' Tan, 'Boredom'; (Redacted) Interview, CPT U.S. Army, 7 July 2022.

14. Counts Interview, 7 September 2022.

15. 5/2 SBCT, 'Special Assessment.'

16. Michael Hastings, 'King David's War,' *Rolling Stone*, 2 February 2011.

17. Kirk Johnson, 'Guilty Plea by Sergeant in Killing of Civilians,' *New York Times*, 5 June 2013; Ernesto Londono, 'US soldier charged in Kandahar massacre showed no remorse, comrade says,' *Washington Post*, 5 November 2012; Bill Chappell, 'US Soldier Sentenced to Life in Afghan Village Attacks,' *National Public Radio*, 23 August 2013; Ali Latifi and Abdullah Shahood, 'Afghan rage over Kandahar massacre sentence,' *Al Jazeera*, 1 September 2013.

18. Robinson, *One Hundred Victories*, 147, fn. 8.

19. Fritz Interview, 27 June 2021; Flannery Interview, 18 March 2022; Aggus Interview, 12 April 2022; Davis Interview, 16 September 2022.

20. 'Canadian Forces in Afghanistan: Report of the Standing Committee on National Defence,' 39th Canadian Parliament, 1st session (June 2007), 67; The Canadian government owned the Tim Horton's franchise, which had cost $1.2 million to install, 'but profits have been coming in at a rate much higher than expected' (67).

21. For 'end of the line,' see Elliot Ackerman, *The Fifth Act: America's End in Afghanistan* (New York: Penguin, 2022), 8; for 'Alamos,' see Johnny Rico, *Blood Makes Grass Grow Green: a Year in the Desert with Team America* (New York: Random House, 2007), 1.

22. Edwards Interview, 25 March 2021; Joseph LaPlante Interview, 1LT U.S. Army, 8-1 CAV, 5 May 2021; Robert Kaplan, 'Indian Country,' *Wall Street Journal*, 21 September 2004; Stephen Silliman, 'The 'Old West' in the Middle East: U.S. Military Metaphors in Real and Imagined Indian Country,' *American Anthropologist*, 110, no. 2 (June 2008), 237-47.

23. Barack Obama, 'The New Way Forward - The President's Address,' White House Archives, 1 December 2009.

24. Ackerman, *Fifth Act*, 38.

25. Rogers Interview #2, 1 September 2022; Naqib Mirzada Interview #2, MAJ ANSF Special Operations, 14 October 2022.

26. James Fortune Interview, 1LT U.S. Army, 4-2 CAV, 7 April 2021; Slade Lerch Interview #2, 20 March 2022.

27. Counts Interview, 7 September 2022; Rogers Interview, 28 July 2022.

28. Johnson Interview, 9 April 2021; (Redacted) Interview, CPT U.S. Army 1, 21 April 2021,.

29. W. Clark Interview, 26 March 2021.
30. W. Clark Interview, 26 March 2021; Fazel Interview, 26 March 2021.
31. Jalali, *Military History of Afghanistan*, 310-12.
32. Fazel Interview, 26 March 2021.
33. KIFC, 'Taking Stock of COL Abdul Razziq,' 3-5.
34. TF Saint, 'Non-Combat Event,' Wikileaks, 16 December 2009.
35. Kirby Interview, 19 March 2021; Whitlock, *Afghanistan Papers*, 183.
36. W. Clark Interview, 26 March 2021.
37. Fox Interview #2, 14 August 2021.

Chapter 11: Peak of the Surge (2010–11)

1. Green Interview, 22 March 2021; Fox Interview #2, 14 August 2021.
2. Fox Interview #2, 14 August 2021; Dustin Carroll Interview, SFC U.S. Army, 4-2 CAV, 13 October 2021; Kenneth Reed Interview, MAJ U.S. Army, 4-2 CAV, 15 June 2022.
3. Green Interview, 22 March 2021.
4. Beckman, Sr. Interview, 12 May 2021; David Sanger, 'A Test for the Meaning of Victory in Afghanistan,' *New York Times*, 13 February 2010; Noah Shachtman, 'Marjah's 'Government in a Box' Flops as McChrystal Fumes,' *Wired*, 25 May 2010; Robert Cassidy, *War, Will, and Warlords: Counterinsurgency in Afghanistan and Pakistan, 2001-2011* (Quantico: Marine Corps University Press, 2012), 135.
5. Diplomatic (Washington) cable, 'Afghan Border Police in the Spin Boldak District, Kandahar Province,' 26 November 2010.
6. Chayes Interview, 23 June 2021; Rajiv Chandrasekaran, *Little America: The War Within the War for Afghanistan* (New York: Vintage, 2012), 162-4.
7. Christopher Kolenda, SIGAR Lessons Learned Interview, *Washington Post Afghanistan Papers*, 5 April 2016, 2-3; Chayes Interview, 23 June 2021; Noah Coburn, 'Merchant-Warlords: Changing Forms of Leadership in Afghanistan's Unstable Political Economy,' in *Modern Afghanistan: The Impact of Forty Years of War*, ed. Nazif Shahrani (Bloomington: Indiana University Press, 2018).
8. *Enduring Voices*, ed. Koontz, 206, 249-251. There were initially just three regional commands: East, South, and West (the North, where there was little resistance to NATO occupation, was known as 'AO ISAF' before becoming the fourth regional command). A fifth RC emerged in 2010, as Helmand and Nimruz Provinces left RC-South to form RC-Southwest, which was dominated by the U.S. Marine Corps.
9. Beckman, Sr. Interview, 12 May 2021.
10. Achakzai elders mentioned in intelligence reports as possible replacements for Raziq were Haji Abdul Karim Khan and Haji Wali Shah; ABP Kandak

Commanders included COL Ayub Khaki of Shorabak, COL Makhmud of Arghestan, and COL Anwar of Maruf; 5/2 SBCT 'Special Assessment,' 13 March 2010, 6; see also KIFC, 'Taking Stock of COL Abdul Razziq,' 19 November 2009; CTF Lightning Intelligence, 'Spin Boldak Corruption,' 12 September 2010.

11. 5/2 SBCT, 'Special Assessment,' 3-4; the Finance Minister in question was Hajji Faiz Mohammad. Andrew Green, correspondence with author, 5 April 2025.

12. Beckman, Sr. Interview, 12 May 2021.

13. 5/2 SBCT 'Special Assessment,' 4; Fox Interview #2, 14 August 2021.

14. Green Interview, 22 March 2021; (Redacted) Interview, COL U.S. Army, 9 July 2021.

15. Kenneth Scheidt Interview, LTC U.S. Army, AfPak Hands, 29 June 2021; Robinson, *One Hundred Victories*, 32.

16. Chandrasekaran, *Little America*, 275-7; (Redacted) Interview, COL U.S. Army, 9 July 2021.

17. Green Interview, 22 March 2021; Fox Interview #2, 14 August 2021.

18. Fortune Interview, 7 April 2021.

19. Rajiv Chandrasekaran, 'The Afghan Robin Hood,' *Washington Post*, 4 October 2010; Green Interview, 22 March 2021; (Redacted) Interview, Senior U.S. Government Official 1, 22 June 2021; (Redacted) Interview, CPT U.S. Army 1, 21 April 2021; (Redacted) Interview, U.S. Special Forces Officer, 15 February 2022.

20. For the concept of the bandit as prospective government agent and the violence of European state-making in the early modern era: 'A king's best source of armed supporters was sometimes the world of outlaws. Robin Hood's conversion to royal archer may be a myth, but the myth records a practice.' Charles Tilly, 'War Making and State Making as Organized Crime,' in *Bringing the State Back In*, ed. Theda Skocpol et. al. (Cambridge, 1985), 173. For more on the myth and Hood as 'treacherously slain,' see David C. Fowler, 'Rymes of Robin Hood,' in *Literary History of the Popular Ballad* (Duke, 1968). For a bizarre op-ed that advocated 'strategic bombing' of opium, while comparing the asymmetric nature of combat in Afghanistan to the Robin Hood story, see Reese Schonfeld, 'Afghanistan: Robin Hood and the Sheriff of Nottingham,' *Huffington Post*, 29 November 2009.

21. CTF Lightning Intelligence, 'Spin Boldak HUMINT,' 5 October 2010; M/4-2 CAV Intelligence, 'Recent Interactions with ANSF,' 22 September 2010; M/4-2 CAV Intelligence, 'Spin Boldak Inbrief,' 25 September 2010, 4, 7-8; M/4-2 CAV Intelligence, 'Bismillah Arghestani Interview,' 13 November 2010; M/4-2 CAV Intelligence, 'M Troop 4/2 Personalities,' undated c. 2010, 5-6; 525 BfSB OPSUM, 9 September 2011, 10.

22. Green Interview, 22 March 2021.

23. Fritz Interview, 27 June 2021.

24. Green Interview, 22 March 2021.

25. (Redacted) Interview, Senior U.S. Government Official 1, 22 June 2021; 5/2 SBCT, 'Special Assessment,' 2.

26. (Redacted) Interview, Linguist 3, 16 April 2022; Hastings, *The Operators*, 362.

27. Gall, *Afghan Napoleon*, Chapter 3.

28. Carroll Interview, 13 October 2021; Fox Interview #2, 14 August 2021.

29. Carroll Interview, 13 October 2021; Fox Interview #2, 14 August 2021.

Chapter 12: How Spin Boldak Works (2010–11)

1. M/4-2 CAV Intelligence, 'M Troop 4/2 Personalities.'

2. Green Interview, 22 March 2021; Fox Interview #2, 14 August 2021.

3. M/4-2 CAV Intelligence, 'How Spin Boldak Works,' 6; Diplomatic (Washington) cable, 'Relationship Dynamics, Afghan Border Police Colonel Abdul Razaq,' Wikileaks, 16 November 2010; for the high estimate, see Blum and Conway, *Finance Analysis*, 130; Aikins, 'Master of Spin Boldak.'

4. M/4-2 CAV Intelligence, 'Recent Interactions with GIRoA,' 27 September 2010.

5. M/4-2 CAV Intelligence, 'M Troop 4/2 Personalities,' 2-4; M/4-2 CAV Intelligence, 'Notes from Recent Interactions with ANSF,' 22 September 2010; Diplomatic (Washington) cable, 'Afghan Border Police in the Spin Boldak District, Kandahar Province,' 26 November 2010.

6. M/4-2 CAV, 'How Spin Boldak Works.'

7. Gregory Interview, 13 May 2021; Kelley Interview, 19 March 2021; Green Interview, 22 March 2021.

8. Fortune Interview, 7 April 2021.

9. 4-2 CAV, 'Spin Boldak Inbrief,' 25 September, 2010, 11; Kelley Interview, 19 March 2021.

10. 'How Spin Boldak Works,' 10, fns. 15-17: discoveries of ammonium nitrate on 19 April 2010, 4 October 2010, and 11 October 2010 by Sadullah Khan followed direct U.S. pressure on Raziq to produce Taliban caches of IED materials, and explosives arrived with little evidence that the materials had been carried across the border by insurgents.

11. Fortune Interview, 7 April 2021.

12. Annie Jacobsen, *First Platoon: a Story of Modern War in the Age of Identity Dominance* (New York: Penguin 2021).

13. Bass Interview, 16 April 2021; Browne Interview, 11 May 2021; Scheidt Interview, 29 June 2021.

14. Fortune Interview, 7 April 2021; Arian Interview, 9 April 2021; US Embassy (Kabul) cable, 'Spin Boldak Powerbroker Encourages Modernization of Customs Operations,' 3 February 2010.

15. Gelareh Kiazand, 'Inside the Afghan National Army, Part 4/5, Killing Time in Kandahar,' *Vice News*, 27 February 2014.
16. 525 BfSB OPSUM, 10-11.
17. Kirby Interview, 19 March 2021.
18. Arian Interview, 9 April 2021; Arian Interview #2, 10 May 2021; (Redacted) Interview, Linguist 1, 2 November 2021.

Chapter 13: Surveillance Brigade (2010–11)

1. James Edwards, Contemporary Operations Study Team Interview, 13 February 2013; Edwards Interview, 25 March 2021; Gary Johnston Interview, COL U.S. Army, 504 BfSB 16 November 2021; Davis Interview, 16 September, 2022.
2. Kelley Interview, 19 March 2021; Browne Interview, 11 May 2021.
3. James Edwards, 'Brigade Commander's After Action Notes,' 525 BfSB, 9 September 2011, 2-3; 525 BfSB, OPSUM, 16.
4. 525 BfSB, OPSUM, 7; Edwards Contemporary Ops Interview, 13 February 2013.
5. Tou Xiong Interview, SPC U.S. Army, 525 BfSB, 26 May 2022.
6. Michael T. Flynn, Matt Pottinger, Paul Batchelor, 'Fixing Intel: A Blueprint for Making Intelligence Relevant in Afghanistan,' Center for a New American Security, January 2010.
7. Edwards, email correspondence with author, 21 March 2021.
8. Arian Interview #3, 12 August 2021; Fox Interview #2, 14 August 2021; Carroll Interview, 13 October 2021.
9. Edwards Interview, 25 March 2021; Forsberg, 'Counterinsurgency in Kandahar,' 47.
10. Yaroslav Trofimov and Matthew Rosenberg, 'In Afghanistan, US Turns 'Malignant Actor' Into Ally, *Wall Street Journal*, 18 November 2010; see also Chandrasekaran, *Little America*, 259-67.
11. Forsberg, 'Counterinsurgency in Kandahar,' 47.
12. Robinson, *One Hundred Victories*, 42-3; LTC Chris Riga was Raziq's Special Forces partner at the time.
13. Green Interview, 22 March 2021; Edwards Interview, 25 March 2021; 525 BfSB OPSUM, 9 September 2011, 10.
14. Diplomatic (Washington) cable, 'Afghan Border Police in the Spin Boldak District, Kandahar Province,' 26 November 2010.
15. Kirby Interview, 19 March 2021; Bass Interview, 16 April 2021; David Crow Interview, CPT U.S. Army, 8-1 CAV, 29 April 2021; (Redacted) Interview, CPT U.S. Army 1, 21 April 2021.
16. Adamec, *Gazetteer*, 81.
17. (Redacted) Interview, CPT U.S. Army 1, 21 April 2021.

18. Diplomatic (Washington) cable, 'Afghan Border Police in the Spin Boldak District, Kandahar Province,' 26 November 2010; M/4-2 CAV Intelligence, 'Notes from Recent Interactions with GIRoA,' 27 September 2010; Fox Interview, 28 February 2021; Kelley Interview, 19 March 2021; Green Interview, 22 March 2021.

19. M/4-2 CAV, 'Notes from Recent Interactions with GIRoA,' 27 September, 2010; Green Interview, 22 March 2021; Fortune Interview 7 April 2021; Bass Interview, 16 April 2021; Aadland Interview, 4 May 2021; Scheidt Interview, 29 June 2021.

20. Diplomatic (Washington) cable, 'Afghan Border Police in the Spin Boldak District, Kandahar Province,' 26 November 2010.

21. Fox Interview, 28 February 2021; Bass Interview, 16 April 2021.

22. M/4-2 CAV Intelligence, 'Bismillah Arghestani Interview,' 13 November 2010.

23. Bass Interview, 16 April 2021.

24. 525 BfSB, OPSUM, 9 September 2011, 10.

25. Edwards Interview, 25 March 2021.

26. Gregory Interview, 13 May 2021; Kohler Interview, 19 May 2021; Leydet Interview, 28 May 2021.

27. Edwards Interview, 25 March 2021; Bass Interview, 16 April 2021; Gregory Interview, 13 May 2021.

28. 525 BfSB OPSUM, 9 September 2011, 13; Elena Becatoros and Tarek El-Tablawy, '17 killed in suicide blast in southern Afghanistan,' *Denver Post*, 7 January 2011; 'Deadly suicide bombing wrecks Afghan bathhouse,' *France24*, 7 January 2011.

29. Fox Interview #2, 14 August 2021; Xiong Interview, 26 May 2022.

30. Arian Interview #3, 12 August 2021.

31. Edwards Interview, 25 March 2021.

32. Afridi Interviews, 28 and 31 May 2022; Saqib Interview, 8 August 2022; (Redacted) Interview, Linguist 3, 16 April 2022.

33. Joshua Partlow, *A Kingdom of Their Own*, 305-314; Malkasian, *American War*, 289.

34. Gul Agha Sherzai quoted in Declan Walsh, 'Powerful Afghan Police Chief Puts Fear in Taliban and Their Enemies,' *New York Times*, 8 November 2014.

35. Kris Kough Interview, LTC California NG, 29 January 2022.

36. Tom Peter, 'Assassinated Kandahar Police chief was optimistic about security,' *Christian Science Monitor*, 15 April 2011; Sally Sara, 'Taliban claims Afghan bomb attack,' *Australian Broadcasting Corporation*, 15 April 2011.

37. Green Interview, 22 March 2021; Arian Interview, 9 April 2021.

38. SIGAR, 'Lessons Learned: Police in Conflict,' June 2022, 178-81; 'Treatment of Conflict-Related Detainees in Afghan Custody, UNAMA

report, October 2011; 'Treatment of Conflict-Related Detainees in Afghan Custody: One Year On,' January 2013, 4-5, 49, 52; see also State Department, 'Afghanistan 2012 Human Rights Report,' Country Reports on Human Rights Practices for 2012, 3; State Department, 'Afghanistan 2013 Human Rights Report,' Country Reports on Human Rights Practices for 2013, 2-3, 8. The report for next year specified: 'In August, Raziq told the media he had ordered his forces to execute militants on the spot, rather than take them prisoner. While Raziq later retracted his comments, Kunduz Provincial Chief of Police Mustafa Moseni and Baghlan Provincial Chief of Police Aminullah Amarkhel, among others, echoed his statements.' (State Department, 'Afghanistan 2014 Human Rights Report,' 2).

39. UNAMA, 'One Year On,' 80-1, fn. 277.
40. UNAMA, 'One Year On,' cites eighty-one missing persons from September 2011-October 2012, and thirteen bodies delivered to Mirwais hospital with gunshot wounds from April-August 2012 (5, 53). One journalist with extensive experience in Afghanistan documented another ten bodies delivered to Mirwais hospital in October 2013 (Anand Gopal, 'Kandahar's Mystery Executions,' *Harper's Magazine*, September 2014); Twenty-six more individuals disappeared after ANP arrests in 2013 and 2014 (State Department, 'Afghanistan 2015 Human Rights Report,' 4).
41. Reed Interview, 15 June 2022; Joseph Duwors Interview, Chaplain U.S. Army, 4-2 CAV, 5 August 2022.
42. Green Interview, 22 March 2021; Reed Interview, 15 June 2022.

Chapter 14: Drawdown (2012–13)

1. Edwards, Contemporary Ops Interview, 13 February 2013, 9.
2. Malkasian, *American War*, 290-292; Terry Nihart Interview, LTC U.S. Army, 503 MP, 5 November 2021; Nihart Interview #2, 24 November 2021; (Redacted) Interview, U.S. Special Forces Officer, 15 February 2022.
3. Nihart Interview, 5 November 2021; Davis Interview, 20 October 2022.
4. Patrick Michaelis Interview, LTC U.S. Army, 8-1 CAV, 13 August 2021.
5. Nihart Interview, 5 November 2021; Nihart Interview #2, 24 November 2021; Kincy Clark Interview, LTC California NG, 15 December 2021; (Redacted) Interview, Senior U.S. government official, 23 December 2021.
6. Nihart Interview, 5 November 2021; (Redacted) Interview, Law Enforcement Professional, 2 February 2022; Scheidt Interview, 29 June 2021; Thomas Feltey Interview, LTC U.S. Army, 2-23 IN, 26 October 2021.
7. Counts Interview, 7 September 2022.
8. Nihart Interview #2, 24 November 2021; SSG Bryan Dominique, 'Unit gives women voice in Southern Afghanistan,' *Fayetteville Observer*, 23 August 2012.

9. Nihart Interview, 5 November 2021; Counts Interview, 7 September 2022; Michaelis Interview, 13 August 2021.

10. Nihart Interview, 5 November 2021; David Cloud, 'Letting Go in Afghanistan as Mission Winds Down,' *Los Angeles Times*, 9 December 2012.

11. 'Department of Defense Contractor and Troop Levels in Afghanistan and Iraq: 2007-2020,' Congressional Research Service report, Updated 22 February 2021, 7.

12. David Kilcullen and Greg Mills, *The Ledger: Accounting for Failure in Afghanistan* (London: Hurst, 2021), 197.

13. President Obama on *BBC Persia*, October 2010: 'We're not going to suddenly leave, turn off the lights, and go home...What will happen is, as we are training up more and more Afghan security forces, they're becoming more effective. We will transition so that they are starting to take over more responsibility for security, and slowly, the United States troop presence, as well as coalition troop presence, will diminish.' Cited in Robert Cassidy, *War, Will, and Warlords: Counterinsurgency in Afghanistan and Pakistan, 2001-2011* (Quantico: Marine Corps University Press, 2012), 232. For West Point speech, see Barack Obama, 'The New Way Forward - The President's Address,' 1 December 2009.

14. Giulia Minoia and Adam Pain, "90% Real' – The Rise and Fall of a Rentier Economy: Stories from Kandahar, Afghanistan,' AREU working paper 38, November 2015, 11; Wolusmal Interview, 10 July 2021.

15. Wesa Interview #2, 5 August 2021; Saqib Interview, 8 August 2022; Ashley Jackson, 'Politics and Governance in Afghanistan: The Case of Kandahar,' AREU working paper 34, June 2015; Aikins, 'Contracting the Commanders'; Astri Suhrke, *When More is Less: The International Project in Afghanistan* (New York: Columbia University Press, 2011).

16. Minoia and Pain, '90% Real,' 20.

17. Daniel Markert Interview, MAJ California NG, 27 January 2022.

18. Miranda Summers Lowe, 'The Gradual Shift to an Operational Reserve: Reserve Component Mobilizations in the 1990s,' *Military Review*, May-June 2019, 120-126; Lowe, 'The National Guard and Reserves,' in *Understanding the U.S. Military*, ed. Katherine Carroll and William Hickman (Routledge, 2023), 127-8.

19. (Redacted) Interview, U.S. Special Forces Officer, 15 February 2022; Mark Tomola Interview, MAJ U.S. Army, 7 SF, 23 February 2022.

Chapter 15: Advisers (2013–18)

1. MSG Paul Hughes, 'Engineers generate power at FOB Walton,' *DVIDS*, 11 August 2011; SSG Whitney Houston, 'FOB Walton closes: A step in the right direction,' *DVIDS*, 20 July 2014.

2. (Redacted) Interview, Linguist 4, 26 April 2022.

3. Saqib Interview, 8 August 2022; (Redacted) Interview, U.S. Special Forces Officer, 15 February 2022; (Redacted) Interview, Senior U.S. Government official, 23 December 2021.

4. Raziq in 2010: 'We don't take prisoners – if they are trying to kill me, I will try to kill them. That's how I order my men. If they submit, and say they made a mistake, then yes, we will take them prisoner.' (Hastings, *The Operators*, 361); an Afghan linguist sympathetic to Raziq: 'He was against the Taliban. He was killing them, too, instead to detain them. Because he was thinking, this is not good. And honestly, he had his reason. He said they are killing my soldiers. And when I get them, I will kill them, too.' (Fazel Interview, 26 March 2021).

5. (Redacted) Interview, Senior U.S. Government official, 23 December 2021.

6. Ahmed and Aikins, 'America's Monster.'

7. UNAMA Reports on the Protection of Civilians in Armed Conflict, 2010-2014.

8. Human Rights Watch, 'World Report 2014: Afghanistan'; Frud Bezhan, 'Afghans Laud, Rights Groups Concerned By 'Take No Prisoners' Orders,' *Radio Free Europe*, 24 August 2014.

9. Scheidt Interview 31, 29 June 2021; Feltey Interview, 26 October 2021.

10. Scheidt Interview 31, 29 June 2021.

11. 2-23 IN, 'WARNO 4 to OPORD 13-01: Tomahawk Freedom, 31 October 2012,' 7; Feltey Interview, 26 October 2021; Freakley Interview #2, 15 November 2022.

12. Feltey Interview, 26 October 2021.

13. 'Taliban Admit Covering Up Death of Mullah Omar,' *BBC News*, 31 August 2015; Jibran Ahmad, 'Taliban's Mullah Omar Died of Natural Causes in Afghanistan, Son Says,' *Reuters*, 14 September 2015; 'Taliban Leader Mullah Akhtar Mansour Killed, Afghans Confirm,' *BBC News*, 22 May 2016; Adam Entous and Jessica Donati, 'How the U.S. Tracked and Killed the Leader of the Taliban,' *Wall Street Journal*, 25 May 2016.

14. (Redacted) Interview, Senior U.S. government official 2, 20 December 2021.

15. Carter Malkasian, Jerry Meyerle, Megan Katt, 'The War in Southern Afghanistan, 2001-2008,' *Strategic Studies*, July 2009, 40-1.

16. Stephen Griffiths Interview, CPT U.S. Army, 1-26 IN, 13 October 2021.

17. Giustozzi, *Taliban at War*, 200-1, fn. 14.

18. (Redacted) Interview, U.S. Special Forces Officer, 15 February 2022.

19. Haqmal Daudzai, *The State-Building Dilemma in Afghanistan: The State Governmental Design at the National Level and the Role of Democratic Provincial Councils in Decentralization at the Sub-National Level* (Berlin: Budrich Academic Press, 2021), 156.

20. Feltey Interview, 26 October 2021; Walsh, 'Powerful Afghan Police Chief'; Malkasian, *American War*, 306.

21. Grenier Interview, 11 October 2022; S. Rebecca Zimmerman, 'The Afghan Warlord with a Cheshire Cat Grin,' *Newsweek*, 29 April 2015; Mujib Mashal, 'Afghan Police Chief, Long a Taliban Target, Faces a New Emotion: Fear,' *New York Times*, 31 May 2015; Paul McGeough, 'Who Killed Australia's Warlord in Afghanistan?' *Sydney Morning Herald*, 26 June 2015.

22. Tomola Interview, 23 February 2022; Walsh, 'Powerful Afghan Police Chief'; 'Afghan Forces Battle Taliban in Uruzgan,' *BBC News*, 8 September 2016; Aikins, 'America's Monster.'

23. (Redacted) Interview, Senior U.S. government official 3, 23 December 2021; K. Clark Interview, 15 December 2021.

24. Markert Interview, 27 January 2022.

25. David Craig Interview, LTC California NG, 14 January 2022.

26. K. Clark Interview, 15 December 2021; (Redacted) Interview, Law Enforcement Professional, 1 February 2022.

27. (Redacted) Interview, Senior U.S. Government Official 1, 22 June 2021; Jean-Christophe Peuch, 'Afghanistan: Warlord's Role as Political Leader Remains Questionable,' *Radio Free Europe*, 12 April 2001; 'Commander Massoud to visit European Parliament in Strasbourg on 5 April 2001,' Press Release, President of the European Union; Tamim Hamid, 'Paris Unveils Plaque in Honor of Ahmad Shah Massoud,' *Tolo News*, 27 March 2021.

28. Green Interview, 22 March 2021; (Redacted) Interview, Senior U.S. Government official, 22 June 2021; Fox Interview #2, 14 August 2021; Feltey Interview, 26 October 2021; Malgarai Interview, 11 June 2022; (Redacted) Interview, Linguist 1, 2 November 2021; (Redacted) Interview, Linguist 2 #2, 28 March 2022; U.S. Embassy (Kabul), 'Spin Boldak Powerbroker Encourages Modernization of Customs Operations,' Wikileaks, 3 February 2010.

29. Kough Interview, 29 January 2022.

30. Afridi Interviews, 28 and 31 May 2022; Malgarai Interview, 11 June 2022; Saqib Interview, 8 August 2022.

31. Markert Interview, 27 January 2022.

32. K. Clark Interview, 15 December 2021.

Chapter 16: Ghost Town (2015–21)

1. Markert Interview, 27 January 2022; Davis Interview, 16 September 2022.

2. Rogers Interview, 28 July 2022; Rogers Interview #2, 1 September 2022; SIGAR 23-16-IP, 'Why the Afghan Security Forces Collapsed,' February 2023, 27-8.

3. (Redacted) Interview, Linguist 4, 26 April 2022; Rangina Haimidi Interview, Afghan Education Minister, 30 June 2022; Savage Interview, 15 July 2022.

4. Diplomatic (Washington) cable, 'Afghan Border Police in the Spin Boldak District, Kandahar Province,' 26 November 2010; (Redacted) Interview, Linguist 2 #2, 28 March 2022; Malkasian, *American War*, 306.

5. (Redacted) Interview, Law Enforcement Professional, 1 February 2022, pp. 18-20; (Redacted) Interview, Linguist 2 #2, 28 March 2022,; 'UAE confirms five officials killed in Afghan attack,' *BBC*, 11 January 2017; Masood Saifullah, 'Who Carried Out the Kandahar Bombing?' *Deutsche Welle*, 11 January 2017; Jibran Ahmad, 'Taliban seeks to reassure UAE over Afghanistan attack,' *Reuters*, 19 January 2017; Ayesha Tanzeem, 'Afghan Intel Chief: Suspects that Killed UAE Ambassador Living in Pakistan,' *Voice of America*, 15 June 2017.

6. Ali Yawar Adili and Thomas Ruttig, 'The 'Ankara Coalition': Opposition from within the government,' Afghan Analysts Network, 25 July 2017; Clayton Thomas, 'Afghanistan: Background and U.S. Policy: In Brief,' Congressional Research Service Report, 1 November 2018.

7. Gordon Lubold, 'In Afghanistan's Troubled South,' *Christian Science Monitor*, 30 April 2008; Sami Sadat, 'I commanded Afghan troops this year. We were betrayed,' *New York Times*, 25 August 2021.

8. Freakley Interview, 3 November 2022; (Redacted) Interview, Linguist 2, 21 March 2022.

9. Bill Roggio, 'General Raziq's assassin trained at a Taliban camp,' *Long War Journal*, 21 October 2018; Mujib Mashal and Thomas Gibbons-Neff, 'How a Taliban Assassin Got Close Enough to Kill a General,' *New York Times*, 2 November 2018; Sharif Amiri, 'Documentary on Gen. Raziq's Assassination,' *Tolo News*, 9 November 2018.

10. Michael Semple, 'Not Everybody's Hero,' *Afghan Analysts Network*, 31 October 2018.

11. K. Clark Interview, 15 December 2021; Jeffrey Smiley Interview, BG California NG, 12 January 2022; (Redacted) Interview, Linguist 2 #2, 28 March 2022.

12. 'Afghan-Pakistani border crossing closed after clashes,' *Radio Free Europe*, 15 October 2018; Sharif Amiri, 'Documentary on Gen. Raziq's Assassination,' *Tolo News*, 9 November 2018; Mujib Mashal and Thomas Gibbons-Neff, 'How a Taliban Assassin Got Close Enough to Kill a General,' *New York Times*, 2 November 2018.

13. Philip Walter Wellman, 'Conspiracy theories abound over US role in Kandahar police chief's killing,' *Stars and Stripes*, 26 October 2018. To believe these stories, you would have to believe, incidentally, that the U.S. government had been willing to risk life and limb of one of its Brigadier Generals, along with theater commander GEN Scott Miller, in the process. Due to the clandestine way the army handled casualty reporting, outsiders

accused the U.S. of covering up BG Jeffrey Smiley's gunshot injury. Smiley's busted hand and hushed evacuation from the country became another plank of suspicion in the platform against the United States, rather than contrary evidence to an American role in Raziq's murder plot.

14. Arian Interview #2, 10 May 2021; the rival general was Northern Zone Police Chief Mohammad Daud Daud.

15. Ghafoor Saboory, 'Raziq Says Government Cannot Remove Him from His Post,' *Tolo News*, 2 January 2018; 'Afghan Provincial Police Chief Says Government Cannot Fire Him,' *Radio Free Europe*, 3 January 2018.

16. One Bamiyan resident claimed: 'Atta Mohammad Noor is the brightness of our eyes; General Abdul Raziq is in our heart.' Samim Faramarz, 'Noor Receives Huge Support from Kabul Gathering,' *Tolo News*, 29 December 2017; Thomas Ruttig, 'The Killing of Razeq: Removing the Taleban's strongest foe in Kandahar, an indirect hit at elections,' *Afghanistan Analysts Network*, 19 October 2018; SIGAR, Quarterly Reports to Congress, 30 January 2018, 121-122.

17. Barfield, *Afghanistan*, 235-6.

18. Steve Coll and Adam Entous, 'The Secret History of the U.S. Diplomatic Failure in Afghanistan,' *The New Yorker*, 10 December 2021.

19. (Redacted) Interview, Linguist 4, 26 April 2022; (Redacted) Interview, Linguist 5, 20 September 2022.

20. 'Top US general says Afghan collapse can be traced to Trump-Taliban deal,' *The Guardian*, 29 September 2021.

21. MOAB was dropped on a cave complex occupied by the Islamic State-Khorasan (ISIS-K), a tiny terrorist cell, an estimated 700 fighters at the time, rather than the more numerous Taliban; Shannon Collins, 'What to Know About the GBU-43/B, 'Mother of All Bombs,'' *DVIDS*, 14 April 2017; Robin Wright, 'Trump Drops the Mother of All Bombs on Afghanistan,' *The New Yorker*, 14 April 2017; Ali M. Latifi, 'Mother of All Bombs,' *New York Times*, 20 April 2017.

22. (Redacted) Interview, CPT U.S. Army 2, 6 July 2022; Mirzada Interview, 6 October 2022; Mirzada Interview #2, 14 October 2022.

23. Ackerman, *Fifth Act*, 146-7; Michael Crowley, 'Trump's Deal with the Taliban Draws Fire from his Former Allies,' *New York Times*, 19 August 2021.

24. K. Clark Interview, 15 December 2021.

25. Johnston Interview, 16 November 2021; Mirzada Interview #2, 14 October 2022; Safi Interview, 10 February 2022; (Redacted) Interview, Linguist 2, 21 March 2022; (Redacted) Interview, Linguist 3, 16 April 2022.

26. Asfandyar Bhittani, Twitter @AsfandBhittani, 12 August 2021.

27. 'Afghanistan's Ghani says 45,000 security personnel killed since 2014,' *BBC*, 25 January 2023.

28. Twitter @Yas_Al_Zmn, 29 December 2021, retweet of Pashtana Zalmai Khan Dorani, 29 December 2021.

29. Abubakar Siddique, "Afghanistan Is Hell': Supporters of Late Afghan General Claim Taliban Killings, Persecution,' *Radio Free Europe*, 2 November 2022; (Redacted) Interview, Linguist 4, 26 April 2022.

30. Modaser Islami, 'Afghans demand justice for war victims after mass grave discovery,' *Arab News*, 27 September 2022.

Epilogue

1. State Department, 'Dissent Channel Cable,' 7 January 2021: 'The Department of State should explicitly denounce President Trump's role in this violent attack on the U.S. government. Just as we routinely denounce foreign leaders who use violence and intimidation to interfere in peaceful democratic processes and override the will of their voters.'

2. Devlin Barrett, et al, 'A Sprawling Investigation: What we know so far about the Capitol mob arrests,' *Washington Post*, 13 May 2021; Tom Dreisbach and Meg Anderson, 'Nearly 1 in 5 Defendants in Capitol Riot Cases Served in the Military,' *NPR*, 21 January 2021.

3. Renee Crisostomo, 'Abdul Raziq in 2012,' 18th Wing Public Affairs, U.S. Air Force photo, 7 June 2012.

4. (Redacted) Interview, Linguist 5, 20 September 2022.

5. Raziq Showqi, 'Shaheed General Raziq,' *YouTube*, available https://www.youtube.com/watch?v=OjlX4SKRo5w; the video had 82,000 views as of February 2024.

6. Obeid Tukhi, 'Shahed General Raziq,' *YouTube*, available at https://www.youtube.com/watch?v=zq7qXMnPxYg; the video had 96,000 views as of February 2024.

7. (Redacted) Interview, Linguist 2, 21 March 2022.

8. Akbar Shah Nikzad, 'Da Pashtani Mor (The Pashtun Mother).' This video had 1.2 million views as of January 2023, but has since been removed from *YouTube*. Other versions of the song are available online by searching 'Pashtani Mor,' such as the one at: https://www.youtube.com/watch?v=AYZWnBZ548s.

INDEX